D0456778

INSPIRE / PLAN / DISCOVER / EXPERIENCE

NEW YORK CITY

NEW YORK CITY

CONTENTS

DISCOVER 6

EXPERIENCE 62

NEED TO KNOW 304

Left: A bustling street in Manhattan's Times Square
Previous page: Sunset over the East River

DISCOVER

Sun rises over the Brooklyn Bridge

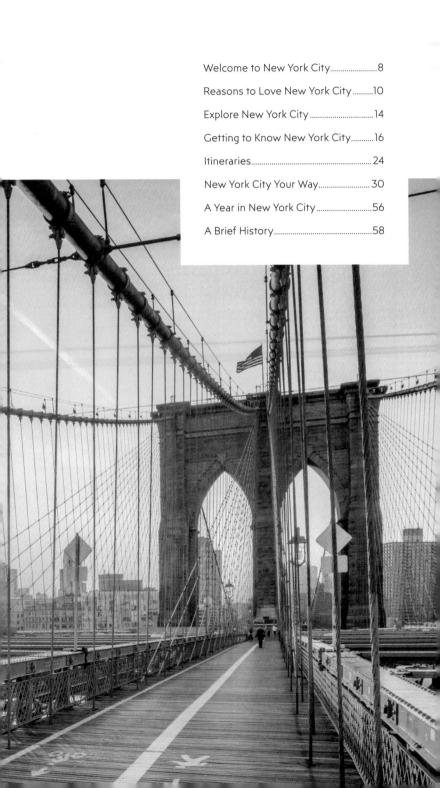

WELCOME TO
NEW YORK
CITY

Stately museums and soaring skyscrapers. Blissful parks and bustling stores. Sultry bars and sublime cocktails. Whatever your dream trip to NYC entails, this DK Eyewitness Guide is the perfect companion.

1 Bartender prepares a cocktail

2 Spectacular interior of the Metropolitan Museum of Art

3 Greenery and skyscrapers converge at 230 Fifth Avenue's rooftop bar

Dynamic and diverse, New York offers everything in abundance; it's no wonder that, as the saying goes, it's a city so nice, they named it twice. The gateway to America, you can follow in the footsteps of millions at Ellis Island and get a sense of 19th-century life at the Lower East Side Tenement Museum, or remember modern history at the National September 11 Memorial. Art is everywhere in New York: goggle at the bounty of Old Masters in the Met and check out street art in Harlem. As for food and drink, you're spoiled for choice. New York has a plethora of superlative bars and restaurants, not forgetting a wealth of cuisines in neighborhoods like Nolita and Chinatown. Bucks burning a hole in your pocket? Go window-shopping along Fifth Avenue, run amok in Bloomingdale's, and find vintage gems at Brooklyn Flea.

You'll love New York's outer boroughs, each with their own distinct personality, too. Catch a Yankees game in The Bronx, board the Staten Island Ferry for unmissable views, try assorted craft beers in Queens, and snap that perfect photo on Brooklyn Bridge after exploring trendy Williamsburg.

From Lower Manhattan to the Bronx, and everything in between, we break New York City down into easily navigable chapters full of expert knowledge. If you're not sure where to begin, we include detailed itineraries and comprehensive maps to help plan the perfect adventure. Add insider tips, and a Need To Know guide that lists all the essentials to be aware of before and during your trip, and you've got an indispensable guidebook. Enjoy the book, and enjoy New York City.

REASONS TO
LOVE NEW YORK

It's undeniably spectacular. It's a world in a city. It never sleeps. Ask any New Yorker and you'll hear a different reason why they love their city. Here, we pick some of our favorites.

1 SHAKESPEARE IN THE PARK

In warm summer twilight actors entertain audiences at Central Park's Delacorte Theater with free performances of the Bard's greatest plays.

STATUE OF LIBERTY *2*

Looming over the harbor, Lady Liberty holds her beacon to light the world - the greatest symbol of the American dream. Climb to her crown for spine-tingling views of Manhattan.

3 JEWISH FOOD IN THE LOWER EAST SIDE

Mountainous pastrami, chewy bagels, freshly baked challah breads; Jewish life in the Lower East Side lives on in its delis, bakeries, and cafés.

HIGH LINE 4

Gliding through Chelsea's rooftop gardens, this stunning transformation of an elevated railroad into a tranquil, tree-lined walkway offers tantalizing perspectives of the city below.

CATCHING A GAME AT YANKEE STADIUM 5

Watching America's most famous baseball team battle with arch-rivals the Boston Red Sox – or cross-town adversaries the Mets – is electric.

BROOKLYN FLEA AND SMORGASBURG 6

Artsy crafts, antique stalls, and artisanal food sellers have made these weekend markets, across the East River, New York institutions.

LIVE JAZZ 7
Live jazz is flourishing in NYC. The legacy of legends lives on at the iconic Village Vanguard, Blue Note, and Birdland clubs, while smaller, intimate venues in Harlem host new talent.

THE METROPOLITAN 8
MUSEUM OF ART
Simply one of the greatest caches of art in the world, with over two million artifacts spanning 5,000 years housed beneath its grand ceilings.

9 EMPIRE STATE BUILDING
King Kong clung to it. Tom Hanks and Meg Ryan kissed on top of it. Still the most elegant skyscraper of them all, the Empire State has been a symbol of New York City since 1931.

10 OPERA AND BALLET AT THE LINCOLN CENTER

Casts of sopranos, tenors, and baritones; achingly beautiful ballet dancers; extravagant sets and costumes. Welcome to the Lincoln Center.

11 HARLEM GOSPEL AND SOUL FOOD

Join the flock and belt out hymns at Harlem's Abyssinian Baptist Church on Sundays. Afterwards schlep to Sylvia's and sample the justly celebrated BBQ ribs and candied yams.

12 BAR-HOPPING IN WILLIAMSBURG

After exploring ever-so-trendy Brooklyn head for once-shabby, now-chic Williamsburg - or Billyburg to locals. Meander from bar to bar, sipping on craft cocktails and bitters.

EXPLORE
NEW YORK CITY

This guide divides New York City into 15 color-coded sightseeing areas, as shown on the map below. Find out more about each area on the following pages. Away from the city, Beyond the Center *(p286)* covers Upper Manhattan, the Bronx, Queens, and Staten Island.

UNION CITY

WEEHAWKEN

Hudson River

NEW JERSEY

THE HEIGHTS

HOBOKEN

NEWPORT

PAULUS
HOOK

MIDTOWN WEST AND
THE THEATER DISTRICT
p172

MoMa
Rockefeller Center
St. Patrick's
Cathedral

CHELSEA AND THE
GARMENT DISTRICT
p160

Grand Central
Terminal

Empire State
Building

LOWER
MIDTOWN
p184

GRAMERCY AND THE
FLATIRON DISTRICT
p150

GREENWICH
VILLAGE
p124

SOHO AND
TRIBECA
p114

EAST VILLAGE
p138

CHINATOWN,
LITTLE ITALY,
AND NOLITA
p102

World Trade
Center

City Hall

LOWER EAST
SIDE
p90

East River

Williamsburg
Bridge

Ellis
Island

Battery
Park

Brooklyn
Bridge

Manhattan
Bridge

Statue of
Liberty

LOWER
MANHATTAN
p64

BROOKLYN
HEIGHTS

WILLIAMSBURG

Governors
Island

BOERUM
HILL

BROOKLYN
p268

PROSPECT
HEIGHTS

RED HOOK

GETTING TO KNOW
NEW YORK CITY

Global capital of finance and culture, New York is a vast city of over 8 million people. For many, the island of Manhattan *is* New York, with its permanent purr of traffic and bounty of diverse restaurants, not to mention its dizzying assemblage of signature sights and characterful neighborhoods.

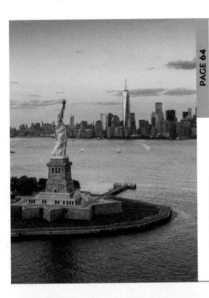

PAGE 64

LOWER MANHATTAN

Lower Manhattan's regeneration since 9/11 has been remarkable, and the island's southern tip continues to pulse with industrious energy. It remains the financial center of the world and, as the oldest part of the city, has plenty of historic appeal, with Ellis and Liberty islands looming large in the harbor.

Best for
History and skyscrapers

Home to
Statue of Liberty, Ellis Island, National September 11 Memorial and Museum

Experience
A scenic cruise around New York harbor

PAGE 90

LOWER EAST SIDE

Once the most impoverished of New York's immigrant neighborhoods, the Lower East Side is now known for its hip bars and varied restaurants. Delis are a legacy of its Jewish heritage, while Latino and Chinese eateries have added to its culinary appeal. Prepare for an assault on the senses when walking these clamoring streets.

Best for
Bars and cocktails, Jewish food

Home to
Lower East Side Tenement Museum, Katz's Deli

Experience
Jewish history on a guided tour of the neighborhood

CHINATOWN, LITTLE ITALY, AND NOLITA

PAGE 102

These vibrant enclaves are among the city's most colorful. Swarms of shoppers hungry for a bargain comb Chinatown's stores and sidewalk markets, which overflow with exotic fruits, potent herbs, and Asian antiques. Little Italy has dwindled to a few blocks, but the tempting scents from its old-fashioned bakeries, Sicilian cafés, and red-sauce joints linger. Nolita offers a wholly different ambience, with chic boutiques and cafés along its gentrified streets attracting well-heeled fashionistas.

Best for
Cheap Chinese and Italian restaurants, Chinese culture

Home to
Museum of Chinese in America, New Museum

Experience
Chinatown by trawling its dumpling and noodle shops for cheap eats

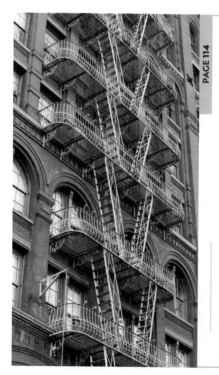

SOHO AND TRIBECA

PAGE 114

SoHo's charming, village vibe is welcome relief from the relentless jostle of Lower Manhattan. The neighborhood is known primarily for one thing: shopping. Its attractive, cobblestone streets are crammed with designer-clothing and home-furnishing boutiques, making use of the stunningly ornate cast-iron architecture that dominates the area. The adjoining neighborhood of Tribeca, meanwhile, shelters homes for wealthy New Yorkers and some of the city's finest restaurants.

Best for
Cast-iron architecture, shopping, fine dining

Home to
New York Earth Room, Children's Museum of the Arts

Experience
Pretty Greene St and admire SoHo's most intricate cast-iron architecture

→

GREENWICH VILLAGE

PAGE 124

Referred to simply as "the Village" by New Yorkers, Greenwich Village has been the artistic heart of the city since the 1920s, and it remains one of the more progressive neighborhoods, with a notable LGBT and New York University student presence. Visitors flock to the Village to admire its famously handsome brownstones and meander around its quaint side streets comprising cafés, restaurants, and nightclubs. This is the perfect area for people-watching – you might even spot a celebrity or two.

Best for
Bars and restaurants, reliable nightlife, gorgeous residential streets

Home to
Whitney Museum of American Art

Experience
Historic Washington Square Park while indulging in cupcakes from Magnolia Bakery

EAST VILLAGE

PAGE 138

The East Village, one of New York's most fashionable neighborhoods, is home to a cache of unmissable bars, restaurants, and independent theaters. More alternative and edgier than Greenwich Village, like its neighbor, it has been transformed in recent years, with an influx of New York University students and new condo developments. This is the haunt of effortlessly cool New Yorkers, thanks to its smattering of independent boutiques, thrift stores, record stores, and artsy performance spaces.

Best for
New York's historic counter culture, dive bars, cheap international restaurants

Home to
St. Mark's Church-in-the-Bowery, Stomp, Little Tokyo, Russian and Turkish Baths

Experience
Lively St. Mark's Place, grabbing snacks to enjoy in Tompkins Square Park

PAGE 150

GRAMERCY AND THE FLATIRON DISTRICT

These once quiet neighborhoods are on the rise. New York's biggest farmers' market fills Union Square with a riot of colorful produce, and is attracting stores and restaurants galore. Development has extended to the Flatiron District, where Madison Square is home to the hottest restaurants and the holy grail of food markets, Eataly. Gramercy remains affluent and residential, known for its London-style private park.

Best for
Escaping the bustle, shopping and food markets, award-winning restaurants

Home to
Flatiron Building, Eataly NYC Flatiron, Union Square Greenmarket

Experience
Madison Square Park while munching on a Shack Burger and slurping chocolate frozen custard

PAGE 160

CHELSEA AND THE GARMENT DISTRICT

Chelsea is an important center for avant-garde culture and a dynamic hub for gay New Yorkers. Art lovers head for the modish galleries in converted warehouses around the High Line, where the high-rise park has sparked a flurry of new buildings. The Garment District attracts shoppers, with Herald Square and Macy's at the heart of the city's busiest shopping area. Soaring over it all, the Empire State Building marks the start of Midtown.

Best for
Contemporary art galleries, designer flagships, LGBT scene

Home to
High Line, Empire State Building, Macy's

Experience
An early morning stroll along the High Line, taking in the local art galleries

→

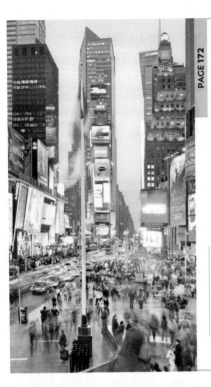

PAGE 172

MIDTOWN WEST AND THE THEATER DISTRICT

Midtown West offers the New York cityscape of popular imagination, best known for the theaters of Broadway. Times Square anchors the neighborhood, a spectacular showcase of garish neon, where impersonators and street musicians vie with hordes of tourists and the roar of traffic. Scattered throughout are famous restaurants and famous cocktail bars – perfect for unwinding in after negotiating the ruckus.

Best for
Modern New York, classic skyscrapers, live theater, old-school bars

Home to
Rockefeller Center, New York Public Library

Experience
The Today Show *live at Rockefeller Center, before taking the NBC Studio Tour*

PAGE 184

LOWER MIDTOWN

Primarily a business district, Lower Midtown contains some of the city's most venerable architecture from New York's golden age. From the iconic spire of the Chrysler Building, to the grand expanse of Grand Central, and the Modernism of the United Nations, it's all here. Midtown's streets are crowded with office workers during the day, though there is less to do at night, and the blocks near the UN are residential districts for rich New Yorkers and diplomats.

Best for
Modern architecture, classic skyscrapers, New York at work

Home to
United Nations, Grand Central Terminal, Morgan Library, Chrysler Building

Experience
Irresistible Scandinavian delicacies at Great Northern Food Hall

PAGE 198

UPPER MIDTOWN

Upper Midtown is the city's richest business and shopping district. Primarily the realm of banks, offices, posh hotels, and expensive condos, this is where Trump Tower rose in the 1980s. Fifth Avenue is lined with super-exclusive boutiques and iconic names such as Saks, Barney's, Cartier, and Tiffany's. Most visitors come here to take in the classic skyscrapers and Instagram-friendly street scenes, but also to pay homage to MoMA, one of the world's greatest modern art galleries.

Best for
Famous bars and department stores, luxury shopping, insight into business in New York City

Home to
MoMA, St. Patrick's Cathedral, Bloomingdale's, Tiffany's, Roosevelt Island

Experience
Some retail therapy at Bloomingdale's and grab an iconic "brown bag"

PAGE 214

UPPER EAST SIDE

This area has long been associated with New York's upper crust, and the likes of Fifth Avenue, Madison Avenue, and Park Avenue remain bastions of old-school wealth. The Beaux Arts mansions flanking Fifth Avenue are occupied by embassies and museums, while Madison Avenue's posh boutiques vie with Fifth Avenue for exclusivity. Further east are remnants of the area's German, Hungarian, and Czech heritage, while a sprinkling of hip gastropubs and cocktail bars, frequented by moneyed New Yorkers, has helped to shed the Upper East Side's stuffy image.

Best for
Beaux Arts architecture, fine art, historic churches

Home to
The Met, Guggenheim, Frick Collection

Experience
Klimt's stunning Woman in Gold at the Neue Galerie

→

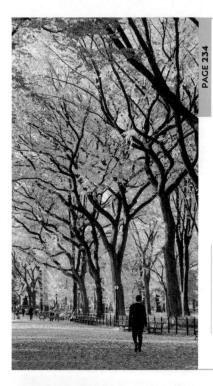

PAGE 234

CENTRAL PARK AND THE UPPER WEST SIDE

Central Park is the city's greatest green space and offers respite from Manhattan's thronging sidewalks and blaring sirens. In summer its lawns, are packed with families, joggers, soccer players, and cyclists, while in winter it's often shrouded in a magical blanket of snow. Next door, the Upper West Side remains a popular residential neighborhood, home to the fabulous American Museum of Natural History and dynamic Lincoln Center.

Best for
Escaping the hustle and bustle of the city, boating and cycling

Home to
American Museum of Natural History

Experience
Cycling in Central Park before refueling with smoked fish and bagels at Barney Greengrass

PAGE 250

HARLEM AND MORNINGSIDE HEIGHTS

This neighborhood, synonymous with the country's most famous African-American community, is thrumming with life. Visitors are greeted by some of the city's prettiest streets and a vibrant culinary landscape; the mouthwatering aromas of soul food, Caribbean, and West African cuisine drift from bustling restaurants, while a burgeoning bar scene and local jazz clubs keep things buzzing at night.

Best for
African-American culture, street art, soul food, live jazz, Sunday gospel

Home to
Schomburg Center, Hamilton Grange, National Jazz Museum in Harlem

Experience
The uplifting and electrifying Sunday gospel choir at the Abyssinian Baptist Church

BROOKLYN

PAGE 268

Across the East River, Brooklyn is a vast city-within-a-city; a patchwork of neighborhoods anchored by a booming downtown, now with its own mushrooming condo skyscrapers. Between the gorgeous brownstones of Fort Greene and Park Slope, and the hip bars of Williamsburg and Bushwick – where the chatter of bar-hoppers drifts along the weathered streets – you'll find the art galleries of Dumbo, vintage treasures at the Brooklyn Flea, and the nostalgic, seaside delights of Coney Island.

Best for
Flea markets, pizza, brownstone rowhouses, farm-to-table restaurants

Home to
Brooklyn Museum, Smorgasburg, Dumbo, Brooklyn Navy Yard, Coney Island

Experience
The hubbub of vintage treasure-trove Brooklyn Flea, before hitting food market Smorgasburg for snacks

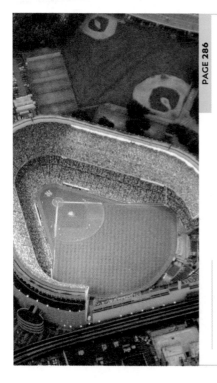

BEYOND THE CENTER

PAGE 286

There's more to New York than Manhattan and Brooklyn; there are, after all, five boroughs that comprise the city. Queens is the most multicultural part of the city, with a dynamic culinary scene, while the Bronx boasts beautiful parks, a world-class botanic garden, and the iconic Yankee Stadium. Even Staten Island, the "forgotten borough" and most suburban part of New York, features a fascinating colonial village and a captivating Tibetan gallery, and more history can be found in Upper Manhattan. Turn to p286 for more about Beyond the Center.

Best for
Immigrant New York, authentic cuisines, contemporary and medieval art, baseball

Home to
The Cloisters, New York Botanical Garden, Noguchi Museum, Yankee Stadium

Experience
Life as a real New Yorker, outside of Manhattan

←

① Pedestrians outside the Stock Exchange

② A ferry nears the Statue of Liberty in New York City's harbor

③ Enjoying the view from Battery Park

④ A performance of Broadway musical *Wicked*

New York City is bursting at the seams with unmissable sights, diverse cuisines, and truly unique experiences. These itineraries will help you make the most of your visit to the magnificent metropolis.

24 HOURS

Morning

Both historic and symbolic, Liberty and Ellis islands are the best introduction to any visit to New York City. Rise early and head down to Battery Park (p84) to book the 8:30am ferry to the Statue of Liberty (p68), the city's enduring symbol of freedom. On arrival, purchase a "pedestal access" ticket, which gives entry to the museum and viewing deck at the base of the statue (skip the walk up to the crown – it's not worth the extra time, and there's much more to do today). Continue on to Ellis Island (p70), where more than 100 million Americans can trace their roots. The Ellis Island Café is fine for a quick, basic lunch but, if you can hold out, we recommend returning to Battery Park on the ferry and heading for Pier A Harbor House (p81). Next to the ferry dock, this place has fabulous views from the outdoor deck and serves excellent oysters and refreshing craft beers.

Afternoon

From Battery Park it's a relatively short walk up Broadway to historic Trinity Church (p79). Be sure to pay your respects at the tomb of Alexander Hamilton in the cemetery outside here. Wall Street (p88) runs east toward the East River from the church and is lined with jaw-dropping, limestone skyscrapers the whole way. Check out the exterior of the world-famous New York Stock Exchange and the statue of George Washington in front of Federal Hall (p78) before jumping on the #6 subway train and heading uptown. Get off at 33rd Street and stroll over to the city's most iconic skyscraper, the Empire State Building (p164). Provided the weather isn't especially bad, the views from the observation deck on the 86th floor are worth the wait. From here, continue on to the 34 St-Herald Square station and proceed to Times Square (p180). Soak up the frenetic scene here before grabbing a pre-theater dinner at Sardi's (www.sardis.com) or Junior's (www.juniorscheesecake.com).

Evening

Enjoy a classic Broadway musical (if you booked tickets in advance), or catch a play in one of the buzzing theaters around Times Square. After the show, jump in a cab or take the #1 subway train down to Christopher St station for dessert and late-night drinks in Greenwich Village (p157).

$\longrightarrow$

① Morning in Central Park

② Artisan cheese sold at
Eataly NYC Downtown

③ The reflective pools of National
September 11 Memorial, overlooked
by One World Trade Center

④ Walkers enjoy the elevated
High Line at dusk

2 DAYS

Day 1

Morning Start your day with a take-away bagel and coffee in Central Park (p238). Try to arrive at the Met (p220) by opening time at 10am (from the southern end of the park, on 59th St, it takes around 40 minutes to walk to the museum). You could spend days marveling at the wonders inside the Met, but focus on the highlights over 2–3 hours; we suggest the European paintings section, plus the Temple of Dendur.

Afternoon Grab a cab or bus on Madison Avenue down to Grand Central (p188) for a quick seafood lunch at the Oyster Bar. From here walk (or take a bus) down to the Empire State Building (p164), to soak up the Art Deco splendor and those magnificent views. If you still have energy left, it's a 15-minute ride on bus #M34 to Hudson Yards and the northern end of the High Line (p166), which makes for a lovely stroll in the late afternoon or early evening light.

Evening Have dinner in the Meatpacking District (p131), at the southern end of the High Line.

Day 2

Morning Grab your camera and jump on a narrated cruise from the Seaport District's Pier 16 (p84) around Liberty and Ellis islands. Afterward, walk or take a cab across to the National September 11 Memorial (p72), taking in the waterfalls and tranquil groves of oak.

Afternoon Have lunch at Eataly NYC Downtown, over in 4 World Trade Center, before walking down Broadway to Wall Street and the Stock Exchange (p88). From Pier 11, where Wall Street meets the East River, take the ferry across to the Fulton Ferry District (p278) in Brooklyn. Grab an ice cream and enjoy wandering the streets of this historic district before strolling back across the Brooklyn Bridge for unmissable views of Manhattan (p272).

Evening From the bridge it's a short walk to Chinatown (p109), where tasty dinners await at Joe's Shanghai. Night owls should continue on to SoHo for evening drinks in one of the neighborhood's fashionable bars (p118).

←

1 Spectacular interior of the Oculus

2 The Guggenheim

3 Breakfast in SoHo

4 Drinkers unwind in Willamsburg, looking over Manhattan

5 DAYS

Day 1

Morning Reserve the first ferry to the Statue of Liberty *(p68)*; once you've admired the iconic statue up close, head back to Battery Park and spend some time at the National September 11 Memorial and Museum *(p72)*.

Afternoon Buy lunch at Le District food hall before strolling through the Oculus to St. Paul's Chapel. Visit Trinity Church *(see p79)* and Wall Street, continuing to Seaport District NYC *(p86)* for some retail therapy.

Evening Stay in Seaport District NYC for aperitifs and then grab dinner in nearby Chinatown *(p109)*.

Day 2

Morning Have breakfast in the Meatpacking District before walking the High Line *(p166)*. At 34th St take a cab or bus across to the Empire State Building *(p164)*, where you can grab a snack on the observation deck.

Afternoon Keep most of the afternoon free for modern art haven MoMA *(p202)* – it's worth reserving tickets to the museum ahead of time to beat the lines.

Evening Aim to hit Times Square *(p180)* as it's getting dark, and the neon lights are particularly spectacular, before ending the day with a Broadway show.

Day 3

Morning Get to the Met *(p220)* right on opening time and focus on just one or two sections, as there's so much to see here. Have lunch at one of the museum's enticing cafés.

Afternoon Wander up to the striking Guggenheim Museum *(p218)* for another hour or so, before heading into Central Park *(p238)* for some fresh air. Grab a snack at the Loeb Boathouse, pay your respects to John Lennon at Strawberry Fields, and stroll toward the Sheep Meadow, where New Yorkers relax on the grass.

Evening Catch an opera, musical performance, or ballet at the Lincoln Center *(p244)*. The excellent restaurants here are perfect for dinner, but try to reserve ahead.

Day 4

Morning Breakfast in SoHo, before walking up to Greenwich Village (follow the route on p136). Take a break and soak up the scene in Washington Square Park *(p134)*.

Afternoon For lunch, head down to Little Italy or Nolita *(p110)* before joining a tour at the historic Lower East Side Tenement Museum *(p94)*. The Museum at Eldridge Street *(p96)* is also worth a look if you have the time (and energy).

Evening Stay in the Lower East Side for dinner and drinks in Ivan Ramen or Mission Chinese Food.

Day 5

Morning Begin the day with a stroll across the Brooklyn Bridge *(p272)*. Stop at the Fulton Ferry District *(p284)* for refreshments before exploring Brooklyn Bridge Park *(p280)*, along the waterfront.

Afternoon Have lunch at Fornino At Pier 6 (www.fornino.com). From here it's an easy hike up to Brooklyn Heights, where you can follow our walking tour *(p228)*. Continue on to trendy Dumbo *(p278)* for the art galleries or a performance at St. Ann's Warehouse.

Evening To end the perfect day in Brooklyn, grab a taxi up to Williamsburg *(p279)* and sample its justly celebrated nightlife.

The New York Deli

A city institution, the deli was traditionally a Jewish affair. Find smoked fish and bagels at Zabar's *(p247)* and Russ & Daughters (179 East Houston St). Katz's Deli is famed for its giant pastrami sandwiches (205 East Houston St). Alleva Dairy (188 Grand St) is a classic Italian deli, while Brooklyn's Sahadi's (187 Atlantic Av,) is a Middle Eastern specialist.

$\leftarrow$

Salami and pickles galore at Katz's Deli in the Lower East Side

NEW YORK CITY FOR
FOODIES

Foodies are in for a treat in New York. Just about every type of cuisine is showcased here, from Colombian and Armenian to Korean and Senegalese, with prices ranging from $1 pizza slices to some of the world's most expensive and prestigious French gourmet and farm-to-table restaurants.

BRUNCH IN NYC

Sunday brunch is a big deal in New York. Special brunch menus (which sometimes include booze) attract long lines at the most popular spots; traditionally in Greenwich Village, Soho, and the Lower East Side, but now just as prevalent in Brooklyn. Carroll Gardens, Cobble Hill, and Williamsburg are especially busy. Reserve a table in advance to avoid disappointment.

America's Fine Dining Capital

Looking to splash out? Thomas Keller's Per Se *(p245)* is always top of a long list of award-winning restaurants, while Eric Ripert's Le Bernardin *(p183)* has three Michelin stars. Chef's Table at Brooklyn Fare (431 West 37th St) and Eleven Madison Park *(p157)* are part of a newer wave of fine dining options.

$\rightarrow$

Irresistible desserts at Le Bernardin, Midtown West and the Theater District

↑ Drinkers and diners at Dekalb Market Hall in Brooklyn

The New York Food Hall

With the success of Eataly *(p154)* and Brooklyn food fair Smorgasburg *(p282)*, gourmet food halls are all the rage in New York. Le District *(p80)* has a French theme, while Great Northern Food Hall in Grand Central Terminal is Scandinavian *(p193)*, and Plaza Food Hall (1 West 59th St) is upscale. Dekalb Market Hall (445 Albee Sq West, Brooklyn) offers everything from dumplings and sushi, to pastrami sandwiches and key lime pie.

💬 INSIDER TIP
Food Tours

Food walking tours are a great way to see the city and fuel up in the process. Top tours include NoshWalks (www.noshwalks.com), and Scott's Pizza Tours (www.scottspizza tours.com).

American Icons

Lombardi's *(p110)*, founded in 1905, was America's first pizzeria, but Patsy's *(p263)* sold the first pizza slice in 1933. Polish-Jewish Nathan Handwerker popularized Coney Island's hot dog, now sold at Nathan's Famous (1310 Surf Av), while German émigré Arnold Reuben invented New York-style cheesecake, best sampled at Junior's *(p282)*. New icon on the block, Dominique Ansel's 'cronut' (croissant-donut pastry) is sold at 189 Spring St.

↑ Nathan's Famous and cronuts *(inset)*, old and new American icons

Parks

New York is home to a number of gorgeous green spaces, ideal for whiling away a morning, afternoon, or entire day. The High Line (p166) and Central Park (p238) are both free and two of the best parks in America. There's also Bryant Park (p184), Washington Square Park (p134), Tompkins Square Park (p142), and Prospect Park (p282).

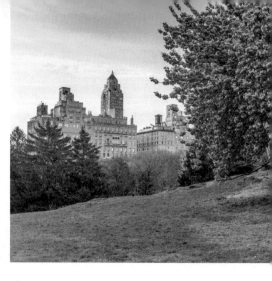

→

A wealth of stunning green spaces awaits in Central Park

NEW YORK CITY ON A
SHOESTRING

New York can be a very expensive place to visit but, with a bit of planning, savvy visitors can find plenty of free or less costly experiences, ranging from free museums to free performances, parks, and art galleries.

PICNICS

An affordable way to enjoy the sights and flavors of the city is with a picnic. Grab all the food you need at Zabar's (p247), one of the best delis in the city, and head for the Great Lawn in Central Park (p238). There's also Governors Island, which shouldn't be missed (p76). Bring sandwiches with you, or buy take-out treats from the food stalls on the island. For a seaside picnic, make for Coney Island (p283). Load up with Eastern European snacks at Brighton Bazaar (1007 Brighton Beach Av), or grab hot dogs at Nathan's Famous (p31).

Brooklyn Brewery Tours

New York's premier micro-brewer offers free tours at 7 & 8pm Fridays; on the half hour from 12:30–6pm Saturdays; and on the half hour from 12:30–4pm Sundays. Tastings aren't part of the free tour, but tokens can be bought without breaking the bank (p279).

Brooklyn Brewery, offering insightful free tours ↑

Free Museums

The American Museum of Natural History *(p242)* is always "pay-what-you-wish," but almost every museum in New York has one day (or evening) where you can do the same. Entirely free museums include African Burial Ground; American Folk Art Museum; The Bronx Museum of the Arts; Hamilton Grange; Museum at FIT; Museum of Reclaimed Urban Space; National Museum of the American Indian; the Schomburg Center; and Theodore Roosevelt Birthplace.

← The American Museum of Natural History is free and great for families

TOP 7 WHAT'S FREE AND WHEN?

Monday
Museum at Eldridge Street (all day)

Tuesday
National September 11 Memorial Museum (4–8pm)

Wednesday
Frick Collection (2–6pm); Museum of Jewish Heritage (4–8pm)

Thursday
Museum of Arts and Design (6–9pm)

Friday
Asia Society (6–9pm); MoMA (4–8pm); Historic Historic Richmond Town (1–5pm)

Saturday
Jewish Museum (all day)

Sunday
New York Hall of Science (10–11am); Studio Museum in Harlem (all day)

Chelsea Art Galleries

It costs nothing to wander around the art galleries of Chelsea, home to some of the world's most cutting-edge contemporary art *(p171)*. Consider combining these wonderful galleries with a day on the High Line *(p166)*, which is completely free and a New York must see, for an affordable day in the city. Be aware that Saturdays can prove very busy.

↑ Chelsea art galleries, home to innovative modern art and design

Contemporary NYC

The High Line *(p166)* has sparked a frenzy of innovative building along its borders: Frank Gehry's IAC Building (2007), the 2015 Whitney museum by Renzo Piano *(p128)*, and Zaha Hadid's 520 West 28th (2017) to name a few. One World Trade Center topped out as the city's tallest building in 2014 *(p74)*, sparking a new bout of "supertall" skyscrapers.

$\rightarrow$
IAC Building
by Frank Gehry,
illuminated at dusk

NEW YORK CITY'S
ARCHITECTURE

Skyscrapers aside, New York is a true architectural showcase – all the significant and influential movements of the last two centuries are represented in the city's magnificent structural landmarks.

The Glory Years

Architects began to design Art Deco sky-scrapers in the 1920s *(p87)*. Some of the city's most impressive structures – such as 1 Wall Street (1931), 70 Pine Street (1930), and the Chrysler Building (1930) – went up just after the 1929 Wall Street Crash. The Rockefeller Center complex *(p176)*, which was worked on throughout the 1930s, is perhaps the zenith of Art Deco style in New York.

↑ Stunning Art Deco skyscraper, the Chrysler Building

The 1950s and 1960s

The Modernist style (the arrival of European architectural movements like Bauhaus and Le Corbusier) influenced the glass-curtain-wall buildings of Mies van der Rohe: the 1950 United Nations *(p190)*, 1952 Lever House *(p211)*, and the 1958 Seagram Building *(p210)*, all in Midtown. This style culminated, perhaps most famously, in the now-destroyed Twin Towers of the World Trade Center (1973).

←

The Secretariat Building within the United Nations complex

The attractive and uniquely shaped Flatiron Building ↓

TOP 6 NEIGHBOR-HOODS FOR BROWNSTONES

Greenwich Village
The Village is home to quiet mews, handsome rowhouses, and elegant apartment blocks.

Upper West Side
Classic brownstones with bay windows can be found at Riverside Drive, between 80th and 81st streets.

Harlem
Some of the most beautiful residential architecture in the city, best exemplified by Strivers' Row.

Brooklyn Heights
Features a wide range of styles, from early Federal rowhouses to large Neo-Romanesque and Neo-Gothic villas.

Fort Greene, Brooklyn
Gorgeous and leafy residential streets, especially South Portland Avenue.

Park Slope, Brooklyn
Some of the finest Romanesque and Queen Anne residences in the U.S. (built in the 1880s and 1890s).

From Cast-Iron to Beaux Arts

It was the advent of cast-iron constructions in the mid-19th century that really thrust New York City to the forefront of architectural sophistication. The 1902 Flatiron Building *(p156)* is regarded as one of the city's first real skyscraper, while the 1913 Woolworth Building *(p87)*, with its decorative Gothic spires and gargoyles, continued the upward trend. The era's Beaux Arts architecture culminated in the 1902 Metropolitan Museum of Art *(p220)*, 1911 New York Public Library *(p178)*, and 1919 Grand Central Terminal *(p188)*.

→

1

2

MANHATTAN'S SKYLINE

The world's most famous skyline is constantly changing. Since the first skyscrapers went up in the 1890s, buildings have become ever taller with the latest boom in 'supertalls' set to make the biggest transformation of New York City since the 1930s. Manhattan has two key clusters of skyscrapers – in Lower Manhattan (sometimes referred to as the Financial District) and Midtown – and its skyline comprises over 260 buildings that reach higher than 500 ft (152 m). Though structures began topping the 300-ft (91-m) mark in the 1890s, the first major skyscraper was the Woolworth Building at 792 ft (241 m), completed in 1913 (p87). These first towers were sheer vertical monoliths, with no regard to how neighboring buildings were affected. Authorities later invented "air rights," a concept limiting a building's height before it had to be set back from its base.

MANHATTAN'S SUPERTALLS

Supertalls are a special class of skyscraper and Manhattan's skyline includes some of the world's most famous. As the name implies, supertalls are colossal in size, standing at over 1,000 ft (305 m), and they are naturally expensive to build. You can learn more supertalls and Manhattan's skyline at the Skyscraper Museum (p81).

One World Trade Center
At 1,776 ft (541 m), this symbolic tower became America's tallest skyscraper on completion in 2013.

Three World Trade Center
This 1,079 ft (329 m) tower topped out in 2016.

Brookfield Place
This office and shopping complex comprises several buildings, the tallest of which reaches 739 ft (225 m).

3

Manhattan's skyline

For the best views of Manhattan's skyline, head to the Top of the Rock *(p176)*, The Hills at Governors Island *(p76)*, the top of the Empire State Building *(p164)*, Roosevelt Island *(p211)*, Brooklyn Bridge Park *(p280)*, or ride the Staten Island Ferry *(p86)*.

 Battery Park, overlooked by 17 State Street.

2 Rebuilt from 1921 to 1928, 26 Broadway was designed to resemble a giant oil lamp.

3 One World Trade Center, an example of Manhattan's evolving skyline, looms large over the city streets.

↓ Manhattan's southern tip as seen from the Hudson River

Woolworth Building
The handsomely decorated "cathedral of commerce," is 792 ft (241 m) tall.

One Wall Street
Art-Deco skyscraper, at 927-ft (282-m), and completed in 1931.

17 State Street
This 541-ft (164-m) building has a distinct curved-glass facade.

26 Broadway
Formerly the Standard Oil Building, 26 Broadway stands at 520 ft (158 m).

One Liberty Plaza
Replacing the former Singer Building, which was the tallest structure ever dismantled, this skyscraper is 743 ft (226 m) tall.

Frick Collection

Henry Clay Frick's personal art collection, displayed in his mansion on the Upper East Side *(p224)*, contains some real gems, not least Holbein's infamous portraits of one-time rivals Thomas More and Thomas Cromwell. Vermeer's *Officer and Laughing Girl*, Bellini's sublime *St Francis in the Desert*, and Rembrandt's enigmatic *Polish Rider* are also on display here.

←

The stunning Garden Court, in the center of the Frick Collection building

NEW YORK CITY FOR
ART LOVERS

New York remains at the center of the global art market, with hundreds of dealers and galleries, illustrious auction houses like Christie's and Sotheby's, and high-profile art colleges attracting some of the best talent in the world. Perhaps best of all is the city's dynamic public art programme.

TOP 5 NEW YORK ARTISTS

Jean-Michel Basquiat (1960-88)
Street artist whose work can sell for $110 million.

Keith Haring (1958-90)
Graffiti mural artist.

Jeff Koons (1955-)
Pop artist known for his steel balloon animals.

Florine Stettheimer (1871-1944)
Ground-breaking painter and art patron.

Andy Warhol (1928-87)
Iconic pop artist.

The Guggenheim

Though Frank Lloyd Wright's seminal building often overshadows the changing exhibitions inside, the Guggenheim contains an exceptional Kandinsky collection, as well as paintings by Picasso, Van Gogh, Monet, and Cézanne *(p218)*.

The striking tiered exterior of the Guggenheim
↓

MOMA

Some of the world's most iconic artwork is preserved here at the Museum of Modern Art, or MoMA for short *(p202)*. From Dali's *The Persistence of Memory* and Van Gogh's *The Starry Night*, to *Dance* by Matisse and *Les Demoiselles d'Avignon* by Picasso, this modern art giant is a must see.

💬 INSIDER TIP
Street art tours

Pioneer graffiti artists started "tagging" in the late 1960s. Graff Tours (www.grafftours. com) and Brooklyn Unplugged (www. brooklynunplugged tours.com) offer highly rated street art tours.

↑ *The Starry Night* (1889), by Vincent Van Gogh, housed at MoMA

The Whitney

At the foot of the High Line, this is New York's premier showcase for modern and contemporary American art *(p218)*. The permanent collection is especially rich in works by Alexander Calder, Jasper Johns, Reginald Marsh, Georgia O'Keeffe, Claes Oldenburg, and Cindy Sherman.

←
The Whitney Museum of American Art, designed by Renzo Piano

The Met

New York's grand dame of art holds massive collections spanning over 5,000 years of world history *(p220)*. Everything from Duccio's priceless *Madonna and Child*, to a ton of French Impressionism and modern work by Clyfford Still, Andy Warhol, and Chuck Close.

→
Water Lilies (1916–19), by Claude Monet, on display at The Met

◁ Museum of the Moving Image

The Museum of the Moving Image in Queens *(p301)* has a popular permanent exhibit relating to all things Muppet-related. More than 300 artifacts are on view, including 47 actual Muppets. Older kids will enjoy the exhibits on film-making, television, and the latest in digital art.

▷ Childrens' Museums

New York is well served by interactive museums dedicated to children. The Children's Museum of Manhattan *(p246)* is packed with toys and games, while the Children's Museum of the Arts *(p118)* encourages kids to get creative with hands-on exhibits. Brooklyn Children's Museum *(p280)* features a fun "block lab", sensory room and special play areas for kids under 6 years.

NEW YORK CITY FOR
FAMILIES

New York is a wonderland for children. From colorful Broadway musicals and thrilling ferry rides, to cavernous stores and expansive green spaces – the Big Apple has something for kids of all ages.

◁ American Museum of Natural History

The city's most popular family destination *(p242)*. Giant dinosaur skeletons, a butterfly conservatory, a simulated African rainforest, 3D IMAX theaters and a massive planetarium await, along with special exhibitions. Head to nearby Central Park afterwards to let off steam.

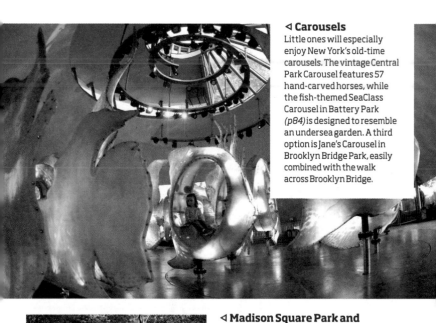

◁ Carousels

Little ones will especially enjoy New York's old-time carousels. The vintage Central Park Carousel features 57 hand-carved horses, while the fish-themed SeaClass Carousel in Battery Park *(p84)* is designed to resemble an undersea garden. A third option is Jane's Carousel in Brooklyn Bridge Park, easily combined with the walk across Brooklyn Bridge.

◁ Madison Square Park and Shake Shack

There's always something happening in Madison Square Park in the summer, from outdoor yoga classes to huge installations of public art. It's also well known for hosting the original Shake Shack burger hut. Grab some Shackburgers, cheese fries, and chocolate frozen custards, and enjoy them in the park.

△ Cycling, Skating or Boating in Central Park

Central Park is fun to tour by bike - pick up some wheels at Bike and Roll *(p240)*. In summer, the Lasker Pool is a great place to swim, while rowboats are available from the Loeb Boathouse *(p241)*. In winter, the Wollman Rink and Lasker Rink both offer ice-skating (and skate rentals).

EAT

Big Daddy's
Brightly colored diner.
◉ E7 ⌂ 239 Park Av S
ⓦ bigdaddysnyc.com

⑤⑤⑤

Bubby's
Great for big breakfasts.
◉ C8 ⌂ 73 Gansevoort St ⓦ bubbys.com

⑤⑤⑤

Ellen's Stardust Diner
Singing wait staff.
◉ D3 ⌂ 1650 Broadway ⓦ ellensstardustdiner. com

⑤⑤⑤

Markets

The weekend Brooklyn Flea (p279) has become the doyen of New York markets, packed with hundreds of furniture, vintage clothing, arts, and antiques stalls. In Manhattan, Chelsea Flea Market features up to 135 vendors, with Hell's Kitchen Flea Market and GreenFlea Market even bigger. The largest farmers' market is at Union Square (p157). Seasonal markets also appear.

←

Fresh produce and flowers at Greenmarket in Union Square

NEW YORK CITY FOR
SHOPPERS

Shops are one of New York's killer attractions, and the city is the undisputed commercial capital of America. Here you'll find flagship stores for every major brand, local boutiques, street markets, and vintage stores, plus the country's most famous department stores – Bloomingdale's and Sak's.

SHOPPING IN SOHO

SoHo is Manhattan's prime clothes-shopping neighborhood, centering on Broadway and Spring St. Popular and affordable brands including Uniqlo, Forever 21, H&M, Nike, Victoria's Secret, and Topshop all have giant emporiums here. High-end designers such as the likes of Marc Jacobs, Balenciaga, Stella McCartney, Paul Smith, Louis Vuitton, and Christian Dior also have boutiques on the side streets here. Aim to shop in SoHo on a weekday if possible as it gets unbearably crowded on weekends.

Department Stores

Bloomingdale's is perhaps New York's most famous department store, though Macy's (p169) is certainly larger (and cheaper). Barneys, Bergdorf Goodman, and Saks Fifth Avenue are all up-scale department stores, famed for their designer fashions and lavish window displays (p208).

Luxury brands

Audrey Hepburn's favorite in *Breakfast at Tiffany's*, Tiffany & Co *(p208)* is still a palace of diamond jewelry. New York designers with flagship stores include Alexander Wang (103 Grand St), Marc Jacobs (113 Prince St), and Vera Wang (991 Madison Av). Prada's lavish store at 575 Broadway is a trend-setter in SoHo, while TV series *Sex and the City* sparked the demand for luxury shoe designers Louboutin (967 Madison Av), and Manolo Blahnik (31 West 54th St).

→

Manolo Blahnik, a New York City landmark to fashionistas

Books and Comics

The Strand *(p147)* is the place for cheap books. In Brooklyn, try indie WORD (126 Franklin St) and Housing Works (126 Crosby St) for second-hand books. Look to St. Mark's Comics *(p147)* or Forbidden Planet (832 Broadway) for comics and Bluestockings (172 Allen St) for LGBT books.

Storefront of Forbidden Planet, a haven for comic fans

Vintage and Thrift Stores

In Brooklyn, head to Beacon's Closet *(p279)*, Amarcord (223 Bedford Av), or Domsey Express (431 Broadway). Across in Manhattan, try Edith Machinist (104 Rivington St), Michael's Consignment (1041 Madison Av), or Resurrection (45 Great Jones St).

→

Vintage treasure trove Beacon's Closet, in Greenpoint, Brooklyn

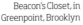

▷ Cheer on the Knicks at Madison Square Garden

The New York Knicks remain a fanatically supported basketball team (with the likes of Spike Lee, Alec Baldwin, and Howard Stern in regular attendence), despite a comically long run of poor form. Games at Madison Square Garden *(p169)* are quite the spectacle, with plenty of music, pageantry, and tasty snacks on offer.

◁ Play Ping Pong

Susan Sarandon is a co-owner (and often appears at) SPiN (48 East 23rd St), a sprawling ping pong club with 19 tables and a restaurant. Open till 2am on weekends, this is more like a lounge bar than a sports club, with high-quality cocktails and snacks.

SPORTING
NEW YORK CITY

New York is one of America's great sports cities, home to iconic teams like the Knicks (basketball) and the Yankees and the Mets (baseball). You can get moving yourself; many of the city's activities are free or surprisingly cheap.

◁ Catch a Baseball Game at Yankee Stadium

Cheering for the most successful baseball team in America is a summer tradition, accompanied by hot dogs and cold beers. Established in 1913, the Yankees have won 27 World Series championships; watch the team yourself.

▷ Cycle in the Park

New York has become a lot more bike-friendly lately. Bike lanes run almost the whole length of Manhattan along the Hudson River, and criss-cross Central Park; both places offer cool breezes and gorgeous views in summer. Check out our list of bike rentals for Central Park *(p240)*, or utilize the Citi Bike bike-share scheme (www.citibikenyc.com).

◁ Go Kayaking on the Hudson River

Kayaking on the Hudson River is a popular and surprisingly tranquil activity, especially in summer, and gives a totally new perspective of New York's famous skyline. Kayaking at the Downtown Boathouse, at Pier 26, is free mid-May to mid-October. The Manhattan Kayak Company at Pier 84, meanwhile, offers lessons and stand-up paddle boarding.

INSIDER TIP
Game tickets

The easiest tickets to get are summer games at Yankee Stadium ($25 for bleachers); buy online or on-the-day. For basketball, it's easiest to see the Brooklyn Nets at the Barclays Center.

▷ Don a Pair of Ice Skates

From November to March, the city opens its outdoor ice rinks. It's hard to beat the magical views from the Lasker and Wollman rinks in Central Park *(p241)*, or the beatiful rink at Rockefeller Center *(p176)*. Seasonal rinks also pop-up at the Standard High Line hotel, and at Bryant Park (which is free).

◁ The Cloisters Museum

It's worth trekking up to the northern end of Manhattan to view the Met's collection of medieval tapestries, paintings, and sculpture. Perched high above the Hudson, with portions of five (real) medieval cloisters incorporated into the structure, it's easy to believe you've left North America altogether (p290).

▷ Hispanic Society, Washington Heights

With its dimly lit main gallery shimmering with the rosy hues of an Andalucían palace, the society owns one of the largest collections of Hispanic art outside Spain. Highlights include Goya's imperious portrait of the Duchess of Alba, and the monumental mural cycle "Vision of Spain," by Joaquín Sorolla y Bastida (p292).

OFF THE
BEATEN PATH

With so many world-famous sights in New York, it can be easy to overlook the city's lesser-visited gems. If here for a longer stay, or visiting for the second or third time, seek out these off-the-beaten track highlights.

◁ Green-Wood Cemetery, Brooklyn

In the 19th-century, Green-Wood Cemetery was the place New York's movers and shakers chose to be buried. Today, the beautifully landscaped site can be toured individually or with guides, taking in the tombs of newspaper editor Horace Greeley, famed preacher Henry Ward Beecher, glass-maker Louis Comfort Tiffany, and composer Leonard Bernstein (p283).

◁ The Rockaways, Queens

Surfing in New York? It's possible in the Rockaways, with a long stretch of lovely sand easily accessible by subway. The beach at Jacob Riis Park is generally tranquil and pristine, though things get lively during the summertime at Riis Park Beach Bazaar, which features live bands and a food market (www.riisparkbeachbazaar.com).

◁ The Jacques Marchais Museum of Tibetan Art, Staten Island

This museum is the most unlikely treasure in New York, clinging to the Staten Island hills like an ancient Tibetan monastery. Founded in the 1940s by Jacques Marchais, a successful art dealer, the complex is full of rare Tibetan artwork, including delicate, colorful prayer flags. This unique museum, which holds the most Tibeten art outside of China, is well worth the excursion (p302).

MICRO-BREWERIES

Some of the city's most highly-prized craft beers come from the outer boroughs, where most of the small-batch producers have tap rooms for sampling brews. Visit the Bronx Brewery (856 East 136th St, Port Morris), or Finback Brewery (7801 77th Av, Ridgewood) and SingleCut Beersmiths (19-33 37th St, Astoria) in Queens. In Brooklyn, Other Half Brewing (195 Centre St, Carroll Gardens) and Threes Brewing (333 Douglass St, Gowanus) compete with Brooklyn Brewery (p279).

△ Greenpoint, Brooklyn

New York's biggest Polish community retains plenty of character. *Kielbasa* and *pierogi* sellers like Polka Dot (726 Manhattan Av) are clustered along the main drag, Manhattan Avenue. Hip Danish brewpub Torst (615 Manhattan Av), and cozy Café Grumpy at 193 Meserole Av (which featured in TV show *Girls*), symbolize the new artsy side of the neighborhood (p279).

On the trail of George Washington

George Washington (1732–99) was a Virginian, but he spent many crucial years in New York during the Revolutionary War. The General requisitioned Morris-Jumel Mansion (p292) in 1776 as army headquarters, returning to the city and Fraunces Tavern (p85) in 1783 to bid farewell to his troops. The Washington Statue outside Federal Hall (p78) commemorates the president's inauguration here in 1789, while his pew is preserved, shrine-like, at St. Paul's Chapel (p80).

→

George Washington's statue standing outside Federal Hall

NEW YORK CITY FOR
HISTORY BUFFS

New York was officially founded by the Dutch (as "New Amsterdam") in 1625, and numerous reminders of the city's relatively short history remain, from old synagogues and churches, to crumbling forts, fine mansions and a host of specialist museums.

 TOP 5 BEST HISTORY MUSEUMS

Museum of the City of New York
The city's history (p231).

New York Historical Society
Changing exhibits on New York themes (p246).

National Museum of the American Indian
A million artifacts are housed here (p85).

Museum of Chinese in America
The Chinese experience since the 1700s (p108).

Italian American Museum
Focuses on the history of Little Italy (p111).

Jewish History

Jewish culture is a key component of New York's identity. The restored synagogue at the Museum at Eldridge Street (p96) is a good introduction to Jewish life in the Lower East Side, where food tours and synagogue tours can enhance the experience. For a fuller understanding of Jewish history, visit the Museum of Jewish Heritage (p81) and the Jewish Museum (p225). The still active Temple Emanu-El (p226) is one of the largest synagogues in the world.

The stunning interior of the Museum at Eldridge Street ↑

African-American History

Colonial New York City was largely built by African-American slaves, remembered at the African Burial Ground in Lower Manhattan (p87). Harlem remains the most famous black community in America, and its legacy is preserved at the likes of the Schomburg Center (p256), Apollo Theater (p264), Studio Museum in Harlem (p262), and Langston Hughes House (p259). Across in Queens, the Louis Armstrong House Museum (p300) commemorates the legendary jazzman and trumpeter, who lived here with his wife for almost three decades.

← The monument at the African Burial Ground, in Lower Manhattan

FOLLOW IN THE FOOTSTEPS OF NEW YORK CITY'S FOUNDING FATHER

Alexander Hamilton (c. 1755-1804) was born on the island of Nevis, in the British West Indies, but spent most of his adult life in New York. His role as first Secretary of the Treasury is commemorated at the Museum of American Finance (p78). His last home, Hamilton Grange (p258), is preserved north of Harlem, while his tomb lies in Trinity Church cemetery (p79). The 2015 smash-hit musical *Hamilton*, written by Lin-Manuel Miranda, shows at the Richard Rodgers Theatre. Tickets are pricey and competitive; try www.hamilton musical.com/lottery.

Immigrant History

Immigrants have always played a crucial role in the history of New York. The enlightening museum on Ellis Island (p70), which served as an inspection station from 1892 until 1954, provides the best introduction. The story continues at the Lower East Side Tenement Museum (p94), where a restored tenement shows how newly arrived immigrants lived and worked.

↑ Photograph showing a slum on East Broadway, c. 1900, where immigrants lived in close quarters

→
Led Zeppelin tribute
concert at prestigious
Carnegie Hall

NEW YORK CITY
LIVE!

Although the glittering lights of Broadway are mesmerizing, New York offers countless forms of live entertainment across the city – from music and comedy, to live TV recordings. Better still, there's something to suit every budget, from lavish concerts at Carnegie Hall to free jazz nights.

Comedy Clubs
New York's comedy clubs often feature stand-up artists you'll recognize, with shows every night. Carolines on Broadway (1626 Broadway) is one of the most famous, while Comic Strip Live (1568 2nd Av) has been around since 1975, and Dangerfield's (1118 1st Av) was founded in 1969. The Gotham Comedy Club (208 W 23rd St) has appeared in many shows and movies.

Sydnee Washington
performs stand-up at ↑
Caroline's On Broadway

Music

You're spoiled for choice when it comes to live music in the Big Apple. Arlene's Grocery (95 Stanton St) offers grungy rock and punk at its Lower East Side venue, which hosted bands such as The Strokes, Lady Gaga, and Arcade Fire in their early years. Prestigious Carnegie Hall *(p181)*, meanwhile, is New York's grande dame of concert venues, and primarily hosts classical music (and some pop concerts). New York is one of the cradles of jazz, with major venues such as the legendary Blue Note (131 West 3rd St) and Village Vanguard (178 7th Av) in Greenwhich Village, and Birdland (315 West 44th St) in Midtown, while Nuyorican Poets Café *(p173)*, in the East Village, is a Latino-oriented venue hosting live hip-hop, performance art, live poetry readings, and other theater performances.

← Live jazz performance at iconic Birdland in Midtown

💬 INSIDER TIP
Free live music

Arlene's Grocery has free punk karaoke with a live band on Mondays. Sidewalk Café, Saint Vitus, and Warsaw & Otto's Shrunken Head are free indie venues. Marjorie Eliot's has free jazz 3.30–6pm Sundays.

Live Late Night TV Show Tapings

To experience American TV up close, apply online for free tickets to be part of the "live audience" at shows taped in New York. Comedy Central's *Daily Show with Trevor Noah* is recorded at 733 11th Av, while the *Late Show with Stephen Colbert* tapes at 1697 Broadway. NBC rival *The Tonight Show with Jimmy Fallon* shows at 30 Rockefeller Plaza. *Late Night with Seth Meyers* is also taped here.

↑ Bryan Cranston with host Stephen Colbert on *The Late Show with Stephen Colbert*

Old-School Cocktails

Vintage cocktails can be enjoyed at Dead Rabbit (30 Water St), while the venerable 21 Club is the place for the "perfect Manhattan" *(p209)*. Maxfield Parrish murals adorn the King Cole Bar *(p210)*, the birthplace of the Bloody Mary, and Ludwig Bemelmans' drawings trim Bemelmans Bar *(p225)*. Black-and-white Bar Pléiades is a stylish homage to Chanel (p225).

→

A bartender mixes a cocktail in The St. Regis Hotel's King Cole Bar

NEW YORK CITY
COCKTAILS

New York is cocktail heaven. This is where the Bloody Mary and the Manhattan were invented, and the Cosmopolitan and Martini were perfected. You'll find "mixologists" everywhere plus a range of ritzy and romanic hangouts; the 21 Club is where Humphrey Bogart took Lauren Bacall on their first date.

Cocktails for Fashionistas

The Fashion Week crowd hang out at Paul's Casablanca *(p118)* and chic Paul's Cocktail Lounge in the Tribeca Grand Hotel (2 Sixth Av). The Standard High Line's (848 Washington St) Boom Boom Room and Top of the Standard are also feted. Apotheke (9 Doyers St) in Chinatown feels like an underground club, while Pegu Club *(p118)* perfected the "Gin-Gin Mule".

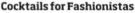

A tempting cocktail, prepared with a theatrical flourish ↑

The Japanese Connection

Japanese owned or themed cocktail bars, in the likes of Chinatown and the Lower East Side, often feature sleek, minimalist decor and sake-based cocktails. A fine example is relative newcomer Bar Goto (245 Eldridge St), while hard-to-find Angel's Share (8 Stuyvesant St) has been a candlelit and atmospheric haven since 1993 (tip: look for the unmarked door in Village Yokocho restaurant). Aside from sake, Decibel (240 East 9th St) also serves lychee martinis and "kamikaze" cocktails.

 ←

Chinatown and the Lower East Side both offer creative and exotic cocktails

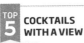

TOP 5 COCKTAILS WITH A VIEW

Loopy Doopy Rooftop Bar
Conrad New York, 102 North End Av; www.conradnyhotel.com

The Ides
Wythe Hotel, 80 Wythe Av, Williamsburg; www.wythehotel.com/the-ides

230 Fifth
230 5th Ave; www.230-fifth.com

Roof Garden Café
The Met, 1000 Fifth Av; www.metmuseum.org/visit/dining

Press Lounge
Ink48 Hotel, 653 11th Av; www.thepresslounge.com

The Speakeasy

The city that tried to ignore Prohibition has revived the "speakeasy," often with concealed entrances. Death & Co *(p143)* has bartenders in bow ties and braces, while a black door marks 124 Rabbit Club (124 Macdougal St). The Back Room (102 Norfolk St) serves cocktails in teacups.

↑ The Night in Tunisia cocktail at 1920's themed bar Death & Co, in the East Village

A YEAR IN
NEW YORK CITY

JANUARY

△ **New York Jewish Film Festival** *(mid–late Jan)*
Showcase of international films at the Lincoln Center exploring the Jewish experience.

FEBRUARY

△ **Westminster Kennel Club Dog Show** *(mid-Feb)*
Some 2,500 canines compete for rosettes and trophies, watched by puppy-dog-eyed fans, at Madison Square Garden.

MAY

△ **Sakura Matsuri** *(early May)* This festival entails events and performances celebrating traditional and contemporary Japanese culture beneath the blooming cherry trees of Brooklyn Botanic Garden.

JUNE

National Puerto Rican Day Parade *(second Sun)*
Some two million spectators gather to watch merrymakers parade along Fifth Av in celebration of all things Puerto Rican.

△ **Pride Week** *(mid-Jun)* New York's annual celebration of LGBTQ culture includes New York City Pride March along Fifth Av (from 37th St and ending at Greenwich St).

Mermaid Parade *(mid-Jun)* Participants dress like mermaids and sea creatures on Coney Island.

SEPTEMBER

△ **West Indian-American Day Parade and Carnival** *(first Mon)* With steel-drum bands providing an irresistible soundtrack, Brooklyn's largest parade takes place on Labor Day in Crown Heights.

Brooklyn Book Festival *(early Sep)* New York's City's largest free literary event can be found at Brooklyn Borough Hall.

Feast of San Gennaro *(ten days in mid-Sep)* The patron saint of Naples is honored with cannoli-eating contests, games, food markets, and a boisterous parade in Little Italy.

New York Film Festival *(late Sep–mid-Oct)* American films and international art films are screened at the Lincoln Center.

OCTOBER

New York Comic Con *(early Oct)* Fans of comics, graphic novels, anime, and manga converge in costume at Jacob K. Javits Convention Center.

Columbus Day Parade *(second Mon in Oct)* Along Fifth Av, this celebrates Italian-American heritage and Columbus's first sighting of America.

△ **Village Halloween Parade** *(Oct 31)* America's largest Halloween celebration, featuring spectacular costumes and giant puppets, takes place along Sixth Av (from Spring St to West 23rd St).

MARCH

△ **St. Patrick's Day Parade** (Mar 17)
Revelers continue to parade along Fifth Av
after Irish militiamen first marched on St.
Paddy's Day in 1762.

Easter Parade (Mar/Apr)
Hundreds of New Yorkers promenade up
Fifth Av (from 49th St to 57th St) in
elaborate, flower-bedecked Easter
bonnets on Easter Sunday.

APRIL

△ **Tribeca Film Festival** (late Apr)
Established by New Yorker Robert De
Niro, this ten-day event screens more
than 100 films from around the world at
Tribeca Film Center and local cinemas.

JULY

△ **Independence Day** (Jul 4) Massive firework
display above either the East River or Hudson
River – head to the waterfront for the best view.

AUGUST

△ **US Open** (last Mon in Aug/first Mon
in Sep) The world's best tennis players
compete at Flushing Meadows–Corona
Park, Queens.

NOVEMBER

△ **New York City Marathon** (first Sun in Nov)
Around 50,000 runners start on Staten Island
and run through all five boroughs.

Macy's Thanksgiving Day Parade (fourth Thu
of Nov) This famous parade sees colossal balloon
characters, spectacular floats, marching bands,
and an appearance from Santa – head for Central
Park West, from West 77th St to Columbus Circle,
and along Broadway down to Herald Square

Rockefeller Center Christmas Tree Lighting
(late Nov) The lighting of the Christmas tree that
overlooks the ice rink at the Rockefeller Center
officially begins the city's holiday season.

DECEMBER

△ **New Year's Eve in Times Square**
(Dec 31) Party-goers drink, dance, and
make merry before counting down the
annual ball drop in Times Square.

A BRIEF
HISTORY

The gateway to America for millions of immigrants, New York has always been a cosmopolitan port city where the only constant is change. Beginning with Dutch fur traders, it has morphed into a financial capital, home to iconic skyscrapers, and an arts scene that produced Beat poets, jazz, and hip-hop.

The Dutch and the British

New York was a forested wilderness populated by the Lenape people when the Dutch West India Company established a fur-trading post on Governors Island, in 1624. The following year the Dutch named their subsequent Manhattan outpost New Amsterdam; it had previously been called *Manna-Hata*, the Lenape word for "Island of the Hills." Peter Stuyvesant arrived in 1647 to bring order to the unruly colony, but in 1664 the Dutch let it fall to the British. They renamed it New York, in honor of Charles II's brother, the Duke of York.

1 New Amsterdam as it appeared in 1660. ↑

2 The Battle of Long Island, in Brooklyn, 1776.

3 Statue of George Washington outside the city's Federal Hall.

4 Manhattan's Times Square, photographed in 1917.

Timeline of events

1624
Dutch colony established on Governors Island.

1653
A wall is built for protection from possible invasions; the adjacent street is named Wall Street.

1664
Dutch surrender to the British, who rename the colony New York.

1776
Revolutionary war breaks out; fire destroys much of the city.

2

3

4

The Revolution

New York did not play a large role in the War of Independence. Citizens fled at the prospect of approaching war and, when battle began in the autumn of 1776, a quarter of troops lost their lives in a matter of days. Though George Washington was in command, the campaign was a disaster, ending with the occupation of the city by the British until 1783, at the conclusion of the war. Soon after, New York became the nation's capital. The seat of the federal government was transferred to Philadelphia a year later.

New York in the 19th Century

In 1825, the completion of the Erie Canal (running from the Hudson River to the Great Lakes) opened up internal trade and created a boom in New York. The first waves of immigrants began to arrive in the mid-19th century; some found prosperity, others crowded into slums in Lower Manhattan. When the Civil War broke out in 1861, New York sided with the Union (North) against the Confederates (South). In 1863, a conscription law provoked the draft riots, with impoverished New Yorkers burning buildings, looting shops, and lynching African-Americans.

ALEXANDER HAMILTON (C. 1755–1804)

Hamilton came to New York in 1772 and served under Washington in the Revolution. Later, as first Secretary of the Treasury, he set up the First Bank of the United States and the US Mint. He was killed in a duel. The musical *Hamilton* is based on his life.

1851
The New York Times first published.

1865
Abraham Lincoln lies in state in City Hall.

1886
The Statue of Liberty, a gift from the French people to America, is unveiled.

1835
"Great Fire of New York" destroys most of the buildings on the southern tip of Manhattan.

1863
Civil War Draft Riots, in which more than 1,000 people are killed.

The Gilded Age

New York's merchant princes grew ever wealthier after the Union won the Civil War, in 1865, and the city entered "The Gilded Age". Cornelius Vanderbilt controlled a vast shipping and railroad empire from here. J.P. Morgan, the banking mastermind, was instrumental in organizing giant financial mergers, and created the country's first major corporations. In 1898, New York City – formerly just Manhattan – assumed its current size by officially intergrating Brooklyn, Staten Island, Queens, and the Bronx.

Between the Wars

In the 1920s, the city entered the Jazz Age in spite of Prohibition, which was a constitutional ban on alcohol. The Harlem Renaissance was propelled by African-American writers like Langston Hughes and Zora Neale Hurston, and music from Duke Ellington, Cab Calloway, and Billie Holiday. The good times ended with the 1929 stock market crash and, as a result of this, the Great Depression. By 1932, one-quarter of New Yorkers were unemployed. With Mayor Fiorello La Guardia's 1933 election, New York began to recover and thrive.

**SHIRLEY CHISHOLM
(1924-2005)**

In 1968, Brooklynite Chisholm became the first African-American woman to be elected to Congress (serving the 12th district of New York). She was post-humously awarded the Presidential Medal of Freedom by Barack Obama, in 2015.

Timeline of events

1929
Wall Street Crash.

1964
Race riots in Harlem and Brooklyn.

1977
The city lights go out for 25 hours; city suffers looting and civil unrest.

2001
Terrorists attack the World Trade Center, causing the Twin Towers to collapse.

1989
David Dinkins becomes first black mayor of New York City.

Post-War New York City

New York became the world's cultural capital in the 1950s, with cutting-edge movements in art and poetry, while the 1960s saw the Stonewall Riots and birth of the Gay Rights Movement. A decade later, punk music developed in the East Village, and hip-hop emerged in the Bronx. In 1975, New York almost went bankrupt, and the tough times continued with the recession of 1989. New York elected Rudolph Giuliani in 1993 – the city's first Republican mayor in 28 years. Giuliani's finest hour came during America's darkest; on September 11, 2001, two hijacked planes crashed into the World Trade Center's Twin Towers.

New York City Today

The city's recovery after 9/11 has been impressive. New sky-scrapers grace the skyline, crime figures continue to fall, and tourist numbers are at their highest. This in spite of the financial crisis of 2008 and the flood waters of Hurricane Sandy in 2012. In 2013, Bill de Blasio became the first Democratic mayor in over 20 years, and he won a landslide re-election in 2017. Despite the growing economy, De Blasio faces an aging transportation infrastructure, unaffordable housing, and a homeless problem.

1 Jazz musician Duke Ellington, a key player in the Harlem Renaissance.

2 The Twin Towers of the World Trade Center after they were hit by two hijacked airliners, September 11, 2001.

3 An aid center set up in repsonse to Hurricane Sandy, 2012.

4 New York City Mayor Bill de Blasio being sworn into office by former U.S. President Bill Clinton, January 1, 2014.

2002

Billionaire Michael Bloomberg becomes mayor; he holds office for an unprecedented three terms.

2008

US mortgage crisis hits Wall Street.

2009

Captain "Sully" Sullenberger makes a miraculous emergency landing on the Hudson River.

2013

Bill de Blasio becomes the first Democratic mayor since 1993.

2016

Local property tycoon and political novice Donald Trump wins the U.S. presidential election.

← Harold Ramis, Dan Aykroyd, Ernie Hudson, and Bill Murray in *Ghostbusters*

A BRIEF HISTORY
ON SCREEN

Parts of New York can feel surprisingly familiar, even for first-time visitors. The city has served a backdrop for thousands of popular movies and TV shows since the 1930s, and it continues to play a starring role on screen.

From Marilyn Monroe's flying skirt in *The Seven Year Itch*, and Macaulay Culkin's friendship with Central Park's Pigeon Lady in *Home Alone 2*, to the exterior of Monica's apartment in *Friends* and the Magical Congress building in *Fantastic Beasts and Where to Find Them*, New York City has been a living and breathing movie since the birth of cinema. Why not pay homage to the city's most iconic scenes, both historic and new, and visit some of its filming locations? We've created a map marking just a few of New York's most famous scenes to get you started.

↑ Melanie Griffith, on the Staten Island Ferry in *Working Girl*

Movie Guide

1933
King Kong

1955
The Seven Year Itch

1961
Breakfast at Tiffany's

1967
Barefoot in the Park

1973
Mean Streets

1976
Taxi Driver

1984
Ghostbusters

1987
Wall Street

FILMING LOCATIONS

① *King Kong*, Empire State Building

② *The Seven Year Itch*, Lexington Av & E 52nd St

③ *Breakfast at Tiffany's*, Tiffany & Co.

④ *Barefoot in the Park*, Washington Sq Park

⑤ *Mean Streets*, St. Patrick's Old Cathedral

⑥ *Taxi Driver*, Times Sq

⑦ *Ghostbusters*, Hook and Ladder Company No. 8

⑧ *Wall Street*, 21 W 52nd St

⑨ *Working Girl*, Staten Island Ferry

⑩ *When Harry Met Sally*, Katz's Deli

⑪ *Home Alone 2*, Central Park

⑫ *Friends*, 90 Bedford St

⑬ *Sex and the City*, 66 Perry St

⑭ *The Devil Wears Prada*, The King Cole Bar

⑮ *Inside Man*, 20 Exchange Pl

⑯ *Girls*, Café Grumpy

⑰ *Fantastic Beasts and Where to Find Them*, Woolworth Building

SEX AND THE CITY

Cult TV series *Sex and the City* was filmed entirely in New York. Guided tours of the gang's favorite hangouts take in "Carrie's Stoop" (66 Perry St), Steve's bar (Onieals, 174 Grand St), Charlotte's gallery (141 Prince St), and Samantha's pad (300 Gansevoort St). Visit www.onlocationtours.com to book.

1988
Working Girl

1989
When Harry Met Sally

1992
Home Alone 2

1994–2004
Friends

1998–2004
Sex and the City

2006
The Devil Wears Prada; Inside Man

2012
Girls

2016
Fantastic Beasts and Where to Find Them

EXPERIENCE

Neon lights light up Man42nd Street

LOWER MANHATTAN

The old and the new converge in Lower Manhattan, where Colonial churches and early American monuments stand in the shadow of skyscrapers. New York was born here in the 1620s, and, with the emergence of Wall Street, it has remained at the heart of the world's financial markets. Since the September 11 attacks, there has been startling regeneration: the new One World Trade Center soars 1,776 ft (541 m) above the city, with a spate of modern office towers, hotels, and transportation hubs dotting the area, including the skeletal Oculus. To the north, the federal goverment's courthouses signal the area's civic role, while nearby South Street Seaport is a restored dock area of stores, restaurants, and old ships.

0 meters 250 N
0 yards 250

F

G

12

WORTH ST

Courthouse District
25

US Court
House

ANDREW'S
PLAZA

CENTRE ST

LAFAYETTE ST

PARK ROW

CATHERINE ST

OLIVER ST

ST JAMES PLACE

MADISON ST

Municipal
Building

Police
Headquarters

S Chambers St
J.Z

S Brooklyn
Bridge-City Hall
4.5.6

AV OF THE FINEST

ROSE ST

WAGNER SR PLACE

R. F. PLACE

BROOKLYN BRIDGE

SPRUCE ST

DOVER ST

BEEKMAN ST

GOLD ST

Southbridge
Towers

PEARL ST

PECK SLIP

WATER ST

FRONT ST

VIADUCT

S Fulton St
2.3

WILLIAM ST

JOHN ST

FULTON ST

BEEKMAN ST

PLATT ST

PEARL ST

SOUTH ST

Seaport District NYC
23 8

PIER 17

LEGION
SQUARE

CEDAR ST

MAIDEN LANE

PIER 16

8 Museum of
American Finance

PINE ST

PIER 15

S
Wall St
.3

WALL ST

STREET

FRONT ST

WATER ST

SOUTH ST

E a s t
R i v e r

HANOVER
SQUARE

STONE ST

PEARL ST

GOUVERNEUR
LAND

OLD SLIP

PIER 11

Wall St Ferry Pier

Elevated
Acre

Fraunces
Tavern Museum
21

16 Vietnam Veterans' Plaza

BROAD ST

New York
Plaza

Downtown
Manhattan
Heliport

PIER 6

Battery
Maritime Building
(BMB)

South Ferry

Staten Island **BMB**
Ferry

22

Staten Island,
Weehawken

Governors
Island

Brooklyn,
Red Hook

F

G

LOWER MANHATTAN

Must Sees

1 Statue of Liberty

2 Ellis Island

3 National September 11 Memorial and Museum

4 World Trade Center

5 Governors Island

Experience More

6 Federal Reserve Bank

7 Federal Hall

8 Museum of American Finance

9 Trinity Church

10 St. Paul's Chapel

11 9/11 Tribute Museum

12 Battery Park City and Irish Hunger Memorial

13 Museum of Jewish Heritage

14 Skyscraper Museum

15 Pier A Harbor House

16 Vietnam Veterans' Plaza

17 Battery Park

18 Charging Bull

19 Bowling Green

20 National Museum of the American Indian

21 Fraunces Tavern Museum

22 Staten Island Ferry

23 Seaport District NYC

24 City Hall and City Hall Park

25 Courthouse District

26 African Burial Ground

27 Woolworth Building

Eat

① Delmonico's

② Nobu Downtown

③ Le District

Shop

④ Brookfield Place

⑤ Century 21

⑥ Fulton Center

⑦ The Oculus

⑧ Seaport District and Pier 17

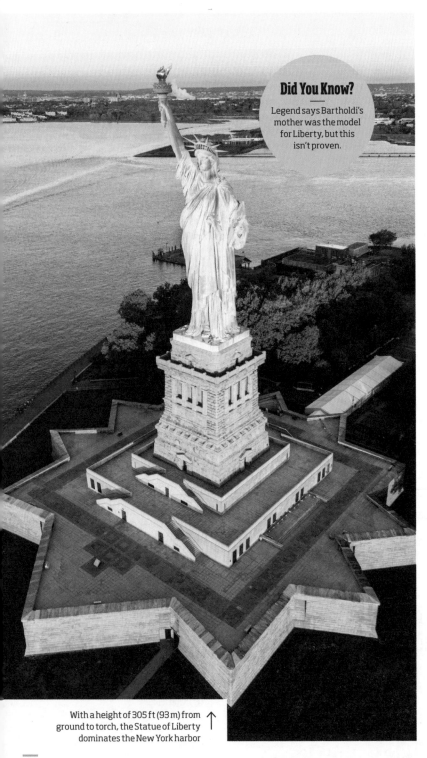

Did You Know?

Legend says Bartholdi's mother was the model for Liberty, but this isn't proven.

With a height of 305 ft (93 m) from ground to torch, the Statue of Liberty dominates the New York harbor ↑

❶ ✏️ 🖥️ 🎒

STATUE OF LIBERTY

📍 C15 🏛️ Liberty Island 🚇 South Ferry (1), Bowling Green (4, 5), Whitehall (R) 🚌 M15, M20, M55 to South Ferry 🕐 9:45am–4:45pm; hours vary during hols 🌐 nps.gov/stli

A gift from the French to the American people, the statue of Liberty has become an enduring symbol of freedom throughout the world.

The Statue

In Emma Lazarus's poem, engraved on the statue's base, Lady Liberty says: "Give me your tired, your poor, Your huddled masses yearning to breathe free." The brainchild of French sculptor Frédéric-Auguste Bartholdi, and the first sight of immigrants upon arrival in New York, the statue was intended as a monument to the freedom Bartholdi found lacking in his own country. Liberty remains an icon today, and visitors can even climb up to her crown (advance booking essential).

The Ferry

Essential to the Statue of Liberty experience is riding the Statue Cruises Ferry across the harbor. The ferry crosses from Battery Park to Liberty Island every 20–30 minutes, 9:30am–3:30pm; the fare includes entry to Ellis and Liberty islands.

FRÉDÉRIC-AUGUSTE BARTHOLDI

Bartholdi devoted 21 years to making the Statue of Liberty a reality, even traveling to America in 1871 to talk President Ulysses S. Grant into funding it and installing it in New York's harbor. A series of graduated scale models enabled Bartholdi to build this, the largest metal statue ever constructed, with 300 copper sheets riveted together making up the statue. The statue's frame was designed by Gustave Eiffel.

←
The Staten Island Ferry offers a great photo opportunity as it passes the Statue of Liberty

Construction Timeline

1874
△ Bartholdi starts construction in Paris, beginning with a terracotta model.

1884
▽ Statue is completed and shipped from Paris to New York in 350 individual pieces.

1886
Lady Liberty is unveiled by President Grover Cleveland.

1916
Public access to the balcony surrounding Liberty's outstretched torch is barred for safety reasons.

1986
△ In celebration of her 100th birthday, Lady Liberty undergoes a $100-million restoration.

② 🔨 🅼 🖵 🍽

ELLIS ISLAND

📍 C15 🚇 Ellis Island 🚇 Bowling Green (4, 5), South Ferry (1), Whitehall (R), then Statue Cruises Ferry from Battery Park ⏰ 9:30am–5:15pm daily (extended hours during Federal hols) 🌐 libertyellisfoundation.org

Around 40 per cent of the country's population can trace its roots to historic Ellis Island, the country's immigration depot from 1892 until 1954. The gateway to America is now a remarkable museum paying homage to the greatest wave of migration the world has ever known.

Ellis Island Immigration Museum

During its tenure, nearly 12 million people passed through Ellis Island's gates and dispersed across the country. Centered on the Great Hall, or Registry Room, the site today houses the three-story Ellis Island Immigration Museum. Its history is told with photographs and the voices of actual immigrants, and an electronic database traces ancestors. Outside, the American Immigrant Wall of Honor is the largest wall of names in the world, with more than 12,000 inscriptions. No other place explains so well the "melting pot" that formed the character of the nation.

Visit early to avoid the crowds. Entry to the museum is included in the ferry fare. The ferry generally departs every 20–30 mins but do check online in advance.

↑ The Medical Examining Rooms, where immigrants with contagious diseases could be refused entry

→ Ellis Island, New York City's immigration depot (1892–1954)

The architects were inspired by the French Beaux Arts style.

The ferry office sold tickets to New Jersey.

← The immigrants' meager possessions were checked in the Baggage Room on arrival

GREAT HALL

Newly arrived immigrants were made to wait for "processing" in the huge, vaulted Great Hall on the second floor. Some days, over 5,000 people would wait to be inspected and registered; if required, medical and legal examinations also took place here. Once the scene of so much trepidation, today the room has been left imposingly bare, with just a couple of inspectors' desks, and original wooden benches.

The railroad office sold onward tickets.

The vast ceiling and large arched windows accentuate the enormity of the complex.

Dormitories were separate for men and women.

Great Hall

The metal-and-glass awning is a re-creation of the original.

Main entrance

Baggage Room

Migrants arrive in America, via Ellis Island.

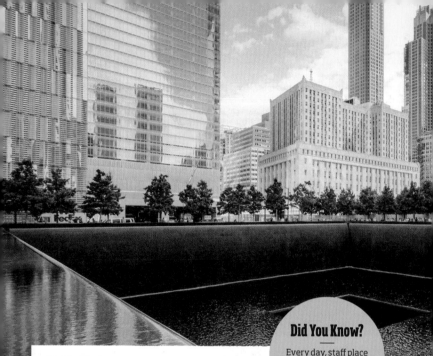

Did You Know?

Every day, staff place white roses by the names of victims who have a birthday that day.

3

NATIONAL SEPTEMBER 11 MEMORIAL & MUSEUM

📍 D13 🏠 180 Greenwich St 🚇 Rector St (R), World Trade Center (E) 🕐 Memorial: 7:30am–9pm daily; Museum: 9am–8pm Sun–Thu, 9am–9pm Fri & Sat 🌐 911memorial.org

The events of 9/11 took a heavy toll on New York City. Poignant and dignified, the National September 11 Memorial and Museum together ensure that the thousands of victims who lost their lives in the worst attack on American soil will never be forgotten.

NATIONAL SEPTEMBER 11 MEMORIAL

Designed by Israeli architect Michael Arad, this moving memorial commemorates the terrorist attacks of September 11, 2001. Two vast memorial pools represent the footprints of the original Twin Towers, with 30-ft (9-m-) waterfalls tumbling down their sides. The bronze parapets that encircle the pools display the names of the 9/11 victims, while the surrounding plaza is studded with 400 white oak trees. Also here is a lone Callery pear tree, or "the Survivor Tree," which miraculously survived the attacks. The tree was planted in the 1970s, and suffered grave damage during 9/11. It was replanted in the Bronx, where it slowly recovered, before it was returned to its original spot in 2010.

> 💬 INSIDER TIP
> **Museum tickets**
>
> To skip the line and ensure admission into the National September 11 Museum, reserve a timed-entry ticket on the website ahead of time (this can be purchased six months in advance). The National September 11 Memorial itself is free with open access.

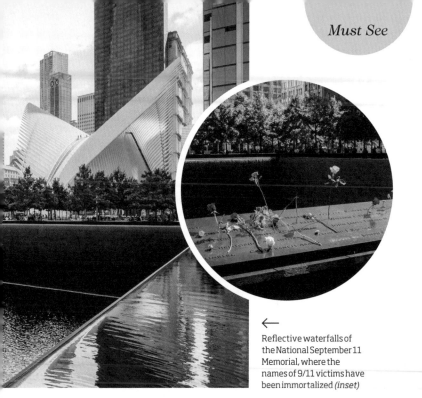

←
Reflective waterfalls of the National September 11 Memorial, where the names of 9/11 victims have been immortalized *(inset)*

NATIONAL SEPTEMBER 11 MEMORIAL MUSEUM

The underground 9/11 Memorial Museum at the heart of the complex chronicles the horrific events of September 11. The museum comprises poignant exhibits, personal accounts, voice recordings, and videos. There is also a crushed FDNY truck, and the iconic final piece of steel to be removed from Ground Zero, referred to as the Last Column. Unlike the memorial, there is an admission charge.

↑ The crushed FDNY fire truck and Last Column, both of which were removed from Ground Zero, are now displayed in the National September 11 Memorial Museum

SEPTEMBER 11, 2001

On September 11, 2001, two hijacked planes flew into the Twin Towers of the World Trade Center. Millions watched in horror, both on the ground and live on TV, as the towers collapsed. In all, 2,977 people perished at the World Trade Center and in a simultaneous attack on the Pentagon. Osama bin Laden's terrorist network, al-Qaeda, claimed responsibility for the attacks. The 1,368-ft (417-m) tall Twin Towers, designed by Minoru Yamasaki, had been a striking and iconic presence on the New York skyline since 1973.

4 🍽️

WORLD TRADE CENTER

📍D13 🚇World Trade Center 🚈Rector St (R), World Trade Center (E) 🕐One World Trade Center Observatory: Sep-Apr: 9am-9pm daily; May-Aug 8am-9pm daily
🌐oneworldobservatory.com

A new World Trade Center has risen from the ashes of 9/11 with America's tallest skyscraper, One World Trade Center, at its heart. The new complex features truly innovative architecture, such as the visionary Oculus terminal, and skyscrapers continue to grow into the skies above the city.

One World Trade Center

The centerpiece of the new World Trade Center, and the tallest skyscraper in the United States, One World Trade Center stands at the symbolic height of 1,776 ft (541 m), reflecting America's declaration of independence in 1776. The soaring tower of glass and steel is a modified version of the "Tower of Freedom" designed by Polish-born architect Daniel Libeskind. Supervised by David Childs, the center finally topped out in 2012. Five high-speed elevators, known as Sky Pods, transport visitors to One World Observatory at the top of the building in just 60 seconds. From here, there are mesmerizing views of the harbor, Staten Island, and Manhattan's rooftops.

Entry to One World Observatory includes access to the upscale One Dine restaurant on the 101st floor, featuring seasonally inspired, contemporary American cuisine (reservations are recommended) and the more casual One Mix bar, along with a number of exhibits.

↓ One World Trade Center looms large over the city skyline

1,362 ft
—
The height of the observation deck; the same height of the Twin Towers (415 m).

← The Oculus, designed by Santiago Calatrava, opened in 2016. Its two spiky steel ribs resemble a dinosaur skeleton, and its futuristic interior *(inset)* comprises a subway station and a Westfield shopping mall.

🔺 GREAT VIEW
World Trade Center

For some of the best views of the whole World Trade Center site, head across to the other side of West Street and stand at the entrance of Brookfield Place. For pictures of One World Trade Center itself, walk north along West Street.

⑤

GOVERNORS ISLAND

📍 D15 🏛 Governors Island ⛴ From Battery Maritime Building, 10 South St 🕐 May-Oct: 10am-6pm Mon-Fri, 10am-7pm Sat & Sun 🌐 govisland.com

Nowhere in New York is quite like Governors Island. A blend of tranquil green spaces and historic buildings cast in the heart of the harbor – this urban park offers a welcome break from the busy pace of city life.

Reminiscent of a college campus, this 172-acre (70-ha) island has been developed into a public space since 2003. There is a wealth of green spaces in which to lounge in the sun, as well as a breezy 2.2-mile (3.5-km) promenade – you can stroll or cycle right down to the southern tip, dubbed Picnic Point, via The Hills, man-made humps rising 80 ft (24 m) above the harbor. En route, Hammock Grove is an enticing space studded with red hammocks. Many of the island's buildings continue to be restored for the public to enjoy. Near the dock, Fort Jay was the island's original late 18th-century fortification, used to deter the British. Completed on the northwest corner of the island in 1811, Castle Williams is a circular brick and sandstone fort that is nearly identical to Castle Clinton in Battery Park. Up to 1,000 Confederate soldiers were held in its cramped cells during the Civil War, and it served as a prison until 1966.

💬 INSIDER TIP
Getting there and around

The ferry from the Battery Maritime Building, in Manhattan, arrives at Soissons Landing, where you'll find the visitors' center. Ferries also run to the island from Brooklyn Bridge Park's Pier 6, Red Hook, and other locations along the East River. The island can be explored on foot or by bike, and two food courts provide a range of eating options.

1699
▽ Under British rule the island is reserved for the "benefit and accommodation of His Majesty's Governors."

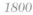

1912
Landfill from the New York subway doubles the size of the island.

2003
▽ Ownership is shared between the City and State of New York, and the National Park Service.

1800
△ New York transfers the island to the US government for military use.

1878
Becomes a major army headquarters and garrison.

↑ Acres of parkland, stunning harbor views, and historic buildings await visitors at Governors Island

NOLAN PARK

Nolan Park is home to some beautifully preserved Neo-Classical and Federal-style mansions (once army officers' homes), including Governor's House and Admiral's House (the site of the Reagan-Gorbachev Summit in 1988). Many of these continue to be converted into seasonal art galleries, and studios such as Holocenter House, which specializes in light-based installations.

EXPERIENCE MORE

6

Federal Reserve Bank

📍E13 🏛33 Liberty St
🚇Fulton St (A, C, 2, 4) 🕐1pm
& 2pm Mon-Fri 🚫Federal
hols 🌐newyorkfed.org

Occupying a full city block, this Italian Renaissance-style building is the largest of America's 12 Federal Reserve banks, implementing US monetary policy, regulating financial institutions and maintaining US payment systems. Secured 80 ft (24 m) below street level is ten per cent of the world's gold reserves – a whopping 7,700 tons of it.

Gold Tours are free and last 45 minutes to an hour. Be sure to make an online reservation at least a week in advance. Arrive at 44 Maiden Lane 30 minutes early with your e-ticket and photo ID (a passport is best). Note that taking pictures and videos is forbidden.

↑ The dome of the Federal Hall's Rotunda, recalling the Pantheon in Rome

7

Federal Hall

📍E14 🏛26 Wall St 🚇Wall St (2, 3, 4, 5) 🕐9am-5pm Mon-Fri 🚫Federal hols 🌐nps.gov/feha

A bronze statue of George Washington on the steps of Federal Hall marks the site where the nation's first president took his oath of office in 1789. Thousands of New Yorkers jammed Wall and Broad streets for the occasion, roaring their approval when the Chancellor of the State of New York shouted, "Long live George Washington, President of the United States." The present structure, built between 1834 and 1842 as the US Customs House, is one of the city's finest Greek Revival designs.

Display rooms off the Rotunda include the Bill of Rights Room and illustrate the Washington connection. Tours take place at 10am, and 1, 2, and 3pm.

8

Museum of American Finance

📍E14 🏛48 Wall St 🚇Wall St (2, 3, 4, 5) 🕐10am-4pm Tue-Sat 🌐moaf.org

This informative museum unmasks the workings and history of New York's financial

---

THE NEW YORK STOCK EXCHANGE

Haphazard trading in stocks and shares had become common in New York and so, in 1792, a group of 22 stockbrokers and merchants gathered beneath a button-wood tree on Wall Street to sign the "Buttonwood Agreement". This formed the trading group that would be called the New York Stock Exchange (NYSE) in 1817.

The NYSE has since weathered a succession of slumps ("bear markets") and booms ("bull markets"), growing from a local marketplace into the world's financial heart. The stock exchange's public viewing galleries were closed indefinitely after 9/11, so it can only be admired from its exterior at 18 Broad Street.

LOWER MANHATTAN'S SKYLINE

125 Broad Street

55 Water Street

One Financial Square

NYSE

↑ Warm hues and historic lines of Trinity Church amid modern architecture

district. Located in the former main hall of the lavish Bank of New York & Trust building, the museum covers and explains all aspects of stocks, bonds and futures trading, with multi-media displays and exhibits explaining all there is to know about the city's financial trading rooms. There are also a number of rare artifacts on display, including a bond signed by George Washington in 1792, a gold ingot from the 1850s, and ticker-tape from the opening moments of the Great Crash in 1929.

Fans of the hit musical *Hamilton* should head for the Alexander Hamilton room. The first Secretary of the Treasury (c. 1755–1804), Hamilton was a financial pioneer in his time, and this room is dedicated to his legacy. The museum also screens documentary films on Wall Street through the day.

9 Ⓜ ☐ ☐

Trinity Church

📍E14 🏠79 Broadway at Wall St Ⓢ Wall St (4, 5), Rector St (R) 🕐7am-6pm daily 🔤trinitywallstreet.org

This square-towered Episcopal church incongruously situated at the head of Wall Street is reminiscent of an English parish church, thanks to its English architect Richard Upjohn. Designed in 1846, it was among the grandest churches of its day, heralding America's best period of Gothic Revival architecture. Richard Morris Hunt's sculpted brass doors were inspired by Lorenzo Ghiberti's *Gates of Paradise* at the Baptistery in Florence.

Restoration has uncovered the original rosy sandstone, long buried beneath layers of city grime. The 280-ft (85-m) steeple, the tallest structure in New York until 1890, still commands respect despite its modern, towering neighbors.

Many prominent early New Yorkers are buried in the graveyard, including statesman and Founding Father Alexander Hamilton, steamboat inventor Robert Fulton, and William Bradford, founder of New York's first newspaper in 1725.

SHOP

Brookfield Place
Mall on the Hudson River, featuring the stunning Winter Garden.

📍D13 🏠230 Vesey St 🔤brookfieldplaceny.com

Century 21
Designer discount store, usually offering 40-60 per cent off retail prices.

📍E13 🏠22 Cortlandt St 🔤c21stores.com

Fulton Center
Stylish mall in Westfield World Trade Center.

📍E13 🏠200 Broadway 🔤westfield.com

The Oculus
Vast subterranean mall within the striking, modern building by Santiago Calatrava.

📍D13 🏠185 Greenwich St 🔤westfield.com

Seaport District and Pier 17
Range of stores in the old seaport and renovated pier.

📍F13 🏠Fulton St, at South St 🔤southstreetseaport.com

Historic St. Paul's Chapel, survivor of 9/11, surrounded by modern architecture

EAT

Delmonico's

One of America's oldest restaurants (est. 1837) has a grand portico atop columns from Pompeii. Signatures include the Delmonico Steak (boneless ribeye), Lobster Newburg, and Baked Alaska. The last two of these dishes were created here.

📍E14 🏛56 Beaver St 🕐Sun 🌐delmonicos restaurant.com

$$$⑤

Nobu Downtown

Lauded Japanese chef Nobu Matsuhisa's iconic restaurant features an elegant bar and lounge, with a stunning, calligraphy-inspired sculpture. Reservations are recommended.

📍E13 🏛195 Broadway 🕐L Sat, L Sun 🌐noburestaurants.com

$$⑤⑤

Le District

The French food court at Brookfield Place has four restaurants and three themed areas: "market", "café," and "garden." Eat in the nearby Winter Garden or at the outdoor tables overlooking North Cove on the Hudson River.

📍D13 🏛225 Liberty St 🌐ledistrict.com

$⑤⑤

10

St. Paul's Chapel

📍E13 🏛209-211 Broadway 📞(212) 602-0800 🚇Fulton St (A, C, 2, 3) 🕐10am-6pm Mon-Sat, 7am-6pm Sun 🕐Most Federal hols

A Georgian gem dating back to 1766, St. Paul's is Manhattan's only extant church pre-dating the Revolutionary War. It was miraculously untouched when the World Trade Center towers collapsed in 2001, and the chapel acted as a sanctuary for rescue workers at Ground Zero for eight months after the tragic event. One of the main attractions here is *Unwavering Spirit*, a moving exhibition on the September 11 attacks. The pew where George Washington prayed in 1789–90 is also part of the exhibition. Akin to a shrine, it has been preserved since New York was the capital of the US, and became a foot-treatment chair for firefighters during the attacks of 9/11.

11

9/11 Tribute Museum

📍E14 🏛92 Greenwich St 🚇Cortlandt St (R), World Trade Center (E), Rector St (1) 🕐10am-6pm Mon-Sat, 10am-5pm Sun 🌐911tributemuseum.org

The 9/11 Tribute Museum was established by the September 11th Families' Association, an organization set up by the victims' families, and gives a personal perspective on the attacks. Opened in 2006, while the nearby National September 11 Memorial was under development, the museum stands separately and houses five small galleries.

Exhibits include a model of the Twin Towers and a section on the day of the attacks, with videos and recorded accounts of the survivors. Daily walking tours led by family members, rescue workers, survivors, civilian volunteers, and local residents take in the National September 11 Memorial.

⓬
Battery Park City and Irish Hunger Memorial

📍 D13 🏠 7 Battery Park City 🚇 Rector St (1)

Construction of the former World Trade Center, in the 1970s, created a million cubic yards of landfill. This was poured into the Hudson to form a neighborhood of restaurants, apartments, sculptures, and gardens. The 1.2-mile (2-km) Battery Park City esplanade offers amazing views of the Statue of Liberty.

Overlooking the Hudson at the end of Vesey Street, the **Irish Hunger Memorial** is a monument to the Irish who starved to death during the Great Famine of 1845–52. The centerpiece is an abandoned stone cottage and stone walls containing rocks from each of Ireland's 32 counties.

⓭
Museum of Jewish Heritage

📍 D14 🏠 36 Battery Pl
🚇 Bowling Green (4, 5)
🚌 M5, M15, M20 🕐 10am–6pm Sun-Tue, 10am–8pm Wed & Thu, 10am–5pm Fri (Nov-Mar: to 3pm) 🚫 Jewish holidays, Thanksgiving
🌐 mjhnyc.org

This museum stands as a memorial to the victims of the Holocaust. The core exhibition, covering three floors, occupies a remarkable six-sided building symbolizing the six million Jews who died under the Nazis and the six points of the Star of

David. The collection begins with the rituals of everyday Eastern European Jewish life pre-1930, moves on to the Holocaust, and ends with the 1948 establishment of the state of Israel and subsequent achievements. Audio tours and lectures are offered – check the website.

⓮
Skyscraper Museum

📍 D14 🏠 39 Battery Pl
🚇 Bowling Green (4, 5)
🕐 noon-6pm Wed-Sun
🌐 skyscraper.org

This museum celebrates New York's architectural heritage and examines the historical forces and individuals that shaped its iconic skyline. Exhibits include a digital reconstruction of the ways in which the city has changed and a collection of hand-carved models of Manhattan. Temporary exhibitions analyze various definitions of tall

buildings: as objects of design, products of technology, construction sites, real-estate investments, and places of work and residence.

⓯
Pier A Harbor House

📍 D15 🏠 22 Battery Pl
🚇 Bowling Green (4, 5)
🕐 11am–midnight daily (until 2am Thu-Sat)
🌐 piera.com

Facing the harbor on the western side of Battery Park, Pier A Harbor House is an ornate pier dating from 1886, and was originally the head-quarters of the New York Harbor Police. After extensive renovation, the structure now contains bars and restaurants. The Long Hall and the Oyster Bar incorporate the original searchlight and restored gauges, while outdoor tables allow guests to admire those fine harbor views over a plate of oysters or a craft beer.

> ### STONE STREET
>
> Tucked away between Hanover Square and Coenties Alley is narrow, cobblestone Stone Street. Many of its atmospheric Greek Revival-style houses were built in the wake of the Great Fire of 1835, which destroyed much of the area. Today, this is a great place to eat and drink. On summer nights it's a vast open-air beer garden, with bars like Ulysses and restaurants such as Adrienne's Pizzabar covering the street with picnic tables.

Skyscrapers loom large on the southern tip of Manhattan

Vietnam Veterans' Plaza

E14 Between Water St and South St **S** Whitehall (R), South Ferry (1)

This multilevel brick plaza features, in its center, an enormous wall of translucent green glass. This glass is engraved with excerpts from speeches, news stories, and moving letters to families from servicemen and women who died in the Vietnam War, between 1959 and 1975.

Battery Park

E14 Battery Pl **S** Whitehall St (R, W), South Ferry (1), Bowling Green (4, 5) **W** nps.gov/cacl

This is one of the best places in the city for views of the harbor. Named for the British cannons that once protected New York, it has more than 20 statues and monuments, such as the Netherlands Monument and memorials to the Korean War, World War II, immigrants, and the Coast Guard. Newer attractions include the SeaGlass Carousel, an aquatic-themed merry-go-round.

Castle Clinton was built just offshore in 1811 as an artillery defense post, but landfill gradually linked it to the mainland. In 1824 it reopened as Castle Garden, containing a theater, beer garden, and an opera house, where Phineas T. Barnum introduced "Swedish nightingale" Jenny Lind in 1850. In 1855 it preceded Ellis Island as the immigration point, and, by 1890, had processed over 8 million newcomers. There's a small exhibit and a section of the original "Battery Wall." Tickets to Ellis Island and the Statue of Liberty are also available.

Charging Bull

E14 Broadway at Bowling Green **S** Bowling Green (4, 5) **W** charging bull.com

At 1am on December 15, 1989, Italian sculptor Arturo Di Modica (b. 1941) and 30 friends unloaded his 7,000-lb (3,200-kg) *Charging Bull* bronze statue in front of the New York Stock Exchange. The group had eight minutes between police patrols, but managed it in just five. The bull was removed for obstructing traffic and lacking a permit, but public outcry ensued. The Parks Department gave it a "temporary" permit on Broadway, where it remains to this day as the unofficial Wall Street mascot.

Di Modica created the sculpture after the 1987 stock-market crash, to

↑ Battery Park's wonderful waterfront offers views

symbolize the "strength, power, and hope of the American people for the future." It took two years, and cost him $350,000.

Bowling Green

E14 **S** Bowling Green (4, 5)

This triangular plot north of Battery Park was the city's earliest park, originally a cattle market and later

---

FEARLESS GIRL AND THE BULL

In 2017, Wall Street's famous *Charging Bull* was challenged by another bronze sculpture dubbed the *Fearless Girl*. Designed by Kristen Visbal, the image of a small girl defiantly staring down the beast quickly became a feminist icon, despite being commissioned as part of a marketing campaign for a gender-diverse index fund. Mayor De Blasio agreed that *Fearless Girl* could stay for 11 months; in 2019, she is slated to move to a more accessible location in front of the New York Stock Exchange as the crowds milling around the statues on Broadway pose a traffic hazard.

ARTURO DI MODICA'S CHARGING BULL

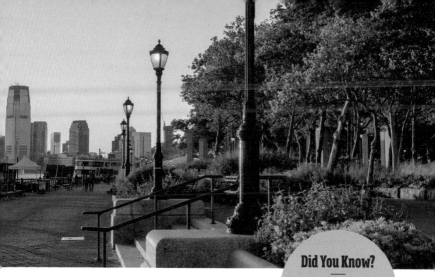

Did You Know?

Battery Park is an annual stopover for thousands of migrating birds and Monarch butterflies.

used as a bowling ground. A statue of King George III stood here until the signing of the Declaration of Independence, when, as a symbol of British rule, it was hacked to pieces and smelted for ammunition. The governor of Connecticut's wife is said to have melted down enough pieces to mold 42,000 bullets.

Beyond the green is the start of Broadway, which runs the length of Manhattan and, under its formal name of Route 9, north to the state capital in Albany.

National Museum of the American Indian

📍E14 🏛1 Bowling Green
🚇Bowling Green (4, 5)
🕐10am–5pm daily (to 8pm Thu) 🌐nmai.si.edu

Cass Gilbert's stately US Custom House now houses the Smithsonian National Museum of the American Indian. The outstanding collection of about a million artifacts, along with an archive of many thousands of photographs, spans the breadth of the native cultures of North, Central, and South America. Exhibitions include works by contemporary

Native American artists as well as changing displays drawn from the museum's permanent collection.

Completed in 1907, and in use until 1973, the Beaux Arts Custom House is also a part of the attraction. The impressive facade, with elaborate statues by Daniel Chester French, depicts the major continents, and some of the world's great commercial centers. Inside, the magnificent marble Great Hall and rotunda are beautifully decorated. The 16 murals covering the 135-ft (41-m) dome were painted by Reginald Marsh in 1937, and show the progress of ships sailing into the harbor.

Fraunces Tavern Museum

📍E14 🏛54 Pearl St
🚇Wall St (2, 3), Broad St (J, Z), Bowling Green (4, 5)
🕐Noon–5pm Mon–Fri, 11am–5pm Sat & Sun
🚫Federal hols 🌐fraunces tavernmuseum.org

New York's only remaining block of 18th-century commercial buildings contains an exact replica of the 1719 Fraunces Tavern where George Washington said a tearful

farewell to his officers in 1783. An upstairs museum displays changing exhibits interpreting the history and culture of early America. George Washington's famous farewell speech took place in the Long Room, which has been recreated in the manner of the time. The adjacent Federal-style Clinton Room is an atmospheric dining room, decorated in rare French wallpaper from 1838. There are galleries of art pertaining to the Revolution, such as the Sons of the Revolution gallery, which gives details about much of the society's history. The restaurant, meanwhile, has wood-burning fires and great charm.

The tavern had been an early casualty of the Revolution: the British ship *Asia* shot a cannonball through its roof in August 1775. The building was bought in 1904 by the Sons of the Revolution and its restoration in 1907 was one of the first efforts to preserve the nation's heritage.

Visitors can join an hour-long tour of the museum at 2pm on Thursday, and at 1 or 2pm Friday through Sunday.

22

Staten Island Ferry

 E15 Whitehall St
South Ferry (1) 24 hrs
siferry.com

With unforgettable views of the harbor and city skyline, this remains the city's best ride – and it's free. The ferry was the first business venture of Cornelius Vanderbilt, in 1810, who later became a railroad magnate. It's popular with tourists and commuters alike.

  23

Seaport District NYC

F13 Fulton St Fulton St (A, C, 2, 3, 4, 5) Museum: Apr-Oct: 11am-5pm Wed-Sun
southstreetseaport.com

Part of New York's original dockyards, the Seaport District has been gradually restored

> **INSIDER TIP**
> ## TKTS box office
>
> The Seaport District's TKTS box, at 190 Front Street, sells same-day, half-price tickets to Broadway shows – like its counterpart in Times Square, but with a fraction of the lines.

since 1966, with a multitude of restaurants and stores replacing its historic warehouses and fish markets. The former Fulton Market Building now contains several posh boutiques and a branch of luxury movie theater chain iPic Theaters, while Pier 17 includes stores, restaurants, and a concert venue. Next door, the refurbished 1904 Tin Building will eventually host a Jean-Georges Vongerichten food market. To enjoy the best views of the Brooklyn Bridge, visit the upper deck of South Street Seaport's Pier 15.

The South Street Seaport Museum has a large collection of maritime art and artifacts, plus several historic ships docked nearby. The main galleries, which are based in Federal-style warehouses dating back to 1812, include the permanent "Street of Ships: The Port and its People." This charts the history of the area and the restoration of the *Wavertree*, a British tall ship built in 1885. Museum admission includes guided tours of the *Wavertree* and the *Ambrose*, a lightship from 1908. The museum also owns the 1893 fishing schooner

↑ The *Ambrose* light-ship in Manhattan's Seaport District

Lettie G Howard and the 1885 cargo schooner *Pioneer*, offering harbor cruises in the summer. Also run by the museum are two historic stores and workshops on Water Street: Bowne Printers at No. 209 and Bowne & Co Stationers at No. 211.

 24

City Hall and City Hall Park

E12 City Hall Park
Brooklyn Bridge-City Hall (4, 5, 6), Park Place (2, 3)
Tour times vary, check website nyc.gov

A gleaming marble palace, New York's Federal-style City Hall is the oldest in the US to retain its original government function. The interior features a spectacular coffered dome, ringed by ten Corinthian columns and a floating marble staircase that spirals up to the second floor, where the city council

To enjoy the best views of the Brooklyn Bridge, visit the upper deck of South Street Seaport's Pier 15.

still meets once a month. Also here is the French Regency-style Governor's Room, with a portrait gallery of early New York leaders. In 1865 Abraham Lincoln's body lay in state here.

Tours of City Hall are free, and generally take place on Wednesday and Thursday. The latter requires advance booking – check the website for all details.

Once a 17th-century communal pasture, City Hall Park has been the seat of New York's government since 1812. An almshouse for the poor stood on this site between 1736 and 1797 and, during the Revolutionary War (1775–83), the British used the nearby debtors' prison to hold and hang 250 prisoners.

㉕

Courthouse District

♀ E12 ♠ Center and Chambers streets ⑤ Brooklyn Bridge-City Hall (4, 5, 6)

Grand Neo-Classical buildings dominate New York's court-house district, the inspiration for many movie settings. The pyramid-topped Thurgood Marshall US Courthouse, designed by Cass Gilbert in 1936, soars at 590 ft (180 m), and continues to serve as a federal courthouse today. The adjacent New York County Courthouse (1927) is a state supreme court, and its elaborate rotunda has Tiffany lighting fixtures and murals by Attilio Pusterla.

Surrogate's Court (1907), on Chambers Street, has an ornate columned facade and figures by Henry K. Bush-Brown, representing life's different stages, from childhood through old age. The ceiling mosaic high above the stunning central hall, meanwhile, was designed by William de Leftwich Dodge, and features the 12 signs of the zodiac.

↑ The Woolworth Building, a stunning monument to an inspired retail giant

㉖

African Burial Ground

♀ E12 ♠ Duane St ⑤ Chambers St (A, C), City Hall (R) ⏰ 9am–4pm Tue–Sat �🌐 nps.gov/afbg

An elegant, black granite monument occupies part of a cemetery that previously lay outside the city. Once the only place African slaves could be buried, the site was discovered by chance in 1991, with the exhumation of 419 skeletons. After being examined, the remains were reinterred here in 2003. Around the corner, the Visitor Center houses an exhibition tracing the history of slavery in New York.

㉗

Woolworth Building

♀ E13 ♠ 233 Broadway ⑤ City Hall (R), Park Place (2, 3) ⏰ daily for tours �🌐 woolworthtours.com

In 1879, sales clerk Frank W. Woolworth opened a new kind of store, where shoppers could see and touch the goods, and everything cost five cents. The chain of stores that followed made him a fortune and changed retailing forever.

His 1913 headquarters set the standard for the great skyscrapers; it was New York's tallest building until 1929. Architect Cass Gilbert's two-tiered design is adorned with gargoyles of wildlife, a pyramid roof, pinnacles, and towers. The interior is rich with sculptured reliefs and a glass-tile mosaic ceiling. Gilbert's sense of humor shows in the bas-reliefs of the founder counting out his fortune in nickels and dimes. Paid for with $13.5 million in cash, the building has never been mortgaged.

Woolworth's went out of business in 1997 but the building is open daily for tours. Book ahead.

ART DECO SKYSCRAPERS

Lower Manhattan boasts some of New York's most iconic Art Deco skyscrapers. The 1931 Bank of New York at 1 Wall Street (654 ft/200 m) has a mosaic lobby. The 1912 Bankers Trust Building at 14 Wall Street (539 ft/164 m) is best known for its step-pyramid top, modeled on the Greek Mausoleum at Halicarnassus. The Bank of Manhattan Trust Building (right) at 40 Wall Street was the world's tallest (at 927 ft/283 m) in 1930. Today, it's known as the Trump Building. Stupendous Art Deco wonder 70 Pine Street (952 ft/290 m), completed in 1932 for the precursor of CITGO, is one of New York's most graceful and iconic Art Deco towers.

A SHORT WALK
WALL STREET

Distance 0.6 mile (1 km) **Nearest subway** Wall St
Time 15 minutes

No intersection has been of greater importance to the city's early evolution than the one at Wall and Broad streets. Federal Hall marks the place where, in 1789, George Washington was sworn in as president. The New York Stock Exchange, founded in 1817, is to this day a financial nerve center whose ups and downs cause tremors globally. Its sights of historical importance aside, this is one of the city's greatest business centers and the very heart of New York's famous financial district. The sense of industry is palpable, with bankers pounding the streets on weekdays.

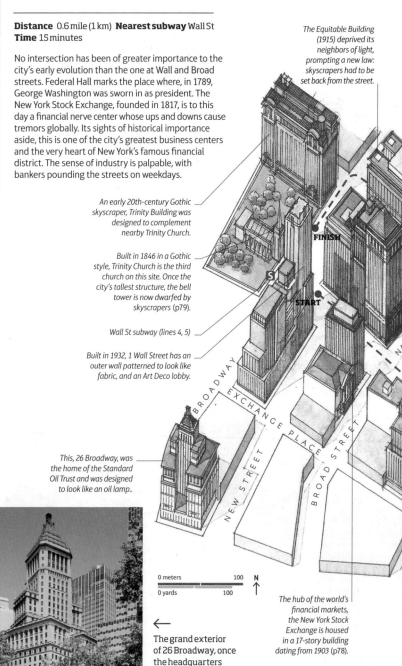

The Equitable Building (1915) deprived its neighbors of light, prompting a new law: skyscrapers had to be set back from the street.

An early 20th-century Gothic skyscraper, Trinity Building was designed to complement nearby Trinity Church.

Built in 1846 in a Gothic style, Trinity Church is the third church on this site. Once the city's tallest structure, the bell tower is now dwarfed by skyscrapers (p79).

Wall St subway (lines 4, 5)

Built in 1932, 1 Wall Street has an outer wall patterned to look like fabric, and an Art Deco lobby.

FINISH

START

This, 26 Broadway, was the home of the Standard Oil Trust and was designed to look like an oil lamp..

BROADWAY

EXCHANGE PLACE

NEW STREET

BROAD STREET

NASSAU

0 meters 100
0 yards 100
N ↑

← The grand exterior of 26 Broadway, once the headquarters of Standard Oil

The hub of the world's financial markets, the New York Stock Exchange is housed in a 17-story building dating from 1903 (p78).

The Marine Midland Building rises straight up 55 stories. This dark glass tower occupies only 40 per cent of its site. The other 60 per cent is a plaza in which a large red sculpture by Isamu Noguchi, *Cube*, balances on one of its points.

The Chamber of Commerce is a fine Beaux Arts building of 1901.

The Liberty Tower is clad in white terracotta and is in the Gothic style. Built in 1910, it was later turned into apartments.

28 Liberty has the famous Jean Dubuffet sculpture *Four Trees* located in the plaza.

In the style of a Renaissance palace, Federal Reserve Bank is a bank for banks. U.S. currency is issued here (p78).

Louise Nevelson Plaza is a park containing Nevelson's sculpture *Shadows and Flags*.

Locator Map
For more detail see p66

MAIDEN LANE

LIBERTY STREET

CEDAR STREET

WALL STREET

Wall Street is named for the wall that kept enemies and hostile Native Americans out of Manhattan – the street is now the heart of the city's business center.

Federal Hall was built as the U.S. Custom House in 1842. The Classical building houses a fascinating exhibit about George Washington (p78).

↑ Federal Reserve Bank rises up over the snowy streets of Manhattan

LOWER EAST SIDE

Nowhere does the strong ethnic flavor of New York come through more tangibly than in the Lower East Side, where the city's first tenement buildings were raised and immigrants began to settle in the mid-19th century. Here Italians, Germans, Chinese, Jews, Irish and, more recently, Dominicans established distinct neighborhoods, preserving their languages, customs, foods, and religions. It wasn't until the 1990s that retro clubs, chic bars, creative restaurants, and boutiques revived the Lower East Side, and today it's this melding of cultures that provides most of area's appeal. The Lower East Side Tenement Museum and Museum on Eldridge Street are the key historic attractions, both paying homage to the area's gritty, immigrant past.

EAST VILLAGE
p138

Angel Orensanz Center

EAST HOUSTON ST

247365 Gallery

Economy Candy ④

Essex Street Market ⑤

Delancey St F

Essex Crossing ⑥

NOLITA

CHINATOWN, LITTLE ITALY, AND NOLITA
p102

Broadway-Lafayette St B.D.F.M

Prince St N.R

Spring St 6

SPRING ST

LITTLE ITALY

Bowery J.Z

Lower East Side Tenement Museum ①

Essex St J.M.Z

DELANCEY

BROOME ②

BROOME ST

GRAND

The Pickle Guys ③③

Grand St B.D

HESTER ST

STRAUS SQUARE

CANAL ST

E Broadway F

Manhattan Bridge Arch

Museum at Eldridge Street ②

DIVISION

MARKET ST

PIKE

HENRY ST

CATHERINE ST

MADISON

MONROE ST

Knickerbocker Village

CHERRY ST

WATER ST

SOUTH ST

LOWER MANHATTAN
p64

LOWER EAST SIDE

Must Sees

① Lower East Side Tenement Museum
② Museum at Eldridge Street

Experience More

③ The Pickle Guys
④ Economy Candy
⑤ Essex Street Market
⑥ Essex Crossing

Eat

① Clinton Street Baking Co
② Dirt Candy
③ Doughnut Plant
④ Ivan Ramen
⑤ Mission Chinese Food

LOWER EAST SIDE

❶ 🤟 Ⓜ️ 🛍️

LOWER EAST SIDE TENEMENT MUSEUM

📍F10 🏠97 Orchard St 🚇Grand St (B, D), Delancey St (F) 🕐10am–6:30pm Fri–Wed, 10am–8:30pm Thu 🌐tenement.org

New York has long been a gateway for immigrants, and this illuminating museum brings the immigrant experience to life. Here, visitors can explore the interior of a 19th-century tenement home in what was once the city's most overcrowded neighborhood.

The Immigrant Experience

Abandoned in 1935, this tenement building was restored by the museum founders in the 1990s. Crumbling and claustrophobic, the tenements lacked any electricity, plumbing, or heating. There were also no indoor toilets – two external toilets would have instead been shared among four families. Apartments were re-created with period furnishings and artifacts found on site, humanizing the lives of those who once lived here.

15,000

immigrants from over 20 countries lived at No. 97 from the 19th to 21st centuries.

Tours of the Tenements

Aided by documents, photographs, and the apartments themselves, guided tours (which are compulsory) provide an insight into the carefully researched lives of several families who once lived here. Tickets are available at the nearby visitor center, where a couple of introductory videos (lasting around 20 minutes) offer context. There is also a great bookstore and art gallery.

These tenements on Orchard Street now house the museum ↓

TOP 5 LOWER EAST SIDE TENEMENT MUSEUM TOURS

Under One Roof
See the post-World War II homes of Jewish, Puerto Rican, and Chinese immigrants.

Shop Life
Stop by the 1870s German saloon, owned by John and Caroline Schneider.

Sweatshop Workers
Visit the Levine family's garment workshop, and the Rogarshevsky family's Sabbath table.

Hard Times
Learn about the lives of the German-Jewish Gumpertz family, and the Italian-Catholic Baldizzi family.

Irish Outsiders
Meet the Irish Moore family in 1869.

1 Worn parlor of the Rogarshevsky family.

2 Actors play the Schneiders at work in their store.

3 Historical photographs of life in the Lower East Side's tenements are shown to a group.

TENEMENTS IN THE LOWER EAST SIDE

New York City's first tenement buildings were constructed in the Lower East Side in 1833, with the development of Little Germany. By 1860, Irish immigrants had started to dominate the neighborhood, but between 1880 and 1920 more than 25 million immigrants, including over 2.5 million Jews, came to the United States. Arrivals in the Lower East Side found low standards of hygiene, abysmal housing, and diseases rife. Reformers like Jacob Riis and Stephen Crane recorded the plight of the city's immigrants in the 1890s, which eventually led to much needed reform in the 20th century.

② 🏛🕍👜
MUSEUM AT ELDRIDGE STREET

📍F11 🏠12 Eldridge St Ⓢ East Broadway (F), Grand St (B, D) 🕐10am–5pm Sun–Thu, 10am–3pm Fri 🌐eldridgestreet.org

The Museum at Eldridge Street showcases the Lower East Side's rich Jewish history in one of the city's most beautiful synagogues. The house of worship is still used by New Yorkers, but visitors are welcome to admire its stunning interiors as part of a guided tour.

Jewish History on the Lower East Side

Constructed in 1887, the Eldridge Street synagogue was the country's first to be built by Eastern European Orthodox Jews. It became part-museum in 2007 after a massive restoration project, but remains a functioning house of worship. The facade is an ornate hybrid of Romanesque, Moorish, and Gothic influences in terra-cotta and brick, but the real attraction is the main sanctuary inside. This features stained-glass windows, a spectacular chandelier, richly carved woodwork, and a beautifully painted ceiling. The rose window, an incredible Star of David roundel, looks stunning on the western wall. There are also displays showing the building's state of dilapidation in the 1970s, and tour guides offer entertaining stories about life in the Lower East Side and the synagogue's role in the local community.

 The intricate exterior of the synagogue, a National Historic Landmark

> **INSIDER TIP**
> **Museum tours**
>
> Note that the main sanctuary of the synagogue can only be visited with a tour guide. Tours of the Museum at Eldridge Street are "pay-what-you-wish" on Mondays, but it's best to arrive as early as possible on the Monday, as the tours can be over-subscribed. Museum tours begin on the hour throughout the week, starting on the lower level, where the Bes Medrash (House of Study) serves as the current synagogue.

Timeline

1887
▽ Synagogue opened by the Kahal Adath Jeshurun, descended from America's first congregation of Russian Jews.

1918
Famed Talmudist Rabbi Aharon Yudelovitch is hired to serve as the first full-time pulpit rabbi.

2014
▽ Seven years after restoration is completed, the visitor center and permanent exhibit are opened.

1940s
After worshiper numbers dwindle, remaining congregation relocates to the lower level; the main sanctuary is closed.

1986
△ Eldridge Street Project established to preserve and restore the virtually derelict synagogue.

Did You Know?

The synagogue took ten months to build and 20 years to restore

↑ The restored synagogue includes spectacular stained-glass windows and a chandelier

Sunrise over a street in the Lower East Side

EXPERIENCE MORE

EAT

Clinton Street Baking Co

Buzzy brunch spot, known for its blueberry pancakes. Walk-in only.

📍G10 🏠4 Clinton St
🌐clintonstreetbaking.com

💲💲💲

Dirt Candy

Stylish vegetarian food; dinner features two set menu choices only.
📍F10 🏠86 Allen St
🌐dirtcandynyc.com

💲💲💲

Doughnut Plant

Doughnuts with seasonal flavors, from pumpkin to chestnut.
📍G11 🏠379 Grand St
🕑D Sun 🌐doughnut plant.com

💲💲💲

Ivan Ramen

Sesame noodles, red chili ramen and steamed pork buns.
📍G10 🏠25 Clinton St
🌐ivanramen.com

💲💲💲

Mission Chinese Food

Danny Bowien's creative take on Sichuan food.
📍G11 🏠171 East Broadway 🌐mission chinesefood.com

💲💲💲

3

The Pickle Guys

📍G11 🏠357 Grand St
🚇Grand St (B, D) 🕑9am–6pm Sat–Thu, 9am–4pm Fri
🌐pickleguys.com

The scent of pickles permeates this little section of Grand Street, just as it did in the early 1900s, when Jewish pickle stores filled the area. True to the traditional Eastern European recipe, The Pickle Guys store their pickles in barrels filled with brine, garlic, and spices; this mixture preserves the pickles for months on end. Pickle varieties include full sour, three-quarters sour, half sour, new, and hot. Chemicals or preservatives are not added, and the store operates to strict Kosher rules.

The store also sells pickled tomatoes, pickled celery, olives, mushrooms, hot peppers, sun-dried tomatoes, sweet kraut, sauerkraut, and herring. It is run like a family business, with a friendly, chatty atmosphere, which perpetuates the neighborhood's traditions.

4

Economy Candy

📍G10 🏠108 Rivington St 🚇2 Av (F) 🕑10am–6pm Mon & Sat, 9am–6pm Tue–Fri & Sun
🌐economycandy.com

A Lower East Side landmark since 1937, this family-owned candy store stocks hundreds of varieties of candy, nuts, and dried fruit. Lined with floor-to-ceiling shelves packed with old-fashioned dispensers, the store is one of the few businesses on the Lower East Side that has remained almost unchanged in name and specialty throughout the neighborhood's fluctuating fortunes over 50 or so years.

This is due in no small part to Jerry Cohen's enterprise in transforming his father's "Nosher's Paradise" from a penny candy store to a national company. The store carries treats from all over the world, as well as gum, no less than 47 types of licorice, all manner of chocolates (including fruit and pretzels covered in the stuff), and even sugar-free candy.

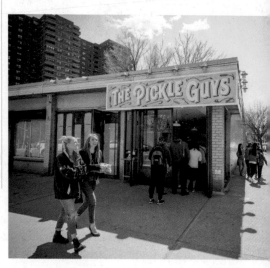

→

Customers lining up for traditional pickles in the Lower East Side

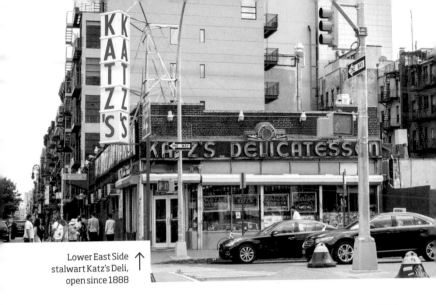

Lower East Side stalwart Katz's Deli, open since 1888

Essex Street Market

📍G10 🏠115 Delancey St
🚇Essex St, Delancey St
(F, M) 🕐8am–7pm Mon–Sat,
10am–6pm Sun 🌐essex
streetmarket.com

The original indoor market was created in 1939 by Mayor Fiorello H La Guardia to bring pushcart vendors together and away from traffic.

In 2018, the Essex Street Market moved to the Essex Crossing complex, taking Saxelby Cheesemongers, Shopsin's iconic diner, and its other tenants to a shiny building that reflects the upwardly mobile character of the neighbor-hood. The move added eleven more vendors, along with two full-service dining options to food hall on the floor below.

Essex Crossing

📍G10 🏠115 Delancey
St 🚇Delancey St (F)
Essex St (J, M, Z) 🌐essex
crossingnyc.com

This vast megaproject covers nine blocks around Delancey and Essex streets, and offers both residential and commercial spaces, plus an expanded Essex Street Market. A movie theater and underground shopping mall, dubbed "The Market Line," should be completed by 2021. In addition, the proposed Lowline would convert a historic trolley terminal into an underground park, lit by solar power. The whole Essex Crossing project is set for completion by 2024.

💬 INSIDER TIP
Deli delights

The Lower East Side is famed for its Jewish delis, which are great for affordable, filling food: on East Houston, head to Katz's Deli for pastrami sandwiches, Yonah Schimmel for potato-and-meat knishes, and Russ & Daughters for bagels.

LOWER EAST SIDE SYNAGOGUES

Jewish heritage is kept alive in the Lower East Side, in part by its historic synagogues. One of the best is the Museum at Eldridge Street (p96), but the Bialystoker (7–11 Willett Street) is another gem. The Kehila Kedosha Janina Synagogue (280 Broome Street) has served the region's Romaniote Jews since 1927, while the section of East Broadway between Clinton and Montgomery streets is known as Shtiebel Row, home to dozens of storefront *shtieblach* (small Jewish congregations).

CHINATOWN, LITTLE ITALY, AND NOLITA

Representing multicultural New York City, these communities have lived here for generations, with Chinese immigrants first arriving in the 1850s. Since the 1980s, Chinatown – Manhattan's most densely populated ethnic neighborhood, and the oldest and largest Chinatown in the Western hemisphere – has pushed into Little Italy, now just a narrow strip along Mulberry Street. Both are colorful neighborhoods with numerous places to eat. To the north is Nolita, home to chic boutiques, restaurants, and bars.

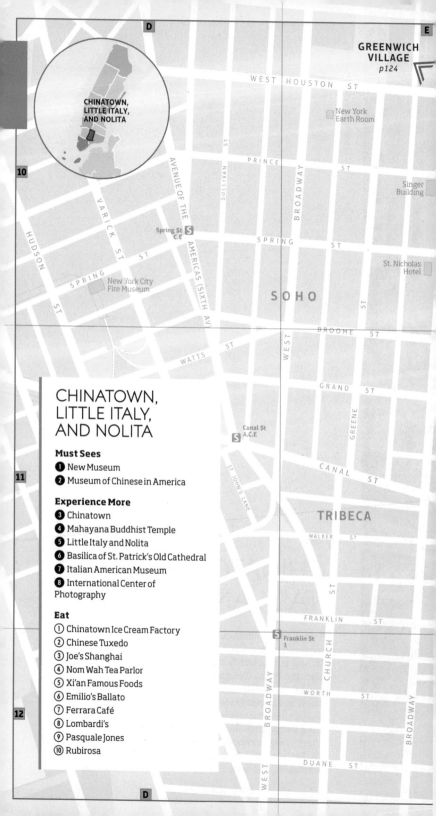

CHINATOWN, LITTLE ITALY, AND NOLITA

Must Sees
1. New Museum
2. Museum of Chinese in America

Experience More
3. Chinatown
4. Mahayana Buddhist Temple
5. Little Italy and Nolita
6. Basilica of St. Patrick's Old Cathedral
7. Italian American Museum
8. International Center of Photography

Eat
1. Chinatown Ice Cream Factory
2. Chinese Tuxedo
3. Joe's Shanghai
4. Nom Wah Tea Parlor
5. Xi'an Famous Foods
6. Emilio's Ballato
7. Ferrara Café
8. Lombardi's
9. Pasquale Jones
10. Rubirosa

EAST VILLAGE
p138

EAST HOUSTON ST

⑥

Puck Building

NOLITA

⑤ Nolita

St. Michael's Church

⑥ Basilica of Saint Patrick's Old Cathedral

International Center of Photography Museum ⑧

STANTON ST

❶ New Museum

FREEMAN ALLEY

RIVINGTON ST

Elizabeth Street Gardens

⑩

Ⓢ Prince St N.R

PRINCE ST

Ⓢ Spring St 6

PETROSINO SQUARE

⑧ SPRING ST

⑨

KENMARE ST

Bowery J.Z Ⓢ

Haughwort Building

BROOME ST

LITTLE ITALY

Old Police Headquarters

⑤ Little Italy

Bowery Savings Bank

SOHO AND TRIBECA
p114

LOWER EAST SIDE
p90

Italian American Museum ⑦

⑦

GRAND ST

Grand St B.D Ⓢ

❷ Museum of Chinese in America

HOWARD ST

HESTER ST

Ⓢ Canal St N.Q.R

Mahayana Buddhist Temple

❹

Ⓢ Canal St 6

CANAL ST

Museum at Eldridge St

Canal St J.Z Ⓢ

WALKER ST

Engine Company No.31

WHITE ST

Civil Court

Criminal Courts Building

Manhattan Bridge Arch

CHINATOWN

❸ Chinatown

Confucius Plaza

MANHATTAN BRIDGE

BAYARD ST

① ⑤

Collect Pond Park

LEONARD ST

HOGAN PL

New York State Building

Columbus Park

MOSCO ST

PELL ST

③

④ DOYERS ST

②

CHATHAM SQUARE

WORTH ST

EAST BROADWAY

LOWER MANHATTAN
p64

NY County Courthouse

PEARL ST

US Courthouse

PACE PLAZA

0 meters   200
0 yards   200

N

Don't miss the museum's rooftop terrace, offering rare panoramas of the Lower East Side. It's open on Saturdays and Sundays during museum hours.

NEW MUSEUM

F10 **235 Bowery** **11am-6pm Tue-Sun (till 9pm Thu)**
2 Av (F, M) **newmuseum.org**

Contemporary art continues to boom in New York, and nowhere more so than at the New Museum. A work of art in itself, this fittingly futuristic space houses quality exhibitions dedicated to cutting-edge art in all mediums.

New York's Contemporary Art Hub

Marcia Tucker left her post as a curator at the Whitney in 1977 to found the cutting-edge New Museum of Contemporary Art, or the New Museum for short. Her aim was to exhibit the work she felt was missing from more traditional museums. The New Museum comprises 60,000 sq ft (5,574 sq m) of exhibition space and the rotating collection features a wide range of art, from photographs of 1960s America to abstract installations. The museum showcases both emerging and established artists, including heavyweights Mark Rothko and Roy Lichtenstein.

↑ The museum's displays are constantly changing, meaning there's always something new to see

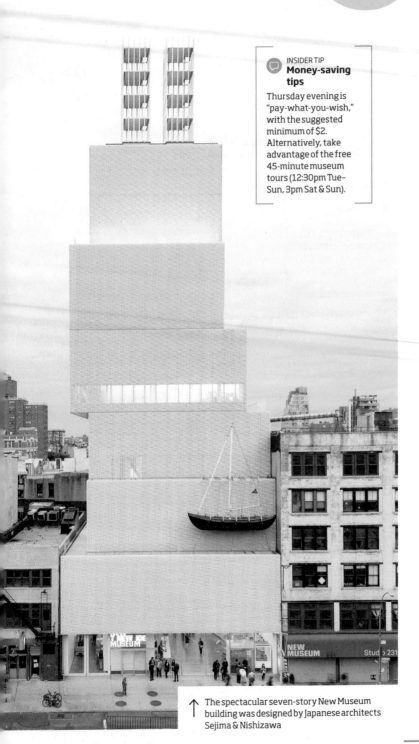

> **INSIDER TIP**
> **Money-saving tips**
>
> Thursday evening is "pay-what-you-wish," with the suggested minimum of $2. Alternatively, take advantage of the free 45-minute museum tours (12:30pm Tue–Sun, 3pm Sat & Sun).

↑ The spectacular seven-story New Museum building was designed by Japanese architects Sejima & Nishizawa

② ⊘ ⊗ 🖐

MUSEUM OF CHINESE IN AMERICA

📍E11 🏠215 Centre St 🚇Canal St (J, N, Q, R, W, Z, 6)
🕐11am–6pm Tue–Sun (until 9pm Thu) 🌐mocanyc.org

Fascinating displays bring past generations back to life at this compelling museum, which honors the legacy of one of New York City's largest immigrant communities, who first settled here in the 19th century.

New York City's Tribute to Chinese-Americans

Visitors can learn about the Chinese-American experience, from the 19th century to the present day, at the engaging Museum of Chinese in America. Issues explored include the Chinese Exclusion Act of 1882, which forbade Chinese workers entry for ten years, and the immigration quotas imposed in the early 20th century, such as the 1924 National Origins Provision (N.O.P.), which restricted entry even further. Via artifacts and multimedia displays, the museum flags various historical and cultural phases in the Chinese-American narrative – from the emergence of "Chop suey" restaurants and so-called "Yellowface" movies in the 1930s, to the evolution of identity for second-generation Chinese-Americans in the 1960s. The museum itself was designed by Maya Lin, who is best known for her creation of the Vietnam Memorial in Washington, D.C. The museum was born from a community-based organization that sought to develop a better understanding of the city's Chinese-American community.

200,000

Chinese immigrants arrived in 1965 after the N.O.P. was abolished.

💬 INSIDER TIP
Money-saving advice

Admission to the Museum of Chinese in America is free on the first Thursday of every month, except for major holidays. The museum doesn't have a café, but it's not far from Chinatown, which has lots of places for an affordable bite to eat.

→
The Museum of Chinese in America, with its striking exterior, is not far from Chinatown

EXPERIENCE MORE

3

Chinatown

🅠 F11 🄰 Streets around Mott St 🅂 Canal St (N, Q, R, 6) 🆆 explorechinatown.com

More than 100,000 Chinese-Americans live in this vibrant neighborhood, one of the biggest and oldest Chinese districts in the West. Since the 1850s, Chinese immigrants have been settling in this part of New York, which today attracts visitors looking to sample the neighborhood's cuisine, visit its galleries, trawl the countless curio stores, and partake in the neighborhood's colorful festivals.

The neighborhood is divided by the east–west Canal Street, with Mott Street cutting north–south. The streets around, which include Pell, Bayard, Doyers, and the Bowery, are lined by fresh fish and fruit stands, dim sum restaurants, souvenir and antiques shops, and tea-and-rice stores.

On the corner of Pell Street and the Bowery lies Huang Daxian Temple, one of the few remaining Taoist temples, with a converted storefront. Farther along Pell Street, No. 16 is the headquarters of the Hip Sing Tong, once a secret society. During an attack in 1924, 70 people were killed when On Leong Tong, part of a criminal fraternity, attacked the building. Halfway along Pell is tiny, crooked Doyers Street, once known as the "Bloody Angle" for its role as a battleground during the Tong Wars in the early 1900s.

To glimpse another side of Chinatown, step into the incense-scented Eastern States Buddhist Temple at 64 Mott Street, where offerings are piled up before tiny golden Buddhas. The temple is open daily.

EAT

Chinatown Ice Cream Factory

Asian flavors, from black sesame and taro, to green tea and lychee.

🅠 F11 🄰 65 Bayard St 🆆 chinatownicecreamfactory.com

Chinese Tuxedo

Hip and contemporary Cantonese restaurant with inventive cocktails.

🅠 F12 🄰 5 Doyers St 🄻 Lunch 🆆 chinesetuxedo.com

Joe's Shanghai

Shrine to American-Chinese cuisine (think deep-fried chicken) and "soup dumplings."

🅠 F12 🄰 9 Pell St 🆆 joeshanghairestaurant.com

Nom Wah Tea Parlor

Elegant and old-fashioned dim sum spot dating back to 1920.

🅠 F12 🄰 13 Doyers St 🆆 nomwah.com

Xi'an Famous Foods

Spicy specialties from northwest China, such as noodles with cumin-spiked lamb.

🅠 F11 🄰 45 Bayard St 🆆 xianfoods.com

4

Mahayana Buddhist Temple

📍F11 🏠133 Canal St
🚇Canal St (N, Q, R, 6)
🕐8:30am–6pm daily
🌐mahayana.us

Larger than its counterpart on Mott Street, this opulent Buddhist temple, at the foot of the Manhattan Bridge, was built by the Ying family, who are from the city of Ningbo, in China. Constructed in 1997, the temple boasts classic Chinese designs, and the main altar contains a massive gold idol of the Buddha. Bathed in blue neon lighting, and surrounded by candles, the statue is 16 ft (5 m) tall. The 32 plaques along the walls tell the story of Buddha's life. A small shrine to Guanyin, the Chinese Goddess of Mercy, stands in the entrance hall. There is a small store upstairs that sells statues, books, and other knick-knacks.

On the other side of the Bowery, the former Citizens Savings Bank is a local landmark, with a Neo-Byzantine bronze dome that was completed in 1924. The building now functions as a branch of HSBC.

TEN REN'S TEA

Founded in Taiwan back in 1953, Ten Ren's Tea remains Manhattan's premier tea merchant. The branch at 75 Mott Street opened in 1984 and quickly developed a cult following. Sample the huge array of teas while you shop, from expensive oolongs and pu'erh teas to simple green varieties. The highly prized Dongfang, or "Oriental Beauty," tea is a heavily fermented oolong with a sweet hint of honey.

↑ The impressive, golden Buddha at the Mahayana Buddhist Temple

5

Little Italy and Nolita

📍F10 & F11 🏠Streets around Mulberry St
🚇Canal St (N, Q, R, 6)
🌐littleitalynyc.com

The most exciting time to visit these neighborhoods is during the 11-day Festa di San Gennaro around September 19. Italians from around the city meet at Mulberry Street for a wild celebration in honor of the patron saint of Naples. The street is full of stands and Italian snack vendors, and there is plenty of lively music and dancing.

Many of Little Italy's restaurants offer simple, rustic food served in friendly surroundings at reasonable prices. Some original cafés and *salumerias* (specialty food stores) still survive, such as Ferrara's at 195 Grand Street. Nolita, meanwhile, is home to stylish boutiques and vintage stores frequented by well-heeled New Yorkers.

Originally inhabited by the Irish, Little Italy and Nolita (or NoLita, shortened from "north of Little Italy") saw an influx of Italian immigrants in the 1800s. Natives of Campania and Naples settled on Mulberry Street, while the Sicilians stayed on Elizabeth Street. Mott Street was divided between people

EAT

Emilio's Ballato
Old-school Italian, with a low-key, clubby atmosphere. Popular with celebrities.

📍E10 🏠55 East Houston St 📞(212) 274-8881 🕐L Sat, L Sun

–––

Ferrara Café
Traditional café, around since 1892, serving cheesecake, cannoli, and gelato.

📍F11 🏠195 Grand St 🌐ferraranyc.com.

–––

Lombardi's
America's oldest pizzeria (1905) offers classic margherita and clam pizzas.

📍F10 🏠32 Spring St 🌐firstpizza.com

–––

Pasquale Jones
Modern diner known for wood-burning ovens, pasta, and pizzas.

📍E10 🏠187 Mulberry St 🕐L Mon–Thu 🌐pasqualejones.com

–––

Rubirosa
A contemporary take on classic red-sauce and pizza restaurants.

📍E10 🏠235 Mulberry St 🌐rubirosanyc.com.

→

Little Italy's colorful streets, lined with countless restaurants

from Calabria and Puglia. However, after World War II, many Italians relocated to the suburbs and today the district is much smaller – Mulberry Street is the only remaining Italian territory. For more about the history of the area, visit the Italian-American Museum, in the building that formerly housed the Banca Stabile.

Basilica of St. Patrick's Old Cathedral

📍E10 **🏛Corner of Mott and Prince sts** **🚇Prince St (R)** **🕐8am–12:30pm & 3:30–6pm Thu-Tue** **🌐oldcathedral.org**

The first St. Patrick's on this site was consecrated in 1815. It was destroyed by fire in the 1860s, but was rebuilt much as it is today. When the arch-diocese transferred the See to the new St. Patrick's Cathedral uptown, Old St. Patrick's became the local parish church, and it has flourished with a constantly changing multicultural congregation.

Below the church are the vaults containing the remains of, among others, one of New York's most famous

families of restaurateurs, the Delmonicos. Pierre Toussaint was also buried here, but in 1990 his remains were moved from the graveyard beside the church to a more prestigious burial place in a crypt in St. Patrick's Cathedral. Born a slave in Haiti in 1766, Toussaint was brought to New York, where he lived as a free man and became a prosperous wig-maker. He was later devoted to caring for the poor and tending cholera victims, and used the money he had made to build an orphanage.

Italian American Museum

📍E11 **🏛155 Mulberry St at Grand St** **🚇Canal St (J, N, Q, R, W, Z, 6)** **🕐For renovation until early 2019** **🌐italianamericanmuseum.org**

Housed in the 1885 Banca Stabile premises (still containing the old bank vault), this museum chronicles the history of Little Italy through original artifacts, rare photo-graphs and documents, including a 1914 extortion note from a "Black Hand" mafia member. One particular

display pays tribute to Giuseppe Petrosino, one of the first Italian-American NYPD officers, murdered working on a mafia case in Sicily in 1909.

The museum is currently undergoing renovation and will open again in early 2019 with additional exhibition and performance space.

International Center of Photography

📍F10 **🏛250 Bowery** **🚇2 Av (F)** **🕐10am–6pm Tue, Wed & Fri-Sun, 10am–9pm Thu** **🚫Federal hols** **🌐icp.org**

All things photography and photojournalism are celebrated at this sleek and dynamic museum. Founded by Cornell Capa in 1974, the ICP aims to conserve the work of photojournalists such as Capa's brother Robert, who was killed on assignment in 1954. The collection of 12,500 original prints includes work by the likes of Ansel Adams, Henri Cartier-Bresson, and W. Eugene Smith.

In addition, special temporary exhibitions are organized from the Center's archive and outside sources.

A SHORT WALK
LITTLE ITALY
AND CHINATOWN

Distance 1.25 mile (2 km) **Nearest subway** Canal St
Time 25 minutes

Manhattan's largest and most colorful neighborhood is
Chinatown, which is growing so rapidly that it is running into
nearby Little Italy as well as the Lower East Side. Streets here
teem with grocery stores, gift shops, and hundreds of Chinese
restaurants; even the plainest offering delicious food and
tempting aromas. What is left of Little Italy can be found at
Mulberry and Grand streets, where old-world flavor abounds.

↑ Vibrant storefronts in New York's
lively Chinatown

Canal St
subway
(lines R, N, Q, 6)

START

FINISH

The market stalls
on Canal Street
have a wide range
of bargains,
including clothes
and fresh produce.

Home to a thriving – and still
expanding – community of Chinese
immigrants, this neighborhood is
famous for its restaurants and hectic
street life (p109).

Once run-down, Columbus Park
now fills with local residents
playing mahjong.

Bloody Angle, where Doyers
Street turns sharply, was the
gruesome site of many gangland
ambushes during the 1920s.

Chatham Square has a memorial dedicated
to the Chinese-American war dead, and to
Lin Zexu, a Qing dynasty official, revered
for his crackdown on the opium trade.

LAFAYETTE STREET

CENTRE STREET

GRAN

BAXTER STREET

CANAL STREET

MULBERRY STREET

BAYARD STRE

PELL STREET

Locator Map
For more detail see p104

CHINATOWN, LITTLE ITALY, AND NOLITA

The dome of the Old Police Headquarters towers over the whole area. In 1973, the police moved out of this Baroque civic building; 10 years later, the building was turned into apartments.

The tantalizing scents of Italy still waft from the traditional restaurants and bakeries of Little Italy, once home to thousands of immigrants (p110).

Umbertos Clam House, known as the place where Mafia boss Joey Gallo was shot in 1972, once occupied this location on Mulberry Street.

Stanford White designed Bowery Savings Bank in 1894. Today it hosts private functions (p192).

The Eastern States Buddhist Temple at 64b Mott Street contains over 100 golden Buddhas.

↑ Old Police Headquarters, now luxury apartments

Confucius Plaza is marked by sculptor Liu Shih's monument to the Chinese philosopher.

Built in 1887, the Museum at Eldridge Street was first the largest synagogue built in the U.S. by European Jews (p96).

0 meters 100
0 yards 100
N ↑

SOHO AND TRIBECA

Stores, eateries, and architecture have transformed these formerly industrial districts. SoHo was threatened with demolition back in the 1960s until preservationists drew attention to its rare and historic cast-iron architecture. The district was saved, and by the 1980s SoHo had developed its own vibrant art scene. It now serves as an enormous outdoor shopping mall, scattered with bars and bistros. Neighboring Tribeca, meanwhile, was once a wholesale food district. When Robert De Niro set up his Tribeca Film Center in 1988, the area became one of the hottest neighborhoods in the city, attracting galleries, boutiques, and restaurants. The Tribeca Film Festival followed in 2002.

SOHO AND TRIBECA

Experience More

❶ Children's Museum of the Arts
❷ New York Earth Room
❸ New York City Fire Museum
❹ 56 Leonard
❺ Hudson River Park
❻ Hook and Ladder Company No. 8
❼ Chocolate Museum and Experience with Jacques Torres
❽ Drawing Center
❾ Leslie-Lohman Museum of Gay and Lesbian Art

Eat

① Balthazar
② Le Coucou
③ The Odeon
④ Grand Banks

Drink

⑤ Paul's Casablanca
⑥ Pegu Club

EXPERIENCE MORE

❶
Children's Museum of the Arts

📍 D10 🏠 103 Charlton St
🚇 Houston St (1) 🚌 M20, M21 🕐 Noon–5pm Mon, noon–6pm Thu & Fri, 10am–5pm Sat & Sun 🌐 cmany.org

Founded in 1988, this innovative museum aims to make the most of children's artistic potential by providing plenty of hands-on activities, sing-alongs, workshops, and performances. Children under 13 can busy themselves with paint, glue, paper, and other messy materials to create their own drawings and sculptures. For inspiration, displays of work by local artists are exhibited alongside examples of children's art from across the world. Kids can play around in the dressing-up room and the ball pond, and the museum also hosts a varied program of events appealing to children and families.

❷
New York Earth Room

📍 E10 🏠 141 Wooster St
🚇 Prince St (R) 🕐 Noon–3pm & 3:30–6pm Wed–Sun 🗓 Mid-Jun–mid-Sep 🌐 diaart.org/sites/main/earthroom

Of the three Earth Rooms created by conceptual artist Walter De Maria (1935–2013), this is the only one still in existence. Commissioned by the Dia Art Foundation in 1977, the interior earth

DRINK

Paul's Casablanca

Opened by Paul Sevigny, this cocktail bar and nightclub has a loyal following among celebs and fashion icons. Open from 10pm until 4am, the interior is decked out like a Moroccan palace, with mosaic tiles, lanterns, and leather beanbag chairs. Staff wear kaftans and DJs spin a different genre every night, from rock to hip hop (The Smiths are featured on Sundays).

📍 D10 🏠 305 Spring St
🗓 Mon, Wed 🌐 pauls casablanca.com

Pegu Club

Elegant cocktail lounge, themed around the original Pegu Club in Burma, a British colonial bar built in the 1880s. Like the original, this lounge serves the gin-based "Pegu Club" cocktail as well as perfecting the Gin-Gin Mule, which consists of ginger beer with Tanqueray gin, fresh mint, and lime juice. Open from 5pm until the very early hours.

📍 E10 🏠 77 Houston St
🌐 peguclub.com

←

Multi-million dollar penthouses, occupying the uppermost floors of 56 Leonard, tower over Tribeca

Cyclists and walkers enjoying the view along Hudson River Park

Did You Know?

The majority of Hudson River Park's total area is located in the river itself.

sculpture consists of 280,000 lb (127,000 kg) of dirt piled 22 inches (56 cm) deep in a 3,600-sq-ft (334-sq-m) room. *The Broken Kilometer*, another sculpture by De Maria, can be seen at 393 West Broadway. It is composed of 500 solid brass rods arranged in five parallel rows.

---

③

New York City Fire Museum

📍 D10 🏛 278 Spring St
🚇 Spring St (6) 🕐 10am–5pm daily ❌ Federal hols
🌐 nycfiremuseum.org

This museum is housed in a Beaux Arts-style 1904 firehouse. New York City's unsurpassed collection of firefighting equipment and memorabilia from the 18th century to 1917 includes scale models, bells, and hydrants. Upstairs, fire trucks are neatly lined up for an 1890 parade. An interactive fire simulation, available for groups, gives an insight into firefighting.

The museum's first floor features an exhibition on 9/11, filled with tributes.

---

④

56 Leonard

📍 E12 🏛 56 Leonard St
🚇 Franklin St (1) ❌ Closed to the public 🌐 56leonardtribeca.com

Completed in 2016, and a new addition to Manhattan's ever-evolving skyline, 56 Leonard comprises a jaw-dropping stack of cantilevered glass blocks. Tribeca's tallest building has been dubbed the "Jenga Building" by local media, thanks to the stack of units designed by Swiss architects Herzog & de Meuron. The interior of the 821-ft (250-m) condominium building is private but you can visit the giant, bean-like object at its base. This highly polished pod by British sculptor Anish Kapoor is similar to his "Cloud Gate" in Chicago.

---

⑤

Hudson River Park

📍 C10 🚇 Houston, Canal or Franklin st (1)
🌐 hudsonriverpark.org

Immediately beyond West Side Highway is the Hudson River Park, a landscaped promenade that stretches north toward Chelsea and Midtown. Visitors can walk to the tip of the island along the shady Battery Park City Esplanade all the way to Battery Park. The once-decaying piers and wharves have been transformed, with fountains, gardens, dog parks, and tennis courts. Pier 25 features Grand Banks, an oyster bar on an old sailing ship, mini-golf and beach volleyball, plus snack stands.

EAT

Balthazar

This brasserie's buzzy atmosphere is hard to resist. Keith McNally's restaurant features ornate Parisian decor and the classics - moules frites, oysters, and Bordeaux wine.

📍E10 🏠80 Spring St 🌐balthazarny.com

💲💲💲

Le Coucou

Highly acclaimed French restaurant featuring oak tables, contemporary chandeliers and French antiques. Great spot for breakfast - don't miss the pancakes.

📍E11 🏠138 Lafayette St 🌐lecoucou.com

💲💲💲

The Odeon

Famously appearing in Jay McInerney's *Bright Lights, Big City*, this iconic bistro offers all the French and American standards.

📍E12 🏠145 West Broadway 🌐theodeon restaurant.com

💲💲💲

Grand Banks

Indulge on oysters and cocktails aboard the 1942 wooden schooner *Sherman Zwicker*, which is now a docked restaurant. Get there before 5pm - limited online reservations.

📍C12 🏠Pier 25, North Moore St 🕐Mid-Apr-Oct only 🚫L Mon-Tue 🌐grandbanks.org

💲💲💲

 Hook and Ladder Company No. 8 firehouse, a popular draw for fans of the *Ghostbusters* movies

6
Hook and Ladder Company No. 8

📍D11 🏠14 North Moore St 🚇Franklin St (1) 🚫To the public

This handsome fire station's claim to fame is revealed by the ghost logos painted on the sidewalk outside. The station starred as the base of the iconic *Ghostbusters* films of the 1980s, and was reportedly chosen by writer and actor Dan Aykroyd, who liked the 1903 Beaux Arts building. The building also featured in the 2016 remake, with its all-female cast.

In real life, Hook and Ladder Company No. 8 played a major role in the rescue efforts following the terrorist attack of September 11, 2001. Today it remains a working firehouse of the New York Fire Department, so it can only be viewed from the outside.

7
Chocolate Museum and Experience with Jacques Torres

📍D10 🏠350 Hudson St 🚇Houston St (1) 🕐10am-5pm Wed-Sun 🌐choco-storyny.com

New York's first chocolate museum opened in 2017, next to one of Jacques Torres' beloved cafés and chocolate shops. The museum features exhibits tracing the history of chocolate, starting with its Mesoamerican roots, but it's the enticing demonstrations held throughout the day (and plenty of free samples) that make visiting a real treat.

Born in the small Provençal town of Bandol, France, chocolatier Jacques Torres (aka "Mr Chocolate") came to New York in 1988 and opened his first chocolate factory in 2000.

Drawing Center

E11 ⊕ 35 Wooster St
S Canal St (A, C, E, N, Q, R, W)
⊙ noon-6pm Wed-Sun (to
8pm Thu) **W** drawing
center.org

SoHo's legacy of fine art
galleries is maintained here
at the Drawing Center, with a
primary focus on changing
exhibitions of historical and
contemporary drawings.
Founded in 1977, the center
has featured masters such as
Marcel Duchamp and Richard
Tuttle, as well as emerging
artists. Each year an artist
is invited to create a wall
drawing in the gallery's

main entryway and stairwell,
with Inka Essenhigh's
Manhattanhenge on display
until early 2019.

Leslie-Lohman Museum of Gay and Lesbian Art

E11 ⊕ 26 Wooster St
S Canal St (A, C, E, F)
⊙ noon-6pm Wed-Sun
(to 8pm Thu) **W** leslie
lohman.org

Founded by J. Frederic "Fritz"
Lohman and Charles W. Leslie
in 1990, this innovative
museum has over 30,000
objects, spanning over three
centuries of LGBTQ art.
Exhibitions have included a
retrospective on the work and
impact of artist and filmmaker
Barbara Hammer, while the
permanent collection contains
works by Berenice Abbott,
David Hockney, Andy Warhol,
Jean Cocteau, Robert Mapple-
thorpe, and many others.

Did You Know?

Though Hook and Ladder
No. 8 featured in 1984's
Ghostbusters, interior
filming took place at a
firehouse in L.A.

CAST-IRON ARCHITECTURE

SoHo is noted for its striking cast-iron
architecture, a style that dominated
construction here from 1860 to the turn
of the 20th century. Molding components
from iron meant cheaper and faster
construction than buildings of brick or
stone. Heavy iron crossbeams could carry
the weight of the floors, allowing greater
space for windows and high ceilings. In
addition, almost any style or decoration
could be cast in iron, painted or plastered,
and bolted to the front of a building to
resemble marble. Some of the best
examples are on Greene Street, where
No. 72-76 is known as the "King of
Greene Street," and No. 28-30, the
"Queen." The Haughwout Building, at
492 Broadway, was erected in 1857 and
the Venetian-style palazzo is considered
the quintessential cast-iron building. The
charmingly ornate Little Singer Building,
at 561-563 Broadway, was designed by
Ernest Flagg, at the very end of the cast-
iron era, in 1904.

A SHORT WALK
SOHO CAST-IRON HISTORIC DISTRICT

Distance 0.16 mile (1 km) **Nearest subway** Canal St, Prince St
Time 15 minutes

The largest concentration of cast-iron architecture in the world survives in the area between West Houston and Canal streets. The heart of the district is Greene Street, where 50 buildings erected between 1869 and 1895 are found on five cobblestoned blocks. Most of their intricately designed cast-iron facades are in the Neo-Classical Revival style. Now they are rare works of industrial art, well suited to the present character of this district, which is largely inhabited by artists, actors, and wealthy New Yorkers. Others visit here for the charming village vibe and cache of excellent bars and restaurants.

↑ Attractive, cobblestoned Greene Street in New York's SoHo

West Broadway, as it passes through SoHo, combines striking architecture with a string of galleries and restaurants.

The Broken Kilometer, at 393 West Broadway, is by Walter De Maria. It plays tricks with perspective (p119).

72–76 Greene Street, the "King of Greene Street," is a splendid Corinthian-columned building, created by Isaac F. Duckworth, a master of cast-iron design.

Performing Garage is a tiny experimental theater that pioneers the work of avant-garde artists.

Of all Greene Street's fine cast-iron buildings, one of the best is 28–30, the "Queen," which was erected by Duckworth in 1872 and has a tall mansard roof.

15–17 Greene Street is a late addition, dating from 1895, in a simple Corinthian style.

START

10–14 Greene Street dates from 1869. The glass circles in the risers of the iron stoop meant daylight could reach the basement.

WEST BROADWAY

WOOSTER STREET

BROOME STREET

GREENE ST

GRAND STREET

Richard Haas, the prolific muralist, has transformed a blank wall into a convincing cast-iron frontage.

Did You Know?

SoHo stands for "South of Houston," and Tribeca for "Triangle Below Canal Street."

Locator Map
For more detail see p116

A terracotta beauty, the Singer Building was built in 1904 for the famous sewing machine company.

0 meters   150   **N**
0 yards   150   ↑

Dean & DeLuca is one of the best gourmet food stores in New York. Its range includes a global choice of coffee beans.

PRINCE STREET

MERCER STREET

FINISH

BROADWAY

CROSBY STREET

Prince St subway station (lines N, R)

101 Spring Street, with its simple, geometric facade and large windows, is a fine example of the style that led to the skyscraper.

During the Civil War, St. Nicholas Hotel was a luxury hotel, and was used as a headquarters for the Union Army.

Dating back to 1857, the Haughwout Building was built for the E.V. Haughwout china and glassware company and featured the first Otis safety elevator.

↑ Shoppers at gourmet food store Dean & DeLuca

GREENWICH VILLAGE

Since the 1920s, Greenwich Village has been the bohemian heart of New York. Popularly known as the West Village, or just "the Village," the area became a sanctuary for city dwellers during the yellow fever epidemic in 1822. The 1950s saw the emerging Beat Movement, while in the 1960s folk singers like Bob Dylan launched their careers here. The Stonewall Riots of 1969, the catalyst for the Gay Rights Movement, began at the Stonewall Inn. With its quaint streets and charming brownstones, Greenwich Village is one of the city's more artistic, liberal neighborhoods. It has steadily become an expensive part of Manhattan, with large expanses owned by New York University.

GREENWICH VILLAGE

Must See

❶ Whitney Museum of American Art

Experience More

❷ Comedy Cellar
❸ Grove Court
❹ Center for Architecture
❺ Renee & Chaim Gross Foundation
❻ Sheridan Square
❼ Meatpacking District
❽ Washington Square Park
❾ West 4th Street Courts
❿ NYU and Grey Art Gallery
⓫ NY City AIDS Memorial
⓬ Keith Haring's Carmine Street Mural

Eat

① Blue Hill
② Chumley's
③ Caffe Reggio
④ Magnolia Bakery

0 meters 200
0 yards 200

N

The cascading levels of the Whitney Museum of American Art, found at the foot of the High Line

WHITNEY MUSEUM OF AMERICAN ART

📍B8 🏠99 Gansevoort St 🚇14 St (A, C, E), 8 Av (L) 🕐10:30am-6pm Mon, Wed-Sun (till 10pm Fri & Sat); Jul & Aug: 10:30am-6pm daily 🚪Some Federal hols 🌐whitney.org

The foremost showcase for American art of the 20th and 21st centuries, the Whitney is housed in a stunning building by architect Renzo Piano.

The Whitney was founded by Gertrude Vanderbilt Whitney after the Met turned down her collection of works by artists such as Bellows and Hopper. The Whitney moved from the Upper East Side to this innovative building in 2015. The sixth and seventh floors showcase pieces from the museum's collection – there isn't a permanent display, rather a constant rotation of works. Temporary exhibits occupy the first, fifth, and eighth floors. The Whitney Biennial, held in even years, is the most significant exhibition of new trends in American art.

↑ *Three Flags* (1958) by Jasper Johns, a key Pop Art influencer

← Tom Wesselman's *Still Life Number 36* (1964), part of an exhibition at the Whitney

→ Detail of George Bellows' *Dempsey and Firpo* (1924), depicting a famous prizefight

GERTRUDE VANDERBILT WHITNEY

Born into the prosperous Vanderbilt family in 1875, Gertrude married wealthy Harry Payne Whitney in 1896. She became an accomplished sculptor and a patron of the arts, promoting female artists in particular. In 1908, she opened the Whitney Studio Gallery in Greenwich Village and, in 1931, she founded the Whitney Museum.

EXPERIENCE MORE

↑ The stunning gardens and desirable real estate of Grove Court

Comedy Cellar

📍D9 🏠117 MacDougal St
🚇W 4 St (A, B, C, D, E, F, M)
🕐For shows only
🌐comedycellar.com

One of the city's most iconic comedy clubs was founded in 1982 by comedian Bill Grundfest, who has since become a TV writer and producer. Shows are held every evening from 7.30pm and normally comprise between five and seven comics performing sets of around 20 minutes each. Regular comics include Todd Barry, Jim Norton, Patrice O'Neal, Michelle Wolf, and Dave Chappelle.

❸ Grove Court

📍C9 🚇Christopher St-Sheridan Sq (1)

An enterprising grocer named Samuel Cocks built the six townhouses here, in an area formed by a bend in the street. (The bends in this part of the Village originally marked divisions between colonial properties.) Cocks reckoned that having residents in the empty passage between 10 and 12 Grove Street would help his business at No. 18. However, residential courts, which are now highly prized, were not considered respectable in 1854, and the lowbrow residents attracted to the area earned it the nickname "Mixed Ale Alley." O. Henry later chose this block as the setting for his 1902 work *The Last Leaf*.

Center for Architecture

📍E9 🏠536 LaGuardia Pl
🚇W 4 St (A, B, C, D, E, F, M)
🕐9am–8pm Mon–Fri, 11am–5pm Sat 🌐centerforarchitecture.org

Established by the American Institute of Architects in 2003, this bold and stylish hub for conferences, lectures, and film screenings also hosts temporary exhibitions highlighting every aspect of architectural design. Topics cover everything from Modernism and the 1964 World's Fair to European social housing projects. The center also leads New York City's annual month-long architecture and design festival, Archtober. Check the website for details of tours of the neighborhood.

❺ Renee & Chaim Gross Foundation

📍E9 🏠526 LaGuardia Pl
🚇W 4 St (A, B, C, D, E, F, M)
🕐Thu & Fri for tours
🌐rcgrossfoundation.org

Born in Austrian Galicia (now Ukraine) in 1904, celebrated Jewish sculptor Chaim Gross emigrated to the United States in 1921. He was a pioneer of the direct carving method, and rose to popularity in the 1930s.

EAT

Blue Hill
Dan Barber's celebrated farm-to-table cuisine.
📍D9 🏠75 Washington Place 🕐Lunch 🌐bluehillfarm.com
💲💲💲

Chumley's
Old speakeasy turned high-end American restaurant.
📍D9 🏠86 Bedford St 🕐Lunch 🌐chumleysnewyork.com
💲💲💲

Caffe Reggio
Open since 1927, this Italian coffee house is crammed with antiques.
📍D9 🏠119 MacDougal St 📞(212) 475-9557
💲💲💲

Magnolia Bakery
Colorful cupcakes, as seen on *Sex and the City*.
📍C9 🏠401 Bleecker St 🌐magnoliabakery.com
💲💲💲

He lived here from 1963 until his death in 1991, and his 1830s townhouse is open for tours. His first-floor sculpture studio remains much as he left it (with a permanent installation of Gross' sculpture next door), while his living quarters upstairs feature works from his personal art collection.

One-hour tours take place at 1 and 3pm, Thu and Fri. Online reservations required.

The Meatpacking District, drawing shoppers by day and club-hoppers by night ↓

6

Sheridan Square

📍 D9 🚇 Christopher St-Sheridan Sq (1)

This square is the heart of the Village. It was named for the Civil War General Philip Sheridan, who became commander-in-chief of the US Army in 1883. His statue stands in nearby Christopher Park.

The Draft Riots of 1863 took place here and, over a century later, another disturbance rocked the square. The Stonewall Inn, at 53 Christopher Street, was a gay bar (the inn here today is not the original). Such establishments were illegal and it had only stayed in business by paying off the police but on June 28, 1969, patrons rebelled, sparking the Stonewall Riots.

7

Meatpacking District

📍 C8 🚇 14th St (A, C, E), 8 Av (L)

Once the domain of butchers in blood-stained aprons, these days (and particularly nights) the Meatpacking District is very different. Squeezed into an area south of 14th Street and west of 9th Avenue, the neighborhood is now dotted with trendy clubs, lounges, and boutique hotels that swell with New Yorkers out for a good time.

Hipsters and fashionistas arrived in droves when Soho House, the New York branch of the London private members' club, moved in. This was followed by the classy Hotel Gansevoort, with its enviable rooftop swimming pool. These institutions aside, fashion designers (including Stella McCartney and Marc Jacobs) have outlets here. There's also upscale restaurants, tempting wine bars, cool nightclubs, and exclusive galleries, with more continuing to pop up.

The greatest allures of the Meatpacking District include the Whitney Museum of American Art (p128) and the High Line (p166), which begins on Gansevoort Street and offers gorgeous views of the neighborhood.

THE STONEWALL RIOTS

The Stonewall Inn dates back to the 1840s, but after becoming a gay bar in 1966 it suffered regular police harassment. During a police raid on June 28, 1969, protestors fought with police for the first time, resulting in several arrests and some injured police officers. The event formally inaugurated the gay-rights movement. In 2016 the "Stonewall National Monument" was dedicated to the LGBTQ-rights movement.

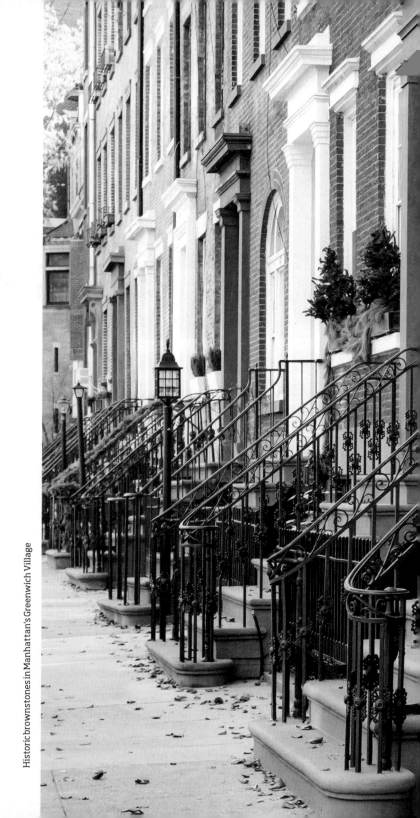

Historic brownstones in Manhattan's Greenwich Village

↑ Leafy Washington Square Park, home to the Washington Square Arch *(inset)*, is a popular place to relax

8
Washington Square Park

D9 **S** W 4 St (A, B, C, D)

This vibrant open space was once marshland through which the quiet Minetta Brook flowed. By the late 1700s, the area had been turned into a public cemetery – when excavation began for the park, some 10,000 skeletal remains were exhumed. The square was used as a dueling ground for a time, then as a site for public hangings until 1819. The "hanging elm" in the northwest corner remains. In 1826 the marsh was filled in and the brook diverted underground, where it still flows; a small sign on a fountain at the entrance to Two Fifth Avenue marks its course. The magnificent marble arch

by Stanford White, at the park's northern entrance, was completed in 1892 to mark the centenary of George Washington's inauguration, replacing an earlier wooden arch that spanned lower Fifth Avenue. A stairway is hidden in the right side of the arch. In 1916, a group of artists led by Marcel Duchamp and John Sloan broke in, climbed atop the arch, and declared the "free and independent republic of Washington Square, the state of New Bohemia."

Across the street is "the Row." Now part of NYU, this block was once home to New York's most prominent families. The Delano family, writers Edith Wharton, Henry James, and John Dos Passos,

and artist Edward Hopper all lived here. No. 8 was once the mayor's official home.

Today, families, joggers, street entertainers, skate-boarders, dog-walkers, and chess-players enjoy the park side by side – particularly when the sun shines.

9
West 4th Street Courts

D9 **A** Sixth Av at West 3rd St **S** W 4 St (A, B, C, D, E, F, M)

These public basketball courts are known as "The Cage" for the physical style of pick-up games typically on display here. Open since 1935, the courts still attract ambitious amateur players from all over the city, hoping to get noticed. Former NBA players Stephon Marbury, Anthony Mason and Smush Parker all played here

Families, joggers, street entertainers, skateboarders, dog-walkers, and chess-players enjoy the park side by side – particularly when the sun shines.

The building was demolished in 1892. The Silver Center now occupies the site and contains NYU's **Grey Art Gallery**, at 100 Washington Square E. Here, exemplary traveling exhibitions are hosted in a wide range of media, such as photography, experimental video art, paintings, and sculpture. There are also temporary exhibits from the permanent collection: American paintings from the 1940s to the present are particularly well represented.

---

11 NY City AIDS Memorial

📍 D8 🚇 West 12th St
🚇 8 Av (L), 14 St (1, 2, 3)
🌐 nycaidsmemorial.org

Inaugurated in 2016, this poignant memorial pays tribute to all the New Yorkers who have died from AIDS since the 1970s – more than 100,000 in total. Designed by New York-based Studio ai, the memorial comprises a giant 18-ft (5.5-m) steel canopy and acts as a gateway to St. Vincent's Park. The granite paving stones below were designed by visual artist Jenny Holzer and are engraved with lines from Walt Whitman's poem *Song of Myself*. The park itself is close to the site of the former St. Vincent's Hospital, which

Did You Know?

Washington Square Park featured in Will Smith's movie *I Am Legend* (2007).

housed the city's first and largest AIDS ward during the 1980s.

---

12 Keith Haring's Carmine Street Mural

📍 D10 🏠 1 Clarkson St at 7th Av 🚇 W 4 St (A, B, C, D, E, F, M)

Pop artist Keith Haring's magnificent Carmine Street mural overlooks the public swimming pool at the back of the Tony Dapolito Recreation Center. Created in 1987, and measuring 18 ft (5.5 m) high by 170 ft (52 m) long, the mural features Haring's trademark colorful, cartoonish designs. The bold, stylized motifs of fish and children, as well as abstract yellow and blue shapes, almost appear to be dancing. You can get a good look from Clarkson Street – or go in for a swim. Haring (1958–90) painted several murals in the city.

in their early years. The courts regularly host high-quality street tournaments; Kenny Graham's West 4th Street summer league usually runs from May through September. Handball is also played here.

---

10 NYU and Grey Art Gallery

📍 E9 🚇 Washington Sq
🚇 W 4 St (A, C, E, F, M), 8 St (N, R, W) 🌐 nyu.edu
🌐 greyartgallery.nyu.edu

Originally named the University of the City of New York, New York University (NYU) was founded in 1831 as an alternative to Episcopalian Columbia University. It is now the largest private university in the US and extends for many blocks around Washington Square. The visitor center is on West 4th Street.

Construction of the school's first building sparked the Stonecutters' Guild Riot of 1833, in which contractors protested against the use of prison inmates to cut stone. The National Guard was brought in to restore order.

↑ The impressive NY City AIDS Memorial at St. Vincent's Hosptial Park

A SHORT WALK
GREENWICH VILLAGE

Distance 0.80 mile (1.25 km) **Nearest metro** Houston St, Christopher St **Time** 15 minutes

A stroll through historic Greenwich Village is a feast of unexpected small pleasures – charming row houses, hidden alleys, and leafy courtyards. The often quirky architecture suits the bohemian air of the Village. Many famous people, particularly artists and writers, such as playwright Eugene O'Neill and actor Dustin

Hoffman, have made their homes in the houses and apartments that line these old-fashioned narrow streets. By night, the Village really comes alive. Late-night coffeehouses and cafés, experimental theaters, and music clubs, including some of the city's best jazz venues, beckon you at every turn.

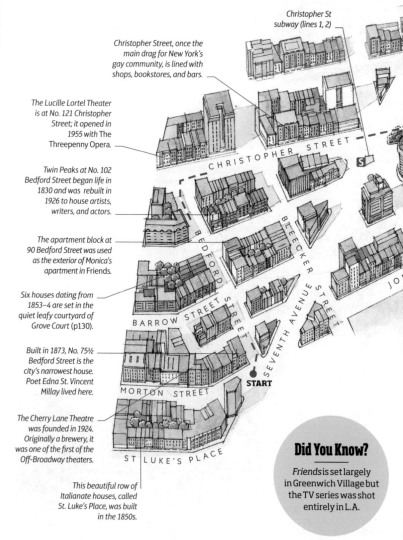

Christopher St subway (lines 1, 2)

Christopher Street, once the main drag for New York's gay community, is lined with shops, bookstores, and bars.

The Lucille Lortel Theater is at No. 121 Christopher Street; it opened in 1955 with The Threepenny Opera.

Twin Peaks at No. 102 Bedford Street began life in 1830 and was rebuilt in 1926 to house artists, writers, and actors.

The apartment block at 90 Bedford Street was used as the exterior of Monica's apartment in Friends.

Six houses dating from 1853–4 are set in the quiet leafy courtyard of Grove Court (p130).

Built in 1873, No. 75½ Bedford Street is the city's narrowest house. Poet Edna St. Vincent Millay lived here.

The Cherry Lane Theatre was founded in 1924. Originally a brewery, it was one of the first of the Off-Broadway theaters.

This beautiful row of Italianate houses, called St. Luke's Place, was built in the 1850s.

CHRISTOPHER STREET

BEDFORD STREET

BLEECKER STREET

BARROW STREET

SEVENTH AVENUE

JON

MORTON STREET

START

ST LUKE'S PLACE

Did You Know?

Friends is set largely in Greenwich Village but the TV series was shot entirely in L.A.

Built in 1848 to house waiters from the Brevoort Hotel, Patchin Place was later home to the poet E. E. Cummings and other famous writers of the 1920s and 1930s.

Locator Map
For more detail see p126

GREENWICH VILLAGE

PERRY ST

CHARLES STREET

GREENWICH AVENUE

10TH STREET

SIXTH AVENUE

WASHINGTON PLACE

FINISH

Jefferson Market Courthouse was built in 1877, and has been voted the fifth most beautiful building in the U.S. It was designed by Calvert Vaux, who co-designed Central Park (p238). The building was converted into a public library in 1967.

Gay Street attracted many aspiring artists, writers, and musicians during the 1920s. It was the setting for Ruth McKenney's novel My Sister Eileen and the film Carlito's Way (1993).

The Northern Dispensary began offering free medical care to the poor in 1831. Edgar Allan Poe (1809–49) was treated for a cold here in 1837. Since 1998, the building has been unoccupied.

0 meters 100
0 yards 100
N

Apartments line Greenwich Village's Gay Street ↓

Bar-hoppers enjoy drinks in the East Village bar, Bua

EAST VILLAGE

Home to a country estate in the 17th century, owned by Peter Stuyvesant, the East Village neighborhood only really took shape in the early 1900s. The Irish, Germans, Jews, Poles, Ukrainians, and Puerto Ricans all left their mark on the area, not least in the form of Manhattan's most varied and least expensive ethnic restaurants. In the 1950s, low rents attracted the "Beat Generation," and, ever since, music clubs and theaters have abounded in the area. From the 1990s, the culinary and bar scene here blossomed, making this one of the city's most fashionable districts. To the west lies NoHo (north of Houston), while to the east, avenues lettered A–D form "Alphabet City," a trendy district of restaurants and gardens.

East

River

FRANKLIN D ROOSEVELT DRIVE

East
River
Park

Athletic
Field

EAST RIVER DRIVE

EAST 14TH ST

EAST 13TH ST

EAST 12TH ST

EAST 11TH ST

EAST 10TH ST

⑨ Museum of Reclaimed Urban Space

EAST 9TH ST

EAST 8TH ST

Square

⑩

VILLAGE

EAST 7TH ST

EAST 6TH ST

EAST 5TH ST

EAST 4TH ST

EAST 3RD ST

❹ Nuyorican Poets Cafe

GUSTAVE HARTMAN SQUARE

EAST HOUSTON ST

AVENUE B
AVENUE C
AVENUE D
SZOLD PLACE

LOWER EAST SIDE
p90

CLINTON ST
PITT ST

DELANCEY ST

DELANCEY ST SOUTH

Harry
Delancey
Plaza

GRAND ST

W H Seward
Park

EAST BROADWAY

EAST VILLAGE

Experience More

❶ Tompkins Square Park
❷ Cooper Union
❸ The Public Theater
❹ Nuyorican Poets Cafe
❺ Merchant's House Museum
❻ St. Mark's Church-in-the-Bowery
❼ Little Toyko
❽ Russian and Turkish Baths
❾ Museum of Reclaimed Urban Space
❿ Orpheum Theatre
⓫ Strand Bookstore
⓬ Ukrainian Museum

Eat

① Artichoke
② Big Gay Ice Cream Shop
③ Momofuku Noodle Bar
④ Veniero's Pasticceria & Café
⑤ Veselka

Drink

⑥ Bua
⑦ Death & Co
⑧ Ghost Donkey
⑨ Proletariat
⑩ Zum Schneider

EXPERIENCE

 Tompkins Square Park

G9 **S** 2 Av (F), 1 Av (L)
M8, M9, M14A

This English-style park has the makings of a peaceful spot, but its past has more often been dominated by strife. It was the site of America's first organized labor demonstration in 1874. Almost 100 years later, during the 1960s, this was the main gathering place for the neighborhood's hippies, and, in 1988, it was an arena for violent riots when the police tried to evict homeless people who had taken over the grounds.

The square also contains a poignant monument to the neighborhood's greatest tragedy. A small statue of a boy and a girl looking at a steamboat commemorates the deaths of over 1,000 local residents in the *General Slocum* steamer disaster. On June 15, 1904, the boat caught fire during a pleasure cruise on the East River. It was crowded with women and children from this then-German neighborhood and many local men lost their entire families and moved away, leaving the area and its memories behind.

 Cooper Union

E9 **7 East 7th St**
S Astor Pl (6) **Sep-May: 11am-7pm Mon-Fri, 11am-5pm Sat** Jun-Aug, Federal hols **cooper.edu**

Peter Cooper had no formal schooling but went on to build the first US steam loco-motive, make the first steel rails, and become a partner in the first transatlantic cable venture. In 1859 the wealthy industrialist founded New York's first free, non-sectarian coeducational college specializing in design, engineering, and architecture. Though no longer free, the college still inspires intense competition for places. The six-story building, renovated in 1973–4, was the first to be constructed with a steel frame, made from Cooper's own rails. The Great Hall, which was inaugurated by Mark Twain in 1859, hosts lectures and concerts.

 The Public Theater

E9 **425 Lafayette St**
S Astor Pl (6) **public theater.org**

This large red-brick and brownstone building began its life in 1854 as the Astor Library, New York City's first free library, made possible through a bequest from millionaire John Jacob Astor. It is one of the foremost examples in the United States of German Romanesque Revival style.

When the building was threatened with demolition in 1965, Joseph Papp, founder of the New York Shakespeare Festival, which became The Public Theater, persuaded New York City to buy it as a home for the company. Renovation began in 1967, and much of the handsome interior was preserved during its conversion into six theaters. Although much of the work shown is experi-mental, the theater was the original home of the hit musicals *A Chorus Line* and *Hamilton* and sponsors the very popular Shakespeare in the Park event (in Central Park) every summer.

Did You Know?
—
The Public Theater's Mobile Unit performs in prisons and homeless shelters.

←

Tompkins Square Park, buzzing with locals enjoying the greenery

DRINK

Bua

Open-fronted (in summer) for people-watching, this bar has a great happy hour.

📍F9 🏠122 St. Mark's Pl
🌐buabar.com

Death & Co

Lauded cocktail bar with a charming, speakeasy theme.

📍F9 🏠433 East 6th St 🌐deathand company.com

Ghost Donkey

Cozy tequila and mezcal cocktail bar.

📍F9 🏠4 Bleecker St
🌐ghostdonkey.com

Proletariat

Long, narrow bar with quality ales and craft beers.

📍F9 🏠102 St. Mark's Pl
🌐proletariatny.com

Zum Schneider

Lively Bavarian *bier-haus*, serving *steins* and *wursts*, with an indoor garden.

📍G9 🏠107 Av C
🌐zumschneider.com

4

Nuyorican Poets Cafe

📍G9 🏠236 East 3rd St
🚇2 Av (F) 🕐For performances only
🌐nuyorican.org

Originally founded in the apartment of Puerto Rican writer and poet Miguel Algarin, in 1973, this seminal Latin American arts venue moved here in 1981. It's a lively hub for live poetry readings, play and film-script readings, open mics, jazz and hip-hop shows, plays, and visual art exhibits.

5

Merchant's House Museum

📍E9 🏠29 East 4th St
🚇Astor Pl (6), Bleecker St (6)
🕐Noon–5pm Mon and Fri–Sun, noon–8pm Thu
🌐merchantshouse.org

This remarkable, Federal-style brick townhouse, improbably tucked away on an East Village block, is a time capsule of a vanished way of life. It retains its original fixtures, and is filled with the actual furniture, ornaments, and utensils of the family who lived here. Built in 1832, it was bought in 1835 by Seabury Tredwell, a wealthy merchant, and stayed in the family until Gertrude Tredwell,

↑ Performance venue and cultural hub Nuyorican Poets Café

the last member, died in 1933. A relative then opened the house as a museum in 1936. The first-floor parlors reveal how well New York's merchant class lived during the 1800s.

6

St. Mark's Church-in-the-Bowery

📍F8 🏠131 East 10th St
🚇Astor Pl (6) 🕐10am–4pm Mon–Fri (hours may vary)
🌐stmarksbowery.org

One of New York's oldest churches, this 1799 building replaced a 1660 church on the *bouwerie* (farm) of Governor Peter Stuyvesant. He is buried here, along with seven generations of his descendants and many other prominent early New Yorkers.

In 1878, a grisly kidnapping took place when the remains of department store magnate A. T. Stewart were removed from the site and held for a $20,000 ransom.

The church rectory at 232 East 11th Street dates from 1900 and is by Beaux Arts architect Ernest Flagg, who achieved renown for his Singer Building.

Weathered apartments in the East Village

EAT

Artichoke

Fabulous late-night pizza slices to go, including the signature artichoke-spinach.

F8 **321 East 14th St** **artichoke pizza.com**

$ $ $

Big Gay Ice Cream Shop

Addictive ice cream with naughty names; try the "salty pimp."

F9 **125 East 7th St** **biggay icecream.com**

$ $ $

Momofuku Noodle Bar

Celebrity chef David Chang's steamed pork buns and pork ramen noodles are not to be missed.

F8 **171 First Av** **momofuku.com**

$ $ $

Veniero's Pasticceria & Café

Old-school Italian gem dating back to 1894; think ricotta cheesecake and cannoli.

F8 **342 East 11th St** **venieros pastry.com**

$ $ $

Veselka

Ukrainian diner offering traditional favorites like *borscht*, *kielbasa* sausage and *pierogi* since 1954.

F9 **144 Second Av** **veselka.com**

$ $ $

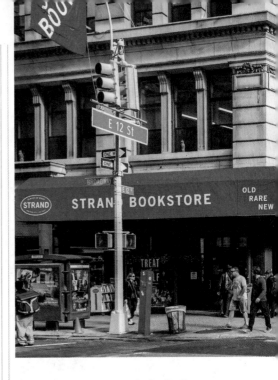

⑦ Little Tokyo

F8 **East 9th and 10th sts (between 3rd and 1st avs)** **Astor Pl (6)**

Located on and around East 9th and 10th streets, this tiny locality is peppered with colorful Japanese stores, steamy noodle shops, packed supermarkets, and quality sushi bars, such as Hasaki at 210 East 9th Street. Sunrise Mart is a popular Japanese supermarket at 4 Stuyvesant Street, while Toy Tokyo at 91 2nd Avenue sells all sorts of Japanese anime figures, collectibles and toys. Top restaurants in the area include Ippudo (at 65 Fourth Avenue), the first overseas outpost of Fukuoka-based "ramen king" Shigemi Kawahara, and Ikinari Steak (90 E 10th Street), a Japanese steakhouse chain. Authentic Tokyo *izakaya* Kenka (25 St. Mark's Place) features wooden benches, small plates of tempting Japanese snacks, and quality sake.

⑧ Russian and Turkish Baths

F8 **268 East 10th St** **1 Av (L), Astor Pl (6)** **Daily (times vary, check website)** **russianturkish baths.com**

One of the few old-school experiences remaining in the East Village, these steam rooms have been active since 1892 and remain popular. There's the Steam Room, the Turkish Room, and the Russian Sauna (the hottest). Admission includes a towel, robe, soap and slippers.

---

⑨ Museum of Reclaimed Urban Space

G8 **155 Av C** **3 Av (L)** **11am-7pm Tue, Thu-Sun** **morusnyc.org**

This tiny museum, housed in a 19th-century tenement and run solely by volunteers, honors the neighborhood's

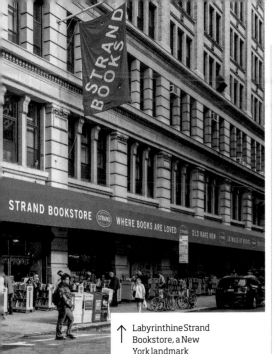

STRAND BOOKSTORE · WHERE BOOKS ARE LOVED · OLD RARE NEW · 18 MILES OF BOOKS

↑ Labyrinthine Strand Bookstore, a New York landmark

This tiny locality is peppered with colorful Japanese stores, steamy noodle shops, packed supermarkets, and quality sushi bars.

long tradition of urban activism and charts its history, covering events such as the Tompkins Square Park riot, development of community gardens, and squatting in the East Village. Check online for guided tour information (usually Sat and Sun at 3pm).

Orpheum Theatre

☉ F9 ☖ 126 2nd Ave
⛎ Astor Pl (6) ⛛ For shows only ⬡ stomponline.com

One of the East Village's biggest (and oldest) theaters has been the home of the innovative percussion group *Stomp* since 1994. The show,

which began in Brighton, England, sees its cast use everyday objects and their own bodies to make music and entertaining, foot-tapping rhythms.

A theater has been on this site since at least 1904, when the whole area became known as the Yiddish Theater District. Years later, several landmark productions had Off-Broadway premieres here, including comedy rock musical *Little Shop of Horrors* (1982), Sandra Bernhard's *Without You I'm Nothing* (1988) and David Mamet's *Oleanna* (1992).

Strand Bookstore

☉ E8 ☖ 828 Broadway
⛎ Union Sq (4, 5, 6, L, N, Q, R)
⛛ 9:30am–10:30pm Mon–Sat, 11:00am–10:30pm Sun
⬡ strandbooks.com

The last remaining bookstore on 'Book Row,' the Strand is a delight, with some 18 miles (29 km) of remaindered, new and used books at discount prices. It's estimated the store contains some 2.5 million books in total. It first opened in 1927 and was named after the London street, before moving into this labyrinthine space in 1957. Authors such as Junot Díaz, Paul Auster and Nicole Krauss regularly hold readings here.

Ukrainian Museum

☉ F9 ☖ 222 East 6th St
⛎ Astor Pl (6) ⛛ 11:30am–5pm Wed–Sun ⬡ ukrainianmuseum.org

Founded in 1976, this small but beautifully maintained museum pays homage to what was once a major Ukrainian enclave in the city. The exhibits primarily comprise folk costumes and textiles, but there is also modern art from lauded Ukrainian artists. There is also a range of traditional crafts, including the famous painted Easter eggs, *pysanky*.

ST. MARK'S PLACE

East 8th Street is known to locals as St. Mark's Place – the cultural, rebellious heart of the 'hood since the 1960s. It's now lined with souvenir stalls, hippie-chic fashion stores, and Asian restaurants. Don't miss St. Mark's Comics, at No. 11, nor Physical Graffiti, at No. 96, which is based in the tenement featured on the eponymous Led Zeppelin album cover.

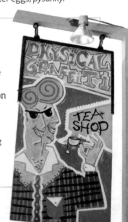

A SHORT WALK
EAST VILLAGE

Distance 1.25 mile (2 km) **Nearest metro** Astor Pl
Time 25 minutes

History abounds in the East Village. At the spot where 10th and Stuyvesant streets now intersect, Governor Peter Stuyvesant's country house once stood, and many other homes were built here between 1871 and 1890. This makes for a picturesque place to explore today – but it's not all beauty and charm. The East Village is one of New York's hottest neighborhoods, and the Manhattan of popular imagination. Here you'll find weathered apartments papered with fliers, locals chatting on stoops, and a buzzing bar and restaurant scene.

Astor Pl subway (line 6)

START

Astor Place saw rioting in 1849. English actor William Macready, playing Hamlet at the Astor Place Opera House, criticized American actor Edwin Forrest. Forrest's fans revolted, and there were 34 deaths.

Alamo is the title of the 15-ft (4.6-m) steel cube in Astor Place designed by Bernard Rosenthal. It revolves when pushed.

Built in the Greek Revival style in the 1830s, the buildings of Colonnade Row were once expensive townhouses. The houses, of which only four are left, are unified by one facade in the European style. The Astor Place Theatre, which is located here, has been home to the Blue Man Group since 1991.

In 1965 the late Joseph Papp convinced the city to buy the Astor Library (1849) as a home for The Public Theater (p142).

The Merchant's House Museum displays Federal, American Empire, and Victorian furniture (p143).

0 meters	100	N
0 yards	100	↑

←

Astor Place, with Astor Place Opera House at its heart

← McSorley's Old Ale House, an East Village icon

EAST VILLAGE

Locator Map
For more detail see p140

Cooper Union is known for its art and engineering programs, and provided free education to its students until 2014 (p143).

Renwick Triangle is a group of 16 houses built in the Italianate style in 1861.

The Stuyvesant-Fish House (1803–4) was constructed out of brick. It is a classic example of a Federal-style house.

St. Mark's Church-in-the-Bowery was built in 1799, and the steeple was added in 1828 (p143).

Stuyvesant Polyclinic was built in 1884 as the German Dispensary and was in use until 2007. The facade is adorned with the busts of famous physicians and scientists.

Little Tokyo is a belt of noodle shops, sushi bars, and Japanese businesses, around East 9th St (p146).

St. Mark's Place was once the epicenter of hippie life and remains an East Village icon. Many shops can now be found here (p147).

McSorley's Old Ale House still serves its own ale in surroundings virtually unchanged since it opened in 1854. There are just two beer options here: "light" and "dark."

Little Ukraine is home to around 25,000 Ukrainians and the Ukrainian Museum (p147).

E 10TH STREET

STUYVESANT ST

FINISH

THIRD AVENUE

ST MARK'S PLACE

E 7TH STREET

E 6TH STREET

SECOND AVENUE

E 9TH STREET

Did You Know?

When you order beer at McSorley's, you get two smallish glass mugs, rather than one.

GRAMERCY AND THE FLATIRON DISTRICT

Four squares were laid out in this area by real estate developers in the 1830s and 1840s to emulate the quiet, private residential quarters in many European cities. Chief among them is Union Square, a bustling space that hosts New York's best farmers' market. To the northeast lies Gramercy, with its private clubs and posh town houses, designed by Calvert Vaux and Stanford White. Gertrude Vanderbilt Whitney's bronze statue of Peter Stuyvesant, overlooked by the stately St. George Episcopal Church, stands in tranquil Stuyvesant Square. Finally, at the north end of the Flatiron District is Madison Square Park.

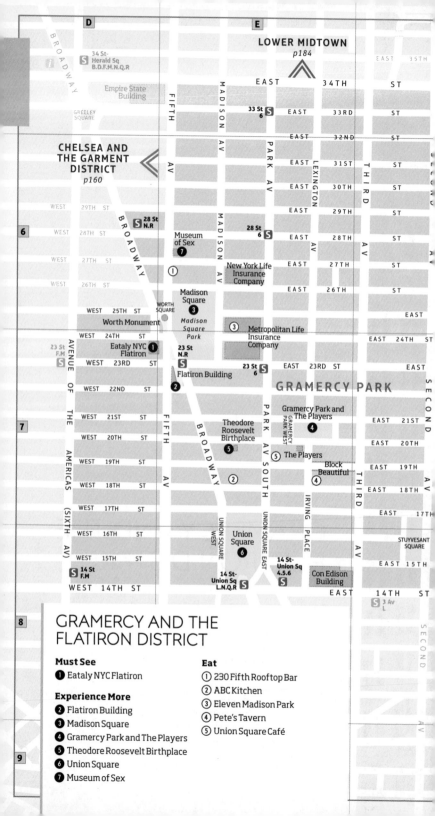

LOWER MIDTOWN
p184

CHELSEA AND
THE GARMENT
DISTRICT
p160

GRAMERCY AND THE
FLATIRON DISTRICT

Must See

① Eataly NYC Flatiron

Experience More

② Flatiron Building
③ Madison Square
④ Gramercy Park and The Players
⑤ Theodore Roosevelt Birthplace
⑥ Union Square
⑦ Museum of Sex

Eat

① 230 Fifth Rooftop Bar
② ABC Kitchen
③ Eleven Madison Park
④ Pete's Tavern
⑤ Union Square Café

TOP 5 EATALY RESTAURANTS

Riso e Risotto
Dedicated to the rich, creamy, rice-based dishes of northern Italy.

Manzo
Butcher-focused restaurant celebrating meat of all kinds, plus a bar specializing in Italian vermouth.

La Pizza & La Pasta
Naples-style pizza and al dente pasta.

Il Pesce
Serves fresh and responsibly sourced fish and shellfish.

La Piazza
Standing-only *enoteca*, with fresh *antipasti*, cured meats, cheeses, and a host of wines.

EATALY NYC FLATIRON

D7 · **200 Fifth Av** · **E 23 St (R, W)** · **7am–11pm daily** · **eataly.com**

Indoor Italian food market Eataly has become a major gastronomic attraction, sparking a New York food hall trend. The market comprises a variety of sit-down restaurants, food and drink counters, and grocery stores, with mouthwatering scents drifting throughout.

Founded by Italian entrepreneur Oscar Farinetti in 2007, the first Eataly debuted in Turin. Part restaurant complex, part food market, Eataly NYC Flatiron opened in 2010, followed by Eataly NYC Downtown in 2016. The market section offers a huge range of rare Italian wines, unusual cheeses, freshly baked breads, and seafood and meats sourced locally or flown in from Italy. Sample fresh *gelato* and *sorbetto* at Il Gelato, sip espresso at Caffè Vergnano, indulge in sweet treats at the Nutella Bar or stand at the tables in La Piazza and nibble on cured meats and cheeses, washed down with a fine Chianti. There's also a cooking school, homewares section, and bookstore, so you can take a little bit of Italy home with you.

1 The entrance to covered food market Eataly NYC Flatiron, just down the block from the Flatiron Building.

2 For those not dining at one of Eataly's self-contained restaurants, the covered food market has places to sit, which get exceptionally busy at peak times.

3 Loaves galore at Eataly's bakery. All of the store's artisanal breads are freshly baked on site in a wood-burning, hand-rotated oven, using natural yeast and stone-ground flour.

↑ Rooftop pop-up SERRA by
Birreria, inspired by the
Italian countryside

EXPERIENCE MORE

Flatiron Building

Q E7 **A** 175 Fifth Av **S** 23 St (N, R) **C** Closed to the public

Possibly one of New York City's most famous sights, the Flatiron's elegant, triangular exterior draws crowds, all vying for that perfect photo. Originally named the Fuller Building after the construction company that owned it, this building by Chicago architect Daniel Burnham was one of the tallest in the world when completed in 1902 and one of the first to use a steel frame. This innovative construction of 20-stories was a precursor to the skyscrapers to come.

Although called the Flatiron for its unusual tapered shape, some called it "Burnham's folly," predicting that the ground level winds created by the building's frame would knock it down. Some even placed bets, convinced it would topple. It has, however, withstood the test of time.

The stretch of Fifth Avenue to the south of the building has chic stores such as Michael Kors and Paul Smith, adding cachet to the area now called the Flatiron District.

Madison Square

Q E6 **S** 23 St (N, R)

Planned as the center of a fashionable residential district, this square became a popular entertainment hub after the Civil War. It was bordered by the elegant Fifth Avenue Hotel, the Madison Square Theater, and Stanford White's Madison Square Garden. The torch-bearing arm of the Statue of Liberty was exhibited here in 1884.

The Shake Shack is a top lunchtime spot for neighborhood office workers, while the surrounding park makes for a leisurely stroll to admire the sculptures. The 1880 statue of Admiral David Farragut, hero of a Civil War sea battle, is by Augustus Saint-Gaudens, its pedestal by Stanford White. Figures representing Courage and Loyalty are carved on the base. The statue of Roscoe Conkling commemorates a US senator who died during the great blizzard of 1888. The Eternal Light flagpole, by Carrère and Hastings, honors fallen soldiers of World War I.

Gramercy Park and The Players

Q E7 **A** Irving Pl, between East 20th and 21st sts **S** 14 St-Union Sq (L, N, R, 4, 5, 6) **W** nationalarts club.org **W** theplayersnyc.org

Laid out in the 1830s and 1840s to attract society residences uptown, this is the city's only private park. Residents of the surrounding buildings have keys to the gate. Famous key-holders have included Uma Thurman, Julia Roberts, and several Kennedys and Roosevelts. The handsome brownstone at 15 Gramercy Park South houses the National Arts Club. Members have included most leading American artists of the late 19th and early 20th centuries, who were asked to donate a painting or sculpture in return for life membership; these gifts form the National Arts Club's permanent collection. The club is open to the public for exhibitions only.

Did You Know?

The Flatiron Building is destined to become a luxury hotel when its current leases expire.

←

Madison Square Park, in the heart of the Flatiron District

Flowers and fresh produce stalls at Union Square Greenmarket

The Players at 18 Gramercy Park South was once the home of actor Edwin Booth, brother of John Wilkes Booth, President Lincoln's assassin. Architect Stanford White remodeled the building as a club in 1888. Intended primarily for actors, members have also included White himself, author Mark Twain, publisher Thomas Nast, and Winston Churchill, whose mother, Jennie Jerome, was born nearby. A statue of Booth playing Hamlet is across the street in Gramercy Park itself.

⑤

Theodore Roosevelt Birthplace

◉ E7 ◫ 28 East 20th St ⬛ 14 St-Union Sq (L, N, R, 4, 5, 6), 23 St (6) ◷ 9am-5pm Wed-Sun (last adm 4pm) ◷ Federal hols ⬚ nps.gov/thrb

The reconstructed boyhood home of the colorful 26th president displays everything from the toys with which the young Teddy played to campaign buttons and emblems of the trademark "Rough Rider" hat that Roosevelt wore in the Spanish-American War. One exhibit features his explorations and general interests; the other covers his political career.

⑥
Union Square

◉ E8 ⬛ 14 St-Union Sq (L, N, R, 4, 5, 6)

Created in the 1830s, this park is an inviting public space, best known for its enormous greenmarket. Held from 8am to 6pm on Monday, Wednesday, Friday, and Saturday, the market sells all sorts of seasonal produce. Statues here include that of George Washington and a Lafayette by Bartholdi, and the square is flanked by restaurants, gourmet supermarkets, and department stores. Nearby is the Decker Building, to which Andy Warhol moved his studio in 1968 and the Union Square Theatre, once headquarters of the Democratic Party.

⑦
Museum of Sex

◉ E6 ◫ 233 Fifth Av at 27th St ⬛ 28 St (N, R, 6) ◷ 10:30am-10pm Sun-Thu, 10:30am-11pm Fri-Sat ⬚ www.museumofsex.com

This is the only New York museum for visitors aged 18 and over. Through thought-provoking changing exhibits, and a permanent collection of over 20,000 artifacts (including works of art, photography, costumes, and technological inventions), the Museum of Sex means to promote serious discourse surrounding sex and sexuality. Temporary exhibits hold court on the first floor.

EAT

230 Fifth Rooftop Bar
Swish bar and roof garden serving international fare. Come for the sensational views of the Empire State Building.

◉ E6 ◫ 230 Fifth Av ⬚ 230-fifth.com

$$ⓈⓈⓈ

ABC Kitchen
New American cuisine from Jean-Georges Vongerichten.

◉ E7 ◫ 35 East 18th St ⬚ abckitchen nyc.com

$$ⓈⓈⓈ

Eleven Madison Park
Gorgeous Art Deco space for contemporary American fine dining.

◉ E6 ◫ 11 Madison Av ◷ L Mon-Thu ⬚ elevenmadison park. com

$$ⓈⓈⓈ

Pete's Tavern
Atmospheric bar, open since 1864, known for being writer O. Henry's local. Serves hearty burgers and Italian staples.

◉ E7 ◫ 129 East 18th St ⬚ petestavern.com

$$ⓈⓈⓈ

Union Square Café
Danny Meyer's famous restaurant produces exquisite contemporary American cuisine.

◉ E7 ◫ 101 East 19th St ⬚ unionsquare cafe.com

$$ⓈⓈⓈ

A SHORT WALK
GRAMERCY PARK

Distance 1.4 mile (2.25 km) **Nearest metro** 23 St
Time 30 minutes

Gramercy Park and nearby Madison Square tell a tale of two cities. Madison Square, ringed by offices and traffic, is used mainly by those working nearby, but the surrounding commercial architecture make it worth visiting. It was once the home of Madison Square Garden, where revelers always thronged. Gramercy Park, meanwhile, retains the air of dignified tranquility it has long been known for. Homes and clubs remain, set around the last private park, accessible only to those living on the square.

The Knickerbocker Club played baseball here, at Madison Square, in the 1840s. Today, office workers enjoy the park's statues (p157).

23 St subway (lines N, R)

START

A sidewalk clock in front of 200 Fifth Avenue marks the end of the once-fashionable shopping area known as Ladies' Mile.

The triangle made by Fifth Avenue, Broadway, and 22nd Street is the site of one of New York's most famous early skyscrapers, the Flatiron Building. When it was built in 1903, the Flatiron was the world's tallest building (p156).

23 St subway (lines N, R)

Broadway from Union Square to Madison Square was once New York's finest shopping area, called Ladies' Mile.

Theodore Roosevelt Birthplace is a replica of the house in which the 26th American president was born (p157).

BROADWAY (LADIES' MILE)

E 23RD STREET
E 22ND STREET
E 21ST STREET
E 19TH STREET
E 17TH STREET

National Arts Club is a private club for the arts, on the south side of the park (p156).

↑ Springtime flowers bloom in Madison Square Park

The grand New York Life Insurance Company building by Cass Gilbert bears his trademark pyramid top.

The small marble Appellate Court is said to be the world's busiest courthouse.

Vast vaulted entrances mark each corner of Metropolitan Life Insurance Company.

23 St subway (line 6)

FINISH

Actor Edwin Booth founded The Players club in 1888 (p156).

↑ Pete's Tavern, a haunt of locals and writers alike

Only residents can Gramercy Park itself, but everyone can enjoy the peace and charm of the area around it (p156).

The Brotherhood Synagogue was a Friends' Meeting House from 1859 to 1975, when it became a synagogue.

Tree-lined Block Beautiful stretches along East 19th Street. Though no particular house is outstanding, the street as a whole is lovely.

Pete's Tavern has been here since 1864. O. Henry wrote The Gift of the Magi in the second booth (p157).

CHELSEA AND THE GARMENT DISTRICT

Developed on former farmland, this area really began to take shape in 1830. This was largely thanks to Clement Clarke Moore, who wrote *'Twas the Night Before Christmas* – his estate comprised most of what is now Chelsea. After a long period as a rather gritty area, a new and fashionable Chelsea emerged. When Macy's arrived at Herald Square, garment and retail districts sprouted around it. Some of New York's best art galleries flourished in the early 1990s, and the transformation of the High Line has triggered the development of major condo conversions, affluent townhouses, and stores of every variety.

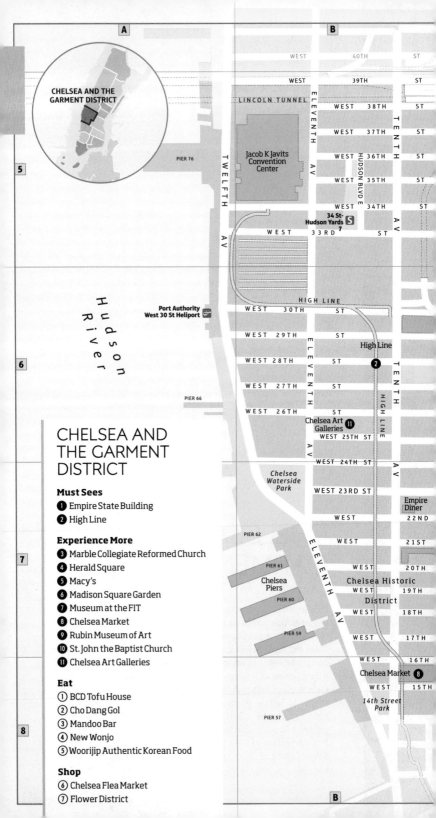

CHELSEA AND THE GARMENT DISTRICT

Must Sees
1. Empire State Building
2. High Line

Experience More
3. Marble Collegiate Reformed Church
4. Herald Square
5. Macy's
6. Madison Square Garden
7. Museum at the FIT
8. Chelsea Market
9. Rubin Museum of Art
10. St. John the Baptist Church
11. Chelsea Art Galleries

Eat
1. BCD Tofu House
2. Cho Dang Gol
3. Mandoo Bar
4. New Wonjo
5. Woorijip Authentic Korean Food

Shop
6. Chelsea Flea Market
7. Flower District

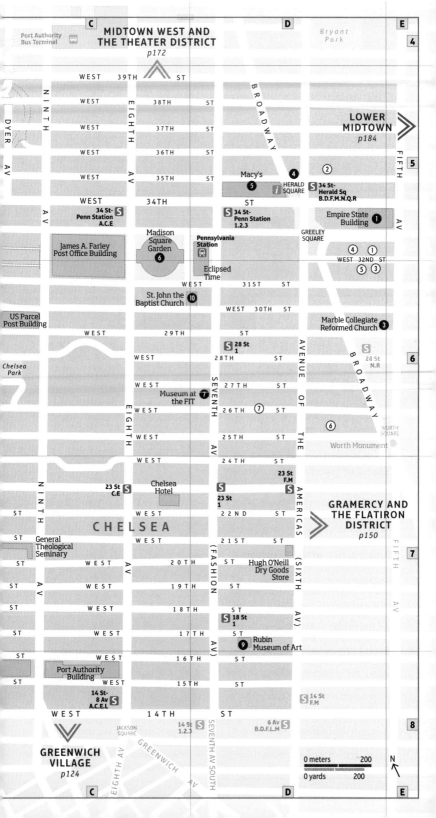

Port Authority Bus Terminal

WEST 39TH ST

NINTH AV
EIGHTH AV
DYER AV

WEST 38TH ST

WEST 37TH ST

WEST 36TH ST

WEST 35TH ST

BROADWAY

LOWER MIDTOWN *p184*

5

FIFTH AV

WEST 34TH ST

Macy's
HERALD SQUARE
4
5
i

②

S 34 St-Herald Sq B.D.F.M.N.Q.R

34 St-Penn Station A.C.E **S**

S 34 St-Penn Station 1.2.3

Empire State Building **1**

GREELEY SQUARE

James A. Farley Post Office Building

Madison Square Garden **6**

Pennsylvania Station

④ ①
WEST 32ND ST
⑤ ③

Eclipsed Time

WEST 31ST ST

St. John the Baptist Church **10**

WEST 30TH ST

Marble Collegiate Reformed Church **3**

US Parcel Post Building

WEST 29TH ST

S 28 St 1

AVENUE OF THE
BROADWAY

S 28 St N.R

6

Chelsea Park

WEST 28TH ST

SEVENTH AV

WEST 27TH ST

Museum at the FIT **7**

WEST 26TH ST **⑦**

EIGHTH AV

WEST 25TH ST

⑥

WORTH SQUARE

Worth Monument

WEST 24TH ST

23 St **S** C.E

Chelsea Hotel

S 23 St 1

23 St F.M **S** **S**

AMERICAS

GRAMERCY AND THE FLATIRON DISTRICT *p150*

CHELSEA
NINTH AV

WEST 22ND ST

General Theological Seminary

WEST 21ST ST

(FASHION (SIXTH AV)

Hugh O'Neill Dry Goods Store

FIFTH AV

7

WEST 20TH ST

WEST 19TH ST

NINTH AV

WEST 18TH ST

S 18 St 1

WEST 17TH ST

Rubin Museum of Art **9**

Port Authority Building

WEST 16TH ST

WEST 15TH ST

S 14 St F.M

14 St-8 Av **S** A.C.E.L

WEST 14TH ST

14 St **S** 1.2.3

6 Av **S** B.D.F.L.M

8

GREENWICH VILLAGE *p124*

JACKSON SQUARE

EIGHTH AV
GREENWICH AV
SEVENTH AV SOUTH

0 meters 200
0 yards 200

N

C **D** **E**

The Empire State Building, dominating the city's skyline ↑

① ⊘ ⑪ ⑪

EMPIRE STATE BUILDING

1,454 ft
—
The height of the Empire State Building with its mast (443 m).

📍 D5 🏠 350 Fifth Ave 🚇 34 St (A, B, C, D, E, F, N, Q, R, 1, 2, 3) 🚌 M1–5, M16, M34, Q32
🕐 8am–2am (last adm: 1:15am) 🌐 esbnyc.com

Named for New York state's nickname, the Empire State Building has become an enduring symbol of the city since its completion in 1931. More than 3.5 million people visit the country's most iconic skyscraper every year to admire the dizzying views from the building's observatories.

Construction of the Skyscraper

Construction of the city's most evocative skyscraper began in March 1930, not long after the Wall Street Crash. The building was designed for ease and speed of construction; everything possible was prefabricated and slotted into place at a rate of about four stories a week. By the time the skyscraper opened in 1931, reaching the heady heights of 102 stories, space was so difficult to rent that it was nicknamed "the Empty State Building." Only the popularity of the observatories saved the building from bankruptcy. Art Deco touches run throughout, such as in the Fifth Avenue Entrance Lobby, which includes a relief image of the building superimposed on a map of New York State. The skyscraper is also a natural lightning conductor and is struck up to 100 times a year.

↑ The 86th-floor observatory offers superb views from its indoor galleries and its outdoor deck. The 102nd-floor observatory requires an extra fee (payable online or at the Visitors' Center).

The mast, which is 204 ft (62 m) tall, transmits TV and radio to the city and four states.

High-speed elevators travel at up to 1,000 ft (305 m) a minute.

The annual Run-Up entails racing up the 1,576 steps from the lobby to the 86th floor.

The framework is made from 60,000 tons of steel.

Ten million bricks were used to line the whole building.

Over 200 steel and concrete piles support the 365,000-ton building.

← The Empire State Building, an icon and a work of art

ENCOUNTERS IN THE SKY

The Empire State Building has starred in many films but the finale from the 1933 classic *King Kong* is easily its most famous guest appearance, as the giant ape straddles its spire to do battle with army aircraft. In 1945, a B-25 bomber flew too low over the city in fog and struck the building just above the 78th floor. The elevator operator made a lucky escape as she plunged 79 floors. The emergency brakes saved her life.

As the building took shape, construction workers often showed great bravery ↑

165

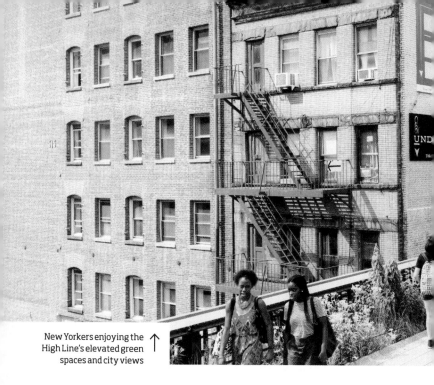

New Yorkers enjoying the
High Line's elevated green ↑
spaces and city views

2

HIGH LINE

 B6 From Gansevoort St (Meatpacking District) to West 34th St (between 10th and 12th avs) 14 St (A, C, E, L), 34 Street-Hudson Yards (7) Jun-Sep: 7am-11pm daily; Apr-May & Oct-Nov: 7am-10pm daily; Dec-Mar: 7am-7pm daily thehighline.org

The High Line has rapidly become one of New York's signature attractions. Once an elevated railroad, now an urban park, this sensational addition to the city offers green spaces and unique perspectives as it cuts through blocks and across streets.

The High Line snaking ↑
through buildings on
Manhattan's west side

New York's Elevated Greenway

An ambitious urban renewal project that links Midtown, Chelsea, and the Meatpacking District, the innovative High Line has transformed a disused railroad into a 1.45-mile (2.33-km) long landscaped park. The railroad had been abandoned for years when, in 1999, two local residents created the Friends of the High Line organization to save the structure from demolition. Extending from Gansevoort Street to 34th Street, the park has since played an important role in the gentrification of the west side of Manhattan. Designed by top architects, the outstanding elevated promenade-cum-public-park stands 30 ft (9 m) high above the streets and cuts through swathes of buildings. At intervals, there are art installations and food vendors, not forgetting water features, areas for seating, and countless attractive flower beds.

🔺 GREAT VIEWS
Viewpoints on the High Line

There are countless stunning views along the High Line, but there are a number of viewpoints that shouldn't be missed. These include the overlook at Gansevoort Street, 15th Street Bridge (which offers views of the 1930 skybridge crossing West 15th Street), 10th Avenue Overlook, 23rd Street Bridge (where the 1931 London Terrace Gardens can be seen), 26th Street Viewing Spur, and the final section along 12th Avenue (which has views of Hudson Yards and the Hudson River).

Timeline

1980
▽ Last train runs on the line; track is abandoned.

2004
James Corner Field Operations, Diller Scofidio + Renfro, and Piet Oudolf selected to lead redevelopment.

2014
▽ Third and final section open.

1934
▲ The High Line opens to trains.

2009
Section 1 opens.

2011
Section 2 opens.

The Marble Church and the Empire State Building reach skyward on Fifth Avenue

EXPERIENCE MORE

Marble Collegiate Reformed Church

◉ D6 ⬠ 1 West 29th St ⬒ 28 St (N, R) ◷ 8:30am–8:30pm Mon–Fri, 9am–4pm Sat, 8am–3pm Sun ◷ Federal hols ⬜ marblechurch.org

This church is best known for its former pastor Norman Vincent Peale, who wrote *The Power of Positive Thinking*. Another positive thinker, future US president Richard M. Nixon, attended services here when he was a lawyer in his pre-White House days.

The church was built in 1854 using the marble blocks that give it its name. Fifth Avenue was then no more than a dusty country road, and the cast-iron fence was there to keep wandering livestock out.

The original white and gold interior walls were replaced with a stenciled gold fleur-de-lis design on a soft rust background. Two stained-glass Tiffany windows, depicting Old Testament scenes, were placed in the south wall in 1900 and 1901.

Herald Square

◉ D5 ⬠ Sixth Av ⬒ 34 St–Penn Station (1)

Named after the *New York Herald*, which occupied a fine arcaded, Italianate Stanford White building here from 1893 to 1921, the square was the hub of the rowdy Tenderloin district in the 1870s and 1880s. Theaters such as the Manhattan Opera House, dance halls, hotels and restaurants kept the area humming with life until reformers clamped down on sleaze in the 1890s. The ornamental Bennett clock, named for James Gordon Bennett Jr., publisher of the *Herald*, is now all that is left of the Herald Building.

The Opera House was razed in 1901 to make way for Macy's and, soon after, other department stores followed, making the square a mecca for shoppers. One such store was the now-defunct Gimbel Brothers Department Store, once arch-rival to Macy's. (The

↑ Macy's storefront, with its famous red star logo

rivalry was affectionately portrayed in the New York Christmas movie *A Miracle on 34th Street*.) In 1988, the store was converted into a vertical mall with a glittery neon front. Herald Square is still a key shopping district, with chain stores and a traffic-free plaza.

⑤
Macy's

📍 D5 🚇 151 West 34th St 🚉 34 St-Penn Station (1), 34 St (A, C, E) 🕐 10am-10pm Mon-Sat, 11am-9pm Sun 🌐 macys.com

The "world's largest store" covers a square block, and the merchandise inside includes any item you could imagine in every price range. Perhaps most famously, the department store sponsors New York's Thanksgiving Day parade, which sees soaring balloons and spectacular floats travel through the streets of Manhattan, along with the Fourth of July fireworks (*p56*). The store's popular Spring Flower Show also draws thousands of visitors.

Macy's was founded by a former whaler named Rowland Hussey Macy, who opened a small store on West 14th Street in 1858. The store's red star logo came from his tattoo, a souvenir of his sailing days.

By the time Macy died in 1877, his little store had grown to a row of 11 buildings, and at the turn of the century it had outgrown its 14th Street

premises. In 1902 it moved to its present site, which covers a staggering 2 million sq ft (186,000 sq m). The eastern facade has a modern entrance but retains the bay windows and pillars of the 1902 design. The 34th Street facade has its original caryatids guarding the entrance, along with the clock, canopy, and lettering. Inside, many of the early wooden escalators are still in working order. Unsurprisingly, Macy's is a designated National Historic Landmark.

---

⑥
Madison Square Garden

📍 C5 🚇 4 Pennsylvania Plaza 🚉 34 St-Penn Station (1), 34th Street (A, C, E) 🕐 Daily (for games, shows, and tours) 🌐 thegarden. com

This is the 20,000-seat home of the NBA's New York Knicks (basketball), Liberty (women's basketball), and New York Rangers (hockey) teams.

 HIDDEN GEM
Eclipsed Time

Look up for Maya Lin's futuristic sculpture in the ceiling of the Long Island Railroad ticket area at Penn Station. Made of glass, steel, and aluminum, it aims to make busy commuters stop and think about time as a part of nature.

A packed calendar of other events includes rock concerts, championship tennis and boxing, outrageously staged wrestling, and the Westminster Kennel Club Dog Show. There is also a 5,600-seat theater. Tours are available daily, except during games and shows.

There's only one good thing to be said for the razing of the extraordinarily lovely McKim, Mead & White Pennsylvania Station building in favor of this undistinguished complex: it so enraged city preservationists that they formed an alliance to ensure that such a thing would never be allowed to happen again.

KNICKS BASKETBALL AT MADISON SQUARE GARDEN

Madison Square Garden is the home of the Knicks, New York's fanatically supported NBA basketball team. Their last championship win was in 1973, despite star players such as Carmelo Anthony and Jeremy Lin. Fans hope Latvian Kristaps Porziņģis will turn things around. Tickets are nonetheless very hard to get and often astronomically expensive, thanks to an enthusiastic fan base that includes a lot of celebrities, such as Tom Hanks and Katie Holmes.

7

Museum at the FIT

📍D6 🏠227 West 27th St
🚇28 St (1) 🕐Noon–8pm
Tue–Fri, 10am–5pm Sat
🌐fitnyc.edu/museum

The Fashion Institute of Technology (FIT) is one of the world's top fashion schools, affiliated with the State University of New York, and Norma Kamali, Calvin Klein, and Michael Kors are among its alumni. In the institute's Shirley Goodman Resource Center, the museum hosts changing exhibits. The Fashion

Gourmet Chelsea Market, selling spices galore (inset) ↑

and Textile History Gallery, on the main floor, rotates selections from its collection of over 50,000 garments and accessories, and 30,000 textiles. All the major designers are here, including Balenciaga, Coco Chanel, Christian Dior, Yves Saint Laurent, Vivienne Westwood, and Manolo Blahnik. The Gallery FIT shows student and faculty exhibitions.

8

Chelsea Market

📍B8 🏠75 Ninth Av
between 15th and 16th sts
🚇14 St (A, C, E) 🕐7am–9pm
Mon–Sat, 8am–8pm Sun
🌐chelseamarket.com

This unmissable destination for foodies incorporates an enclosed food court and shopping mall and the Food Network's TV production facility. A range of gourmet ingredients, exotic food-stuffs, and charming gifts are on offer here, with retail options including Li-lac Chocolates (established in 1923 in the West Village); Chelsea Wine Vault, for a global choice of wines; and Bowery Kitchen Supply, for

---

HOTEL CHELSEA

Arguably Chelsea's most famous building, Hotel Chelsea (222 West 23rd St) was partly converted to a hotel in 1903. It became notorious as the home of literary and music rebels. Jack Kerouac supposedly typed *On the Road* here in 1951, and Dylan Thomas was resident when he died suddenly in 1953. Andy Warhol and protégées Nico and Brigid Berlin holed up here during the filming of *Chelsea Girls* in 1966, and Sid Vicious stabbed Nancy Spungen to death in 1978. It is set to reopen as a luxury hotel by 2019.

> **Attracted by low rents, the many galleries that set up shop in Chelsea during the 1990s were a driving force in this area's resurgence.**

professional-quality equipment. Some high-end purveyors make and bake on site, cooking up only the freshest, most tempting treats.

Rubin Museum of Art

D7 **150 West 17th St** **14 St or 18 St (1)** **11am–5pm Mon & Thu, 11am–9pm Wed, 11am–10pm Fri, 11am–6pm Sat & Sun** **rubinmuseum.org**

This museum may be a lesser-known treasure, but it has a collection of 2,000 paintings, sculptures, and textiles from the Himalayas, Tibet, India, and the neighboring regions. The Tibetan Buddhist Shrine Room recreates an authentic shrine with flickering lamps and an exhibit on the four Tibetan religious traditions, which rotates every two years.

The museum also hosts captivating travel exhibitions and programs, with concerts, debates, and films. Tours take place daily, at 1 and 3pm. Café Serai, on the first floor, serves Himalayan food.

St. John the Baptist Church

D6 **210 West 31st St** **(212) 564-9070** **34 St–Penn Station (1), 34 St (A, C, E)** **6:15am–6pm daily**

Founded in 1840 to serve a congregation of newly arrived immigrants, this small Roman Catholic church, with a single spire, is today almost lost in the heart of the Fur District. Although the brownstone facade on 30th Street is dark with city soot, many treasures

lie within this dull exterior. The entrance is through the modern Friary on 31st Street.

The sanctuary by Napoleon Le Brun is a marvel of Gothic arches in glowing white marble surmounted by gilded capitals. Painted reliefs of religious scenes line the walls and sunlight streams through the stained-glass windows. Also off the Friary is the small Prayer Garden, a peaceful oasis with religious statuary, a fountain, and stone benches.

Chelsea Art Galleries

B6 **Between West 19th St and West 27th St, around 10th and 11th avs** **23 St (C, E)** **Usually 10am–6pm Tue–Sat** **nygallerytours.com**

Attracted by low rents, the many galleries that set up shop in Chelsea during the 1990s were a driving force in this area's resurgence. Some 150 to 200 venues exhibit work from emerging artists in various media. Check out P.P.O.W. or David Zwirner, with reputations for intriguing or provocative work. Avoid Saturdays, when art-crawler traffic is at its heaviest.

↑ Beautiful stained-glass in St. John the Baptist Church

BCD Tofu House
Specializing in home-made tofu – served on its own, in meat dishes, and in soups.

D5 **5 West 32nd St** **bcdtofu.com**

**$**$$

Cho Dang Gol
This place is best known for tofu and *jjigae*, spicy Korean hotpots and soups.

D5 **55 West 35th St** **chodanggolnyc.com**

**$**$$

Mandoo Bar
Mouthwatering, Korean-style "mandoo" dumplings are freshly made all day in the store window up front.

D6 **2 West 32nd St** **(212) 279-3075**

**$**$$

New Wonjo
Korean barbecue is the specialty here, with charcoal-fueled grills under every table.

D5 **23 West 32nd St** **newwonjo.com**

**$**$$

Woorijip Authentic Korean Food
This cafeteria is very popular for its bargain lunch buffets and *bibimbop*.

D6 **12 West 32nd St** **(212) 244-1115**

**$**$$

MIDTOWN WEST AND THE THEATER DISTRICT

At the heart of Midtown lies Times Square, where huge neon displays flash and crowds bustle. The Theater District lies north of 42nd Street, and offers a fabulous concentration of live theater. It was the move of the Metropolitan Opera House to Broadway at 40th Street, in 1883, that first drew theaters and restaurants here. In the 1920s, movie palaces added the glamor of neon to Broadway, the signs getting bigger and brighter, until eventually the street came to be known as the "Great White Way." After World War II, the draw of the films waned, and the glitter was replaced by grime. Fortunately, since the 1990s, regeneration has brought back the public and the bright lights of Broadway.

0 meters   200
0 yards   200

N

PIER 99

PIER 98

WEST

WEST   57TH   ST

PIER 97

WEST   56TH   ST

PIER 96

New York City
Downtown
Boathouse

WEST   55TH   ST

WEST   54TH   ST

De Witt
Clinton
Park

WEST

PIER 94

WEST   52ND   ST

R i v e r

PIER 92

NYC Passenger
Ship Terminal
(Port Authority)

WEST   51ST   ST

3

WEST   50TH   ST

PIER 90

Hell's
Kitchen

WEST   49TH   ST

NYC Passenger
Ship Terminal
(Port Authority)

⓭

PIER 88

HELL'S KITCHEN

WEST   48TH   ST

WEST   47TH   ST

PIER 86

Intrepid Sea, Air,
& Space Museum

WEST   46TH   ST

H u d s o n

⓬

WEST   45TH   ST

WEST   44TH   ST

PIER 84

WEST   43RD   ST

4

HUDSON
RIVER
GREENWAY

PIER 83

WEST   42ND   ST   (THEATER   ROW)

Circle Line
Boat Trip

WEST   41ST   ST

PIER 81

Cardinal
Stepinac Plaza

WEST   40TH   ST

WEST   39TH   ST

LINCOLN TUNNEL

LINCOLN TUNNEL

LINCOLN TUNNEL

Jacob K Javits
Convention
Center

WEST   36TH   ST

5

34 St-
Hudson Yards 7

S

MIDTOWN WEST AND
THE THEATER DISTRICT

WEST   33RD   ST

6

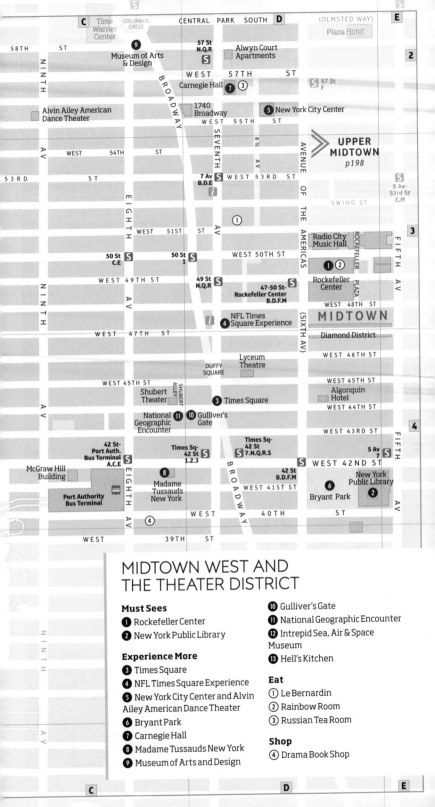

MIDTOWN WEST AND THE THEATER DISTRICT

Must Sees

1. Rockefeller Center
2. New York Public Library

Experience More

3. Times Square
4. NFL Times Square Experience
5. New York City Center and Alvin Ailey American Dance Theater
6. Bryant Park
7. Carnegie Hall
8. Madame Tussauds New York
9. Museum of Arts and Design
10. Gulliver's Gate
11. National Geographic Encounter
12. Intrepid Sea, Air & Space Museum
13. Hell's Kitchen

Eat

1. Le Bernardin
2. Rainbow Room
3. Russian Tea Room

Shop

4. Drama Book Shop

❶ 🖵 🏛

ROCKEFELLER CENTER

📍 D3 🏢 30 Rockefeller Plaza 🚇 47–50 St-Rockefeller Ctr (B, D, F, M) 🕐 8am–midnight daily
🌐 rockefellercenter.com

This massive Art Deco complex has been at the heart of Midtown since the 1930s. Today it's home to TV studios, restaurants, and one of the city's highest observation decks, Top of the Rock, not forgetting the famous ice rink during the holiday season.

The Heart of New York

Today the center encompasses Radio City Music Hall, the 850-ft (259-m) tall 30 Rockefeller Plaza (or "30 Rock"), an underground shopping mall, Rainbow Room, and the sunken Lower Plaza. The Art Deco complex was commissioned by tycoon John D. Rockefeller Jr. and designed by a team headed by Raymond Hood. Rockefeller had leased the site in 1928, seeing it as a new home for the Met Opera, but the 1929 Wall Street Crash scuttled those plans.

↑ Illuminated cityscapes, as seen from the Top of the Rock

Rockefeller went ahead with his own development. The 14 buildings erected between 1931 and 1940 provided jobs for up to 225,000 people during the Depression; by 1973, there were 19 buildings.

The Rink at Rockefeller Center

Every winter since 1936, the Lower Plaza at Rockefeller Center transforms into an ice-skating rink. Skating is on a first-come, first-served basis, so arrive early to avoid a long wait (open daily 8:30am to midnight; www.therinkatrockcenter.com). From late November to early January, the Christmas Tree, known for having featured in a number of shows and movies, overlooks the rink above Paul Manship's *Prometheus* sculpture.

Did You Know?

The Rockefeller Christmas tree is lit by 30,000 environmentally friendly lights.

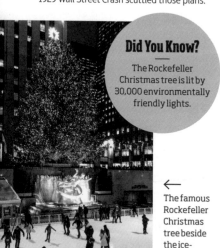

← The famous Rockefeller Christmas tree beside the ice-skating rink

30 ROCK

30 Rockefeller Plaza has long been the home of the NBC television network. See where *Saturday Night Live, The Tonight Show Starring Jimmy Fallon,* and *The Today Show* are filmed on the NBC Studio Tour (www.thetouratnbcstudios.com). You can be a part of *The Today Show* outdoor audience by simply turning up before 7am on a weekday.

Water features lining ↑
the Art Deco Rockefeller
Center complex

② Ⓜ ▭ 🏛

NEW YORK
PUBLIC LIBRARY

📍D4 🏠476 Fifth Av 🚇42 St-Bryant Park (B, D, F, M) 🕐10am-8pm Tue & Wed,
10am-6pm Thu-Sat, 1-5pm Sun 🌐nypl.org

The New York Public Library is one of the city's most beloved public buildings.
It's an attraction as much for its lavish architecture and decor as for its extensive
book collections, changing exhibits, and cultural events.

New York's Beaux Arts Gem

In 1897, the coveted job of designing New York
Public Library Main Branch (now the Stephen
A. Schwarzman Building) was awarded to
architects Carrère & Hastings. The library's first
director envisaged a light, quiet, airy place for
study, where millions of books could be both
stored and available to readers as promptly
as possible. In the hands of Carrère & Hastings,
his vision came true in what is considered
the epitome of New York's Beaux Arts period.
The library opened in 1911 to immediate
acclaim. The vast, paneled Rose Main Reading
Room stretches two full blocks and is suffused
with daylight from the two interior
courtyards. Below it are
88 miles (142 km) of
shelves, holding over
seven million

volumes. The DeWitt Wallace Periodicals Room
is adorned with 13 murals by Richard Haas,
honoring New York's great publishing houses.
The similarly opulent Map Room is home to
one of the largest public map collections in
the world. There are also public exhibitions on
wide-ranging subjects filling several galleries.
Free guided tours (11am and 2pm Mon–Sat)
are a great way to take in these spaces.

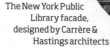

→
The New York Public
Library facade,
designed by Carrère &
Hastings architects

THE REAL POOH BEAR

Visit the Children's Center to see the
real stuffed toy animals that inspired
the beloved Winnie-the-Pooh stories by
A.A. Milne. Pooh, Eeyore, Piglet, Kanga,
and Tigger were originally owned by
Christopher Robin Milne in the 1920s,
and acquired by the Library in 1987.

The Map Room

Aside from its stunning map room, the library's map division houses an astounding 433,000 sheet maps and some 20,000 books and atlases, from the 16th to 21st centuries. Staff are on hand to produce any cartographic print, from British strongholds during the Revolution and German army maps used during World War II to historic maps of New York itself.

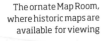

→

The ornate Map Room, where historic maps are available for viewing

↓ The spectacular Rose Main Reading Room

EXPERIENCE MORE

3

Times Square

D4 **S** Times Sq-42 St
(N, R, 1, 2, 3, 7) **i** Broadway
Plaza, between 43rd and
44th sts; 9am-6pm daily
w timessquarenyc.org

Broadway traditions coexist
with modern innovations
here and, thanks to a 1990s
transformation, this is now a
vibrant hub bustling with
activity. Buildings such as
the Bertelsmann and the
fashionably minimalist Condé
Nast offices sit alongside the
classic Broadway theaters.

Although *The New York
Times* has moved from its
original headquarters at the
south end of the Square to
a site opposite the Port
Authority, the glistening ball
(of Waterford crystal) still
drops at midnight on New
Year's Eve, as it has since the
building opened with fanfare
and fireworks in 1906.

Broadway's fortunes have
also revived. Many theaters

 INSIDER TIP
Ticket Bargains

The Times Square
TKTS booth, located
beneath the red steps
at Broadway and West
47th Street, is still the
primary go-to spot for
discounted tickets to
stellar Broadway shows.
Lines are long, but it's
worth it for the disount.

have been renovated and are
again hosting contemporary
productions; theater-goers
throng the area's bars and
restaurants each evening.

One of the landmarks is the
57-story skyscraper, designed
by Miami architects Arquitectonica, that tops the E-Walk
entertainment and retail
complex at 42nd Street
and Eighth Avenue. Other
attractions include a Madame
Tussauds at 42nd Street (*p182*),
a massive Disney Store, a
traffic-free plaza and M&M's
World at 1600 Broadway.

SHOP

Drama Bookshop
Established by the
Drama League in 1917,
this venerable book-
store is one of the city's
few indie booksellers
still going strong. As the
store's name implies, it
specializes in theater
books, scripts, and
publications on all
manner of performance-
related subjects.

C4 **250 West
40th St** **w** dramabook
shop.com

4

NFL Times Square Experience

D3 **20 Times Sq**
S Times Sq-42 St (N, Q, R,
S, 1, 2, 3, 7) **10am-8pm
Fri & Sat, 10am-6pm Sun-
Thu (last adm: 1 hour
before closing)
w nflexperience.com

American football fans of all
ages will enjoy this absorbing
interactive experience.
Touch screens allow visitors
to explore details of all 32
NFL teams, while a 4D special
effects movie theater shows
NFL games close up. Fans
can also test their skills
against professional football
players (the "quarterback
challenge" involves throwing

a real ball at a virtual pitch),
and learn game strategy from
Jon Gruden, the Oakland
Raiders' coach.

5

New York City Center and Alvin Ailey American Dance Theater

D2 **131 West 55th St**
S 57 St (N, O, R, W)
**For performances only
w nycitycenter.org

This highly ornate Moorish
structure, with its dome of
Spanish tiles, was designed
in 1924 as a Masonic Shriners'
Temple. After Mayor LaGuardia
saved it from developers, it
became home to the New
York City Opera (1944–64)
and Ballet (1948–19). City
Center lived on as a key
venue for dance after the
companies moved to the
Lincoln Center, instead
becoming the home base
of the Manhattan Theatre
Club and the highly respected

↑ Alfresco, summer-time dining in pretty Bryant Park

Alvin Ailey American Dance Theater, which specializes in modern dance.

 6

Bryant Park

D4 **S** 5 Av (7), 42 St-Bryant Pk (B, D, F, M) **Daily; hours vary, check website for details** **bryantpark.org**

This park is an oasis of calm wedged between Midtown's skyscrapers. There is a free ice-skating rink in winter, while summer sees open-air screenings of classic movies. Many people don't realise that New York Public Library (*p178*) has over a million books in temperature-controlled storage beneath the park.

In 1853 Bryant Park (then Reservoir Park) housed a dazzling Crystal Palace, built for the World's Fair of the same year. The palace burnt down in 1858. In 1989 the park was renovated and reclaimed for workers and visitors to enjoy.

7

Carnegie Hall

D2 **154 West 57th St** **S** 57 St-7 Av (N, Q, R) **For concerts** **carnegie hall.org**

Financed by millionaire philanthropist Andrew Carnegie, New York's first great concert hall opened in 1891, with guest conductor Tchaikovsky. For many years it was home to the New York Philharmonic, under conductors such as Arturo Toscanini, Bruno Walter, and Leonard Bernstein. Playing Carnegie Hall quickly became an international symbol of success for musicians, and today the corridors are lined with memorabilia of artists who have performed here.

A 1950s campaign by violinist Isaac Stern saved the site from developers, and in 1964 it became a national landmark, planting it firmly in the city's consciousness as a place of cultural importance.

If you aren't able to watch a concert, you can join a tour; check the website for details.

THEATERS OF BROADWAY

Many of Broadway's original theaters have gone, but 25 of those that remain are designated historic landmarks. The 1903 Lyceum (149 West 45th St) was the first to receive the designation and is the city's oldest active theater. When it opened in 1903, the New Amsterdam (214 West 42nd St) was the most opulent theater in the US. The first with an Art Nouveau interior, it was owned by Florenz Ziegfeld, of Ziegfeld Follies fame. The 1912 Helen Hayes (240 West 44th St) is Broadway's smallest theater, while the celebrated Shubert (225 West 44th St) has a magnificent interior that belies its simple exterior.

Madame Tussauds New York

C4 **234 West 42nd St** **Times Sq-42 St (N, Q, R, S, 1, 2, 3, 7)** **9am-10pm Fri, 10am-10pm Sat, 10am-8pm Sun-Thu** **madame tussauds.com/new-york**

This global tourist franchise operates a large branch just off Times Square, with the usual line-up of amazingly realistic wax models of movie stars, celebrities, royalty and politicians. Extras (which you must pay extra for) include the "Ghostbusters: Dimension Virtual Reality Experience," which allows you to dress up like the movie's characters and catch a ghost. There's also the "Marvel 4D Cinema Experience" (where superheroes, including the Hulk, are brought to life in interactive themed areas, with wax figures and 4D film).

Museum of Arts and Design

C2 **2 Columbus Circle** **59 St-Columbus Circle (A, B, C, D, 1)** **10am-6pm Tue-Sun (to 9pm Thu)** **federal hols** **madmuseum.org**

The leading American cultural institution of its kind, this museum, housed in a modern and eye-catching building, is dedicated to contemporary

↑ Waxwork of *Ghostbusters* actress Leslie Jones at Madame Tussauds

DIAMOND DISTRICT

New York's Diamond District (47th Street, between Fifth and Sixth avenues) features window displays of glittering gold and diamonds, the buildings filled with booths and workshops where jewelers vie for customers. The district was born in the 1930s, when Jewish diamond cutters fled Europe to escape Nazism. It deals mainly in wholesale, but individuals are welcome. Bring cash, compare prices, and haggle – but only if you know something about the value of diamonds.

objects, from clay and wood to metal and fiber, in an array of media. The permanent collection has over 2,000 artifacts by international craftspeople and designers.

About four exhibitions a year are complemented by selected pieces from the Tiffany & Co. Foundation Jewelry Gallery. Items by top-class American artisans are for sale in The Store at MAD.

Gulliver's Gate

D4 **216 West 44th St** **Times Sq-42 St (N, Q, R, S, 1, 2, 3, 7)** **10am-8pm daily (last adm: 1 hour before closing)** **gulliversgate.com**

Encompassing some 50,000 sq ft (6,645 sq m), this is a family-friendly, interactive world of miniature cities from five continents. An astounding 102 bridges, 1,000 buildings, and 1,000 trains have been reproduced to mimic real life places. The first exhibit, naturally, is New York City, with its most iconic buildings and landmarks represented. This includes the Brooklyn Bridge, Empire State Building, Central Park, Staten Island Ferry Building, and Grand

Central Station. There are tiny, realistic touches at "street level": familiar graffiti tags, sunbathers on fire escapes, cops investigating crimes, and pigeons fluttering on rooftops.

Latin America features the Panama Canal, Iguazu Falls, Machu Picchu and Chichen Itza, while the Taj Mahal, Angkor Wat, Great Wall and Forbidden City represent Asia. Paris and Venice both feature in Europe's section, and there's a stunning model of Jerusalem's old city. Buy timed tickets online to save time (and money).

National Geographic Encounter

C4 **226 44th St** **Times Sq-42 St (N, Q, R, S, 1, 2, 3, 7)** **10am-9pm Sun-Thu, 10am-10pm Fri & Sat** **natgeoencounter.com**

Opened in 2017, the spectac-ular National Geographic Encounter: Ocean Odyssey is a vast complex that utilizes advanced technology to simulate a walk across the

→

The opulent Russian Tea Room also serves up a sense of history ocean. Specifically, visitors can "walk" from the South Pacific to the coast of California. Immersive sounds, interactive touch screens, and holograms create virtual interaction with sea lions, dolphins, and 50-foot humpback whales. There's even a battle between two Humboldt squids.

Allow at least two hours for this attraction. It's also advisable to buy timed tickets online in advance.

---

12 Intrepid Sea, Air & Space Museum

📍 A4 📍 Pier 86, West 46th St 🚇 Times Sq-42 St (N, Q, R, S, 1, 2, 3, 7) 🚌 M42, M50 🕐 Apr-Oct: 10am-5pm Mon-Fri, 10am-6pm Sat, Sun and hols; Nov-Mar: 10am-5pm daily 🌐 intrepidmuseum.org

Exhibits on board this World War II aircraft carrier include fighter planes from the 1940s; the A-12 Blackbird, the world's fastest spy plane; and the USS *Growler*, a guided-missile submarine launched

in 1958 at the height of the Cold War.

The museum's family-friendly Exploreum Hall contains two G-Force flight simulators, a 4D motion ride theater, a Bell 47 helicopter, and an interactive submarine. There is also the Space Shuttle Pavilion, which houses the historic space craft.

---

13 Hell's Kitchen

📍 B3 🚇 50 St (C, E)

West of Times Square, roughly between 30th and 59th streets, lies Clinton, more commonly called Hell's Kitchen. Known today for its culinary reputation, in the late 1800s the area was a poor Irish enclave, and one of New York's most violent neighborhoods, as Greeks, Puerto Ricans, and African-Americans moved in and

tensions rapidly developed. Such rivalries were glamorized in the musical *West Side Story*, the movie of which was filmed in New York and released in 1957. The area has been cleaned up, with rents sky-rocketing and Ninth Avenue especially crammed with restaurants, bars, and delis. There's also a strong gay community, with as many gay bars as in Chelsea or the East Village. These moved in here as Chelsea and the East Village became gentrified and, as a result, expensive.

EAT

Le Bernardin
This revered and beautifully designed French restaurant has earned three Michelin stars, and serves some of the best seafood in America.

📍 D3 📍 155 West 51st St 🔒 Sun 🌐 le-bernardin. com

$ $ $

Rainbow Room
On the 65th floor of Rockefeller Center, this is not as exclusive as it once was, but the views are magnificent. Jackets are compulsory for men.

📍 D3 📍 30 Rockefeller Plaza 🔒 Sun 🌐 rainbowroom.com

$ $ $

Russian Tea Room
Opened in 1927 by former members of the Russian Imperial Ballet, this venue serves classic Russian dishes in lavish surroundings.

📍 D2 📍 150 West 57th St 🌐 russiantea roomnyc.com

$ $ $

LOWER MIDTOWN

From Beaux Arts to Art Deco, this section of Midtown boasts some fine architecture, chic boutiques, and towering skyscrapers, primarily scattered along Fifth, Madison, and Park avenues. Quiet, residential Murray Hill, between East 34th and East 40th streets, was named for a country estate that once occupied the site. By the turn of the 20th century, it was home to many of New York's first families, including the financier J. P. Morgan, whose library, now a museum, reveals the grandeur of the age. The commercial pace quickens at 42nd Street, near Grand Central Terminal, where tall office blocks line the streets. However, few of the newer buildings have equaled the Beaux Arts Terminal itself or such Art Deco gems as the Chrysler Building, while the Modernist United Nations complex overlooks the East River.

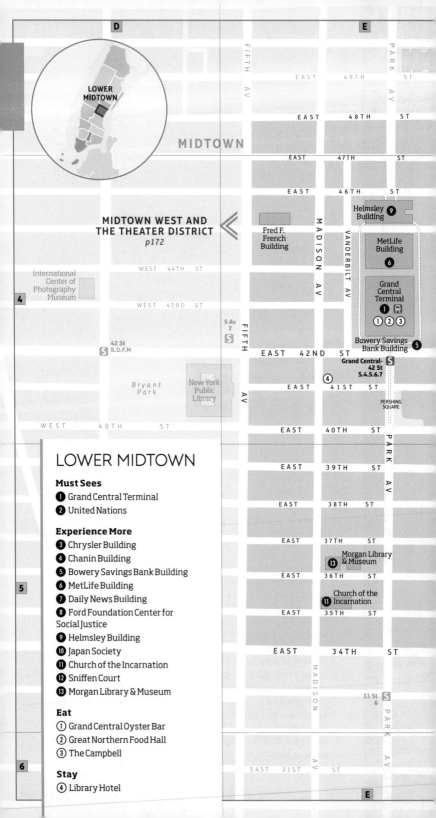

MIDTOWN WEST AND THE THEATER DISTRICT
p172

LOWER MIDTOWN

Must Sees

❶ Grand Central Terminal

❷ United Nations

Experience More

❸ Chrysler Building

❹ Chanin Building

❺ Bowery Savings Bank Building

❻ MetLife Building

❼ Daily News Building

❽ Ford Foundation Center for Social Justice

❾ Helmsley Building

❿ Japan Society

⓫ Church of the Incarnation

⓬ Sniffen Court

⓭ Morgan Library & Museum

Eat

① Grand Central Oyster Bar

② Great Northern Food Hall

③ The Campbell

Stay

④ Library Hotel

GRAND CENTRAL TERMINAL

📍E4 🚇East 42nd St at Park Av Ⓢ Grand Central (S, 4, 5, 6, 7) 🚌M1–5, M42, M50, M101–103, Q32 🕐5:30am–2am daily 🌐grandcentralterminal.com

Since it opened in 1913, this Beaux Arts gem has been a gateway to and symbol of the city. The terminal's glory is its soaring main concourse, along with its fabulous Oyster Bar.

In 1871, Cornelius Vanderbilt (1794–1877) opened a railway station on 42nd Street. Although often revamped, it was never large enough and was finally demolished. Grand Central Terminal as we see it today opened in 1913. The building has a steel frame covered with plaster and marble. Reed & Stern were in charge of the logistical planning; Warren & Wetmore, the overall design. The restoration by architects Beyer Blinder Belle is outstanding, and transports both railway travelers and tourists to a bygone era.

← Sun beams pour through the terminal's main concourse, c. 1930

The 42nd St facade shows Roman gods.

The vaulted ceiling has a zodiac design.

The vast concourse, with arched windows.

Vanderbilt Hall, an example of Beaux Arts architecture.

The Grand Staircase, based on Paris's opera house.

↑ Detail of Grand Central Terminal's interior

EAT

**Grand Central
Oyster Bar**

Sample fresh oysters at
this seafood palace.
Open since 1913, it's
crowned by grand,
vaulted ceilings, below
Grand Central. The
chefs opt for simple
preparation - a squeeze
of lemon or a hand-
plucked garnish -
allowing the fresh fish,
clam chowder, steamed
Maine lobster, and
sweet Kumamoto
oysters to shine on their
own delectable merit.

📍E4 🏠Lower level,
Grand Central Terminal
📅Sun 🕙oyster
barny.com

💲💲💲

↑ The impressive main
terminal concourse
and *(inset)* exterior

Secretariat
Building

The
Conference
Building

Called Colors of the World,
flags of member nations
fly before the UN

Colors of
the World

General
Assembly

Security
Council

Trusteeship
Council

Economic
and Social
Council

WORKS OF ART AT THE UN

The UN Building has acquired numerous works of art; most have either a peace or international friendship theme. These include a mosaic by Norman Rockwell, a Henry Moore sculpture in the grounds, and a Peace Bell gifted from Japan.

Rose
Garden

The United Nations
complex, including
its gardens

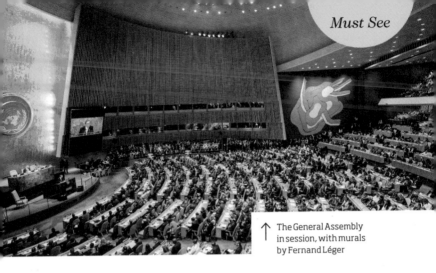

↑ The General Assembly in session, with murals by Fernand Léger

2 🅜 🖥 🛍

UNITED NATIONS

📍 F4 🏛 First Av at 46th St Ⓢ 42 St-Grand Central (S, 4, 5, 6, 7) 🚌 M15, M42, M50 🕐 9am–4:45pm Mon-Fri, 10am–4:30pm Sat & Sun 🚫 Federal hols, Eid 🌐 visit.un.org

Visitors' entrance

Many visitors to New York don't realize that the city is the home of international humanitarian organization the United Nations. The 193 member nations aim to preserve world peace, and aid economic and social well-being around the globe.

The UN was founded in 1945 with just 51 members. John D. Rockefeller Jr. donated $8.5 million for the purchase of the site. Today, the UN comprises five forums. The General Assembly holds regular sessions to discuss international problems September through to December, and all member states are represented with an equal vote. It cannot enact laws, but its recommendations strongly influence world opinion. The most powerful body is the Security Council, which strives to achieve peace and security, intervening in international crises, such as conflict. It is the only body whose decisions member states must obey, as well as the only one in continuous session. China, France, the Russian Federation, the UK, and the US are permanent members of the Council; other nations are elected by the General Assembly.

The 54 members of the Economic and Social Council work to improve the standard of living and social welfare around the world, including economic issues and human rights abuses. The Secretariat has some 16,000 international workers and carries out the day-to-day work of the UN It's headed by the Secretary General, who is a spokesperson in the organization's peace-keeping efforts. Finally, the International Court of Justice settles disputes between member states.

Tours of the UN take place Monday through Friday and booking is essential.

↑ The Security Council, where delegates confer, overlooked by murals by artist Per Krohg

EXPERIENCE MORE

③

Chrysler Building

📍 E4 🏛 405 Lexington Av
☎ (212) 682-3070 🚇 42 St-
Grand Central (S, 4, 5, 6, 7)
🕐 Lobby: 7am–6pm

William Van Alen's 77-story Chrysler Building, topped by its shining crown, is one of New York City's best-known and most-loved landmarks. It was built for Walter P. Chrysler, a former Union Pacific Railroad machinist, whose passion for the motor car helped him rise swiftly to the top of this industry to found the corporation bearing his name in 1925. His wish for a headquarters in New York that symbolized his company led to a building that will always be linked with the golden age of motoring. The stainless-steel Art Deco spire resembles a car radiator grille; the series of stepped setbacks are emblazoned with winged radiator caps, wheels, and stylized automobiles; and gargoyles are modeled on hood ornaments from the 1929 Chrysler Plymouth.

The crowning spire, kept a secret until the last moment, was built in the fire shaft, then raised into position through the roof, ensuring that the 1,046-ft (320-m) building would be higher than the just completed Bank of Manhattan by Van Alen's great rival, H. Craig Severance. Just a few months later, it was overtaken by the Empire State Building.

Van Alen was poorly rewarded. Chrysler accused him of accepting bribes from contractors and refused to pay him. Van Alen's career never recovered from the slur.

The stunning lobby, once a car showroom, is lavish, with patterned marble and granite and a chromed steel trim. A vast painted ceiling by Edward Trumball shows scenes of late 1920s transportation.

Although it was never the Chrysler Corporation's HQ, their name remains.

④

Chanin Building

📍 E4 🏛 122 East 42nd St
🚇 42 St- Grand Central (S, 4, 5, 6, 7) 🕐 Office hours

Once the headquarters of Irwin S. Chanin, one of New York's leading real estate developers and a self-made man, the 56-story 1929 tower, by Sloan & Robertson, was

 ←
The distinctive Chrysler Building, a monument to the early days of motoring

↑ The Chanin Building, a splendid example of Art Deco style

the first skyscraper in the Grand Central area, and is one of the best examples of the Art Deco period. A wide bronze band, with bird and fish motifs, runs the length of the facade and the terra-cotta base features a tangle of stylized plantlife. Sculptor René Chambellan's interior includes reliefs in the vestibule charting Chanin's career.

⑤

Bowery Savings Bank Building

📍 E4 🏛 110 East 42nd St
🚇 42 St-Grand Central (S, 4, 5, 6, 7) 🕐 By appt only
🌐 cipriani.com

Many consider this 1923 building the best work of bank architects York & Sawyer, who chose the style of a Romanesque basilica for the offices of the venerable bank (now part of Capital One Bank). An arched entrance leads into the vast banking room, with a high-beamed ceiling, mosaic floors, and marble columns on which stone arches soar overhead.

Between the columns are unpolished mosaic panels of marble from France and Italy. The building, now an event space, is also home to Cipriani restaurant, whose opulent decor lures high rollers for celebratory dinners.

MetLife Building

E4 **200 Park Av** **S** 42 St-Grand Central (S, 4, 5, 6, 7) **O** Office hours

When this colossus was built, as the Pan Am Building, in 1963, its status as the largest commercial building in the world was somewhat over-shadowed by the loss of the view from Park Avenue of the sculptures atop the Grand Central Terminal. Designed in the Modernist style by Walter Gropius, Emery Roth and Sons, and Pietro Belluschi, it dwarfed the terminal and aroused universal dislike. The building's rooftop heliport was abandoned in 1977 after a freak accident showered debris onto the surrounding streets. In 1981 the building was sold to the Metropolitan Life organization, and then on to Tishman Speyer Properties.

It is ironic that the New York skies were blocked by Pan Am, a company that had opened up the skies as a means of travel. When the company began in 1927, Charles Lindbergh, fresh from his solo transatlantic flight, was one of its pilots and an adviser on new routes. By 1936, Pan Am introduced the first trans-Pacific route, and in 1947 their first round-the-world route was launched.

Great Northern Food Hall

Nordic-inspired food market inside Grand Central, with seasonal menus that showcase the New York region's best produce. Stalls include organic bakery Meyers Bageri, coffee shop Brownsville Roasters, gourmet hot dogs at Danish Dogs, and vegetable-driven menus at Almanak.

E4 **Vanderbilt Hall West, Grand Central Terminal** **W** great northernfood.com

$$$

The Campbell

This is one of New York's most elegant cocktail bars, in the style of a Florentine palace. Serving good lunches and bar food, the real draws here are the drinks and the setting. The adjacent Campbell Palm Court offers views into the terminal. No casual wear after 4pm.

E4 **15 Vanderbilt Av (off 43rd St), Grand Central Terminal** **W** thecampbellnyc.com

$$$

Daily News Building

F4 **220 East 42nd St** **S** 42 St-Grand Central (S, 4, 5, 6, 7) **O** 8am–6pm Mon–Fri

The *Daily News* was founded in 1919 and by 1925 it was a million-seller, known, rather scathingly, as "the servant girl's bible," for its focus on scandals, celebrities and murders, its readable style,

> **William Van Alen's 77-story Chrysler Building, topped by its shining crown, is one of New York City's best-known and most-loved landmarks.**

and heavy use of illustration. Over the years it has stuck to what it does best, and this formula has paid off handsomely. It revealed stories such as the romance of Edward VIII and Mrs Simpson, and has become renowned for its punchy headlines. Its circulation figures are still among the highest in the United States.

Its former headquarters (the offices are now at 4 New York Plaza), designed by Raymond Hood in 1930, have vertical stripes of brown and black brick alternating with windows. Hood's lobby is familiar to many as that of the *Daily Planet* in the 1980s *Superman* movies. It includes the world's largest interior globe, and bronze lines on the floor indicate the direction of world cities and the position of the planets. At night, the intricate detail over the front entrance of the building is illuminated from within by neon. The building has now been designated as a national historic landmark.

Giant globe in the lobby of the Daily News Building ↑

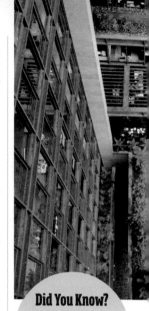

8

Ford Foundation Center for Social Justice

◉ F4 ⌂ 320 East 43rd St S 42nd St-Grand Central (S, 4, 5, 6, 7) ⓘ For renovation

Built in 1968, this building was designed by architect Kevin Roche, and featured the first of the atria now common across Manhattan. The atrium resembles an enormous greenhouse, supported by towering columns of granite, and was one of the first attempts at a natural environment within a building. It is fringed by two walls of offices, visible through windows, and yet the enclave is incredibly tranquil. The din outside disappears and all that remains is the echo of voices, trickle of fountains, and sound of shoes on brick walkways.

The Ford Foundation's staff left the building in 2016 to allow for renovation until 2019. This contemporary workspace will include an art gallery, welcome center, and a number of programs and events.

9

Helmsley Building

◉ E4 ⌂ 230 Park Av S 42 St-Grand Central (S, 4, 5, 6, 7) ⓘ Office hours

One of the great New York views looks south down Park Avenue to the Helmsley Building, straddling the busy traffic flow beneath. There is just one flaw – the monolithic MetLife Building *(p193)* towers behind it, replacing the former backdrop, the sky.

Built by Warren & Wetmore in 1929, the Helmsley Building was originally the headquarters of the New York Central Railroad Company. Its namesake, the late Harry Helmsley, was a billionaire who began his career as a New York office boy for $12 per week. His wife, Leona, was a prominent feature in all the advertisements for their hotel chain – until her imprisonment in 1989 for tax evasion on a grand scale. Many observers believe that the extravagant glitter of the building's facelift was due to Leona's overblown taste in decor.

Did You Know?

When Leona Helmsley died in 2007, she left a $12 million trust fund for her pet Maltese, called Trouble.

10 Ⓜ

Japan Society

◉ F3 ⌂ 333 East 47th St S 42 St-Grand Central (S, 4, 5, 6, 7) 🚌 M15, M50 🌐 japansociety.org

The headquarters of the Japan Society, founded in 1907 to foster understanding and cultural exchange between Japan and the US, was built with the help of John D. Rockefeller III, who underwrote costs of some $4.3 million. The striking black building, with its delicate sun grilles, was designed by Tokyo architects Junzo Yoshimura and George Shimamoto in 1971. It includes a museum gallery, which is open Tuesday to Sunday in October through to June, an auditorium, a language center, a

---

MIDTOWN MANHATTAN

The skyline here is graced with some of the city's most spectacular towers and spires, from the familiar beauty of the Empire State Building's Art Deco pinnacle to the dramatic wedge of Citibank's modern headquarters. As the shoreline progresses uptown the architecture becomes more varied. The United Nations complex dominates a long stretch before, Beekman Place begins a strand of exclusive residential enclaves offering the rich and famous some seclusion in this busy part of the city.

Empire State Building

United Nations

Chrysler Building

The lush atrium of the Ford Foundation Center for Justice brings the outside in

research library, and traditional Oriental gardens.

Changing exhibits include a variety of Japanese arts, from swords to kimonos to scrolls. The society offers programs of Japanese performing arts, lectures, language classes and many business workshops for American and Japanese executives and managers.

---

⑪
Church of the Incarnation

◊E5 ⌂209 Madison Av
Ⓢ42 St-Grand Central (S, 4, 5, 6, 7), 33rd Street (6)
⊙11:30am– 2pm Mon-Fri, 8am-1pm Sun Ⓦchurchof theincarnation.org

This Episcopal church dates from 1864, when Madison Avenue was home to the elite. Its patterned sandstone and brownstone exterior is typical of the period. The interior has an oak communion rail by Daniel Chester French; a chancel mural by John La Farge; and stained-glass windows by La Farge, Tiffany, William Morris, and Edward Burne-Jones.

⑫
Sniffen Court

◊E5 ⌂150-158 East 36th St
Ⓢ33 St (6)

Here is a delightful, intimate courtyard of ten brick Romanesque Revival carriage houses, built by John Sniffen in the 1850s. They are perfectly and improbably preserved off a busy block in modern New York. The house at the south end was the studio of sculptor Malvina Hoffman, whose plaques of Greek horsemen decorate the exterior wall.

---

⑬
Morgan Library & Museum

◊E5 ⌂225 Madison Av
Ⓢ33 St (6) ⊙10:30am-5pm Tue-Thu, 10am-9pm Fri, 10am-6pm Sat, 11am-6pm Sun Ⓦthemorgan.org

One of the world's finest collections of rare manuscripts, drawings, prints, books, and bindings is on display here, accumulated by legendary banker J. P. Morgan (1837–1913). A stunning piazza-style central atrium, created by Renzo Piano, links several Morgan properties. The magnificent palazzo-style building in which Morgan originally stored his collection, completed in 1906, contains his immaculately maintained personal library and study. The 1928 Annex was designed in similar fashion (replacing Morgan's old townhouse) and now houses the Morgan Stanley galleries. The 1850s Italianate brownstone home of J. P. Morgan Jr., who lived here from 1905 to 1943, now features the Morgan Dining Room and Morgan Shop. A 2006 renovation also doubled the exhibition space. The collection has over 10,000 drawings and prints by the likes of Da Vinci and Dürer, rare literary manuscripts by Austen and Dickens, and priceless copies of the Gutenberg Bible (three of the eleven that survive).

A SHORT WALK
LOWER MIDTOWN

Distance 1.25 mile (2 km) **Nearest subway**
Grand Central-42 St **Time** 25 minutes

A walk in Lower Midtown is a great way to fully
appreciate New York's eclectic mix of architectural
styles. Step back to take in the contours of the
tallest skyscrapers, and step inside to experience
the many fine interiors; from modern atriums,
such as those in the Ford Foundation Center for
Social Justice, to the ornate details of the Bowery
Savings Bank Building, and the soaring spaces
of Grand Central Terminal.

*The MetLife Building,
built by Pan Am in 1963,
towers above Park
Avenue (p193).*

*The vast, vaulted interior of Grand
Central Terminal is a splendid
reminder of the heyday of train
travel. This historic building also
features specialty shops and
gourmet restaurants (p188).*

START

S

*Grand Central-42
St subway (lines
S, 4, 5, 6, 7)*

PARK AVENUE

FINISH

E 41 ST ST

LEXINGTON AVENUE

3,862
—
windows on the
Chrysler Building

*Built for self-made
real estate mogul
Irwin S. Chanin
in the 1920s,
the Chanin Building
has a fine Art Deco
lobby (p192).*

*Formerly the headquarters of the
Bowery Savings Bank, this is one
of the finest bank buildings in
New York. Architects York &
Sawyer designed it to resemble a
Romanesque palace (p192).*

*The Mobil Building has
a self-cleaning stainless
steel facade that is
embossed in geometric
patterns to prevent it
from warping. It was
built in 1955.*

←

Magnificent
interior of Grand
Central Terminal

Locator Map
For more detail see p186

LOWER MIDTOWN

Straddling Park Avenue between 45th and 46th, the Helmsley Building has an ornate entrance symbolizing the wealth of its first official occupants, New York Central Railroad (p194).

Ornamented with automotive motifs, the Chrysler Building is an Art Deco delight. It was built in 1930 for the Chrysler car company (p192).

→
Tudor City apartment block, Lower Midtown

The Ford Foundation Center for Social Justice is the headquarters of the philanthropic Ford Foundation. It has a lovely interior garden surrounded by a cube-shaped building made of pinkish-gray granite, glass, and steel (p194).

THIRD AVENUE

E 43RD STREET

E 42ND STREET

SECOND AVENUE

FIRST AVENUE

Ralph J. Bunche Park

Tudor City is a 1928 private residential complex and has 3,000 apartments. Built in the Tudor style, it features fine stonework details.

The Daily News Building, the former home of the eponymous newspaper, is Art Deco in style and has a revolving globe in the lobby (p193).

UPPER MIDTOWN

Upscale New York in all its diversity is here, in
this district of churches and synagogues, clubs
and museums, grand hotels and famous stores,
and trendsetting skyscrapers. Upper Midtown
was once home to society names, such as Astor
and Vanderbilt. The Waldorf Astoria Hotel,
completed in 1931, is where the Waldorf salad
originated and, in 1934, the Bloody Mary was first
served at the King Cole Bar in the St. Regis Hotel.
In the 1950s, architectural history was made when
the Lever and Seagram buildings were erected. The
Museum of Modern Art (MoMA), one of the greatest
art galleries in the world, stands here.

UPPER MIDTOWN

Must Sees
❶ Museum of Modern Art (MoMA)
❷ St. Patrick's Cathedral

Experience More
❸ Fifth Avenue
❹ Waldorf Astoria
❺ Tiffany & Co
❻ Paley Center for Media
❼ Central Synagogue
❽ General Electric Building
❾ St. Bartholomew's Church
❿ Seagram Building
⓫ Citigroup Center

⓬ Lever House
⓭ Roosevelt Island
⓮ Franklin D. Roosevelt Four Freedoms Park

Eat
① The Modern from MoMA
② Palm Court
③ The Pool
④ 21 Club

Drink
⑤ King Cole Bar
⑥ P.J. Clarke's

Central Park Zoo

Bird Sanctuary

DORIS C. FREEDMAN PLAZA

Christ Church United Methodist

S Lexington Av-63 St F

E A S T 61 S T

Lexington Av-59 St N.Q.R S

EAST 60TH

S 5 Av-59 St N.Q.R

Bloomingdale's

WEST 59TH ST

Grand Army Plaza

EAST 59TH ST

59 St 4.5.6 S

Plaza Hotel ②

WEST 58TH ST

MADISON AV

EAST 58TH ST

AVENUE OF THE AMERICAS (SIXTH) AV

FIFTH AV

Fuller Building

WEST 57TH ST

IBM Building

EAST 57TH ST

S 57 St F

WEST 56TH ST

❺ Tiffany & Co

EAST 56TH ST

⑥

WEST 55TH ST

⑤

EAST 55TH ST

Central Synagogue ❼

Museum of Modern Art (MoMA) ❶ ①

Fifth Avenue ❸

Lever House ⓬

EAST 54TH ST

Citigroup Center ⓫

Lexington Av-53 St E.M S

WEST 53RD ST

S 5 Av-53 St E.M

Seagram Building ❿ ③

Villard Houses

❻ ④

SWING ST

Paley Center for Media

WEST 51ST ST

St. Patrick's Cathedral ❷

General Electric Building ❽

51 St 6 S

THIRD AV

EAST

❾ St. Bartholomew's Church

PARK AV

EAST

Waldorf Astoria ④

EAST 49TH

MIDTOWN WEST AND THE THEATER DISTRICT p172

FIFTH AV

MADISON AV

PARK AV

EAST 48TH

MIDTOWN

Helmsley Building

LOWER MIDTOWN p184

D

E

EAST 45TH ST

❶ 🎨 🐚 🖼 ☕ 🍴 🛍

MUSEUM OF MODERN ART (MOMA)

📍 D3 🏛 11 West 53rd St between Fifth Av & Av of the Americas 🚇 5th Av-53rd St (E,M) 🚌 M1-5, M50, Q32 🕐 10:30am–5:30pm daily (till 8pm Fri) 🌐 moma.org

Affectionately shortened to MoMA, this modern art powerhouse contains one of the world's most comprehensive collections of late 19th- and 20th-century art.

Founded in 1929, the Museum of Modern Art set the standard for museums of its kind. The first museum dedicated solely to modern art moved from a small premises on Fifth Avenue to its current location in 1939. Extensions have been added to the building across the decades, the most recent due to be completed in 2019. Stretches of glass across the museum allow for abundant natural light to penetrate the building, and to bathe the Abby Aldrich Rockefeller Sculpture Garden. MoMA houses almost 200,000 works of art by more than 18,000 artists, ranging from Post-Impressionist classics to an unrivaled collection of modern and contemporary art, as well as fine examples of design and early masterpieces of photography and film. Tours are available for groups; check the website for more information.

Gallery Rooms

First Floor

▽ From the entrance on 53rd Street, visitors will find the lobby, store, restaurant, and Sculpture Garden, which contains works by Picasso, Matisse, and Calder. The Sculpture Garden is open free of charge 9–10:15am, though it does close in bad weather.

Second Floor

Aside from a store and café, the second floor houses Contemporary Galleries, Prints and Illustrated Books, Media, and special exhibitions. The Education Center can also be found here.

Third Floor

Galleries here include Architecture and Design, Drawings, and Photography. Special Exhibitions are also displayed here.

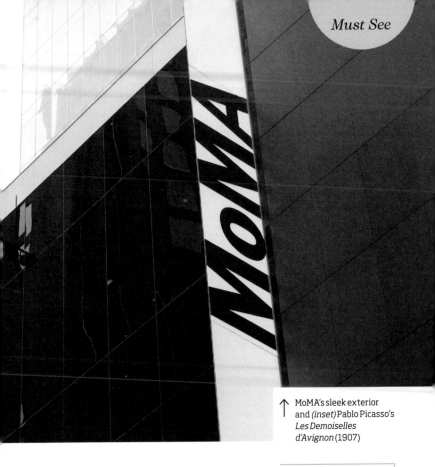

↑ MoMA's sleek exterior and *(inset)* Pablo Picasso's *Les Demoiselles d'Avignon* (1907)

THE DARING LADIES

MoMA was primarily conceived by three remarkable women. Abby Aldrich Rockefeller (wife of John D. Rockefeller Jr.), Lillie P. Bliss, and Mary Quinn had become friends through their love of modern art, but the Met refused to show contemporary artwork in the 1920s. Without J.D's help (he hated modern art), the three women were able to raise the funds and hire the staff for the first modest museum at 730 Fifth Avenue in 1929.

Fourth Floor

The core of the collection, which follows on from the floor above, can be found on the fourth floor. Named Painting and Sculpture II, these galleries are numbered 15-26 and span the 1940s to 1980.

Sixth Floor

Special exhibitions are displayed on the sixth floor. There's also an additional store here.

Fifth Floor

◁ Preceding the fourth floor in years, Painting and Sculpture I displays works from the 1880s through to the 1940s across its galleries numbered 1-14. Along with masterpieces such as *Dance (1)* by Henri Matisse (1909, *inset*), visitors will also find a café here.

MUSEUM'S UPPER LEVELS

MoMA's core collection comprises the Painting and Sculpture galleries, which can be found on the upper levels.

Painting and Sculpture I covers the 1880s through to the 1940s, and can be found on the fifth floor. Paul Cézanne's monumental *The Bather* and Vincent Van Gogh's *Portrait of Joseph Roulin* are two of the seminal works in the museum's collection of late 19th-century painting. Fauvism and Expressionism are well represented with works by Matisse, Derain, Kirchner, and others, while Pablo Picasso's *Les Demoiselles d'Avignon* marks a transition to the Cubist style of painting.

The collection also has an unparalleled number of Cubist paintings, providing an overview of a movement that radically challenged our perception of the world. Among the vast range are Picasso's *Girl with a Mandolin*, Georges Braque's *Man with a*

Guitar and Soda, and *Guitar and Glasses* by Juan Gris. Works by the Futurists, who brought color and movement to Cubism, include *Dynamism of a Soccer Player* by Umberto Boccioni, plus works by Balla, Carrà, and Jacques Villon. The geometric abstract of the Constructivists is included in a strong representation of El Lissitzky, Malevich, and Rodchenko. There is a large body of work by Matisse, such as *Dance (I)* and *Red Studio*. Dalí, Miró, and Ernst feature among the bizarre, strangely beautiful Surrealist works.

Painting and Sculpture II covers the 1940s through to 1980, and can be found on the fourth floor. The postwar art includes works by Bacon and Dubuffet, and has a particularly strong representation of American artists. Abstract Expressionist art here includes Jackson Pollock's *One [Number 31, 1950]*, Willem de Kooning's *Women, I*, Arshile Gorky's *Agony*, and *Red, Brown, and Black* by Mark Rothko. Other notable works include Jasper Johns' *Flag*, Robert Rauschenberg's *First Landing Jump*, composed of urban refuse, and *Bed*. Pop Art here

includes Roy Lichtenstein's *Girl with Ball* and *Drowning Girl*, Andy Warhol's famous *Gold Marilyn Monroe*, and Claes Oldenburg's *Giant Soft Fan*. Works after about 1965 include pieces by Judd, Flavin, Serra, and Beuys.

FILM DEPARTMENT

With more than 22,000 films and four million stills, the collection offers a wide range of programs and exhibits. Film conservation is a key to the department's work and many directors have donated copies of their films to help fund it.

Did You Know?
—
Renovations in 2004, led by Japanese architect Yoshio Taniguchi, doubled exhibition space.

↑ *The Dream* (1910) was painted from Henri Rousseau's imagination

MUSEUM'S LOWER LEVELS

Floors one, two, and three host a number of galleries. The second floor houses a wonderful collection of Prints and Illustrated Books. All significant art movements from the 1880s onward are represented, providing a fascinating overview of printed art. With more than 50,000 items in the department's holdings, there are wide-ranging examples of historical and contemporary printmaking. There are some particularly fine examples of works by Andy Warhol, who is widely considered to be the most important printmaker of the 20th century.

There are also many illustrations and prints by other artists including Munch, Matisse, Dubuffet, Johns, Lichtenstein, Freud, and Picasso.

On the third floor, visitors will find the Architecture and Design galleries. MoMA was the first art museum to incorporate utilitarian objects in its collection. These range from household appliances, such as stereo equipment, furniture, lighting, textiles, and glassware, to industrial ball bearings and silicon chips. Architecture is represented in the collection through photographs, scale models, and drawings of buildings that have been or might have been built.

The photography galleries begin with the invention of the medium around 1840, and include pictures by artists, journalists, and amateur photographers. Highlights include some of the best-known works by American and European photographers including Atget, Stieglitz, Lange, Arbus, Steichen, Cartier-Bresson, and Kertesz.

In the Drawings galleries, more than 7,000 artworks range in size from tiny preparatory pieces to large mural-sized works. Many drawings use conventional materials; however, there are also collages and mixed-media. The collection gives an overview of Modernism, and features drawings by artists such as Picasso, Miró, and Johns, alongside emerging artists.

← *Reflections of Clouds on the Water-Lily Pond* (c. 1920), Claude Monet

EAT

The Modern
Danny Meyer's contemporary, fine-dining restaurant overlooks the Abby Aldrich Rockefeller Sculpture Garden. Its American menu features Maine lobster, beef crusted in aged Comté cheese, and cauliflower roasted in crab butter.

📍D3 🏛First Floor 🚫Sun

⑤⑤⑤

② 🏛

ST. PATRICK'S CATHEDRAL

📍 E3 🏛 Fifth Ave and 50th St 🚇 51 St (6), Lexington Av/ 53 St (E, M) 🚌 M1-5, M50, Q32 🕐 6:30am-8:45pm daily
🌐 saintpatrickscathedral.org

Splendid and Gothic, this is among America's largest Catholic cathedrals. The magnificent house of worship, built during the Civil War, is best appreciated inside, where beautiful details await.

The Roman Catholic Church originally intended this site for use as a cemetery but, in 1850, Archbishop John Hughes decided to build a cathedral instead. Many thought that it was foolish to build so far beyond the (then) city limits, but Hughes went ahead anyway. The result was New York's finest Gothic Revival building, and one of the largest Catholic cathedrals in the US. The cathedral, which seats 2,500 people, was completed in 1878, though the spires were added between 1885 and 1888. It cost a whopping $2 million to build.

The Lady Chapel honors the Blessed Virgin.

The exterior wall is built of white marble. The spires rise 330 ft (101 m) above the sidewalk.

① The facade of St. Patrick's Cathedral.

② The great baldachin, made entirely of bronze, rises over the high altar and is adorned with statues of the saints and prophets.

③ The bronze doors weigh 20,000 lb (9,000 kg) and depict religious figures.

SAINT ELIZABETH ANN SETON

Elizabeth Ann Seton (1774-1821) was the first American to be canonized by the Catholic Church. Born in New York, she lived in Lower Manhattan from 1801 to 1803 and founded the American Sisters of Charity. St. Patrick's houses a statue and screen depicting her life.

A statue of Pietà, created by sculptor William O. Partridge in 1906, can be found by the Lady Chapel.

The baldachin

Catholic house of worship, ↓ St. Patrick's Cathedral

Stations of the Cross reliefs won first prize at the Chicago World's Fair in 1893.

Measuring 26 ft (8 m) in diameter, the rose window shines above the great organ.

The Great Bronze Doors

EXPERIENCE MORE

 3 🛍

Fifth Avenue

📍 E3 🚇 5 Av-53 St (E, M),
5 Av-59 St (N, R, W)

In 1883, when William Henry Vanderbilt built his mansion at Fifth Avenue and 51st Street, he started a trend that led to palatial residences stretching as far as Central Park. One of the few that remains is Cartier at No. 651, once home to millionaire Morton F. Plant, commodore of the New York Yacht Club. As retailers swept north up the avenue – a trend that began in 1906 – high society began to move uptown. In 1917, Plant traded his home to Pierre Cartier for a perfectly matched string of pearls.

Fifth Avenue has long been synonymous with luxury goods. From Cartier to Henry Bendel and Tiffany to Bergdorf Goodman, there are many brands symbolizing wealth and social standing, just as Astor and Vanderbilt once did.

4

Waldorf Astoria

📍 E3 🏠 301 Park Av
🚇 Lexington Av, 53 St
🕐 For renovation
🌐 waldorfnewyork.com

Still deservedly one of New York's most prestigious hotels, this Art Deco classic, which covers an entire city block, is also a reminder of a more glamorous era in the city's history. Designed by Schultze & Weaver in 1931, the 625-ft (190-m) twin towers, where General MacArthur, Cole Porter, Frank Sinatra, and Marilyn Monroe once lived, have hosted numerous celebrities, including every US president since 1931. A huge renovation project, and partial conversion to condos, is underway and the hotel is likely to be closed until at least 2020.

---

5 🖥 🛍

Tiffany & Co

📍 E2 🏠 727 Fifth Av
🚇 5 Av-53 St (E, M), 5 Av-59 St (N, R, W) 🕐 10am-7pm Mon-Sat, noon-6pm Sun
🌐 tiffany.com

Immortalized by Truman Capote in his famous 1958 novel *Breakfast at Tiffany's*, this prestigious jewelry store, founded in 1837, is a must-see for fans of the book and film buffs alike. The famous Tiffany Diamond is usually on display; the 128.54-carat yellow diamond, discovered

---

NEW YORK'S CLASSIC DEPARTMENT STORES

Bloomingdale's, founded in 1872, remains synonymous with the good life, though it had a bargain-basement image until the 1960s. Bergdorf Goodman, luxurious, elegant and understated since 1928, sells contemporary European designer fashions at high prices and is the king of Christmas window decorations. Saks Fifth Avenue has been known for style and elegance since 1924, while Lord & Taylor is the place for classic, conservative fashions.

The Waldorf Astoria, popular with celebrities and dignitaries since the 1930s

and sports documentaries, from radio and television's earliest days to the present. Pop fans can watch the Beatles on the Ed Sullivan Show in 1964 or a young Elvis Presley making his television debut. Comedy fans can enjoy shows such as those made by 1960s television star Lucille Ball, and sports enthusiasts can relive classic Olympic Games moments. World War II footage might be chosen by students of history. Six choices at any one time can be selected from a computer catalog that covers a library of more than 50,000 items. The selections are then played in small private areas. Larger screening rooms are also available, as well as a theater seating 200 for the center's program of retrospectives of artists and directors, and for guest events. There are also photography exhibits and memorabilia.

The museum was the brainchild of William S. Paley, a former head of the CBS TV network. It opened in 1975 as the Museum of Broadcasting on East 53rd Street and was so popular that, in 1991, it moved to this hi-tech $50 million home.

Did You Know?

The 21 Club is where Humphrey Bogart took Lauren Bacall on their first date.

in South Africa in 1877, was acquired by founder Charles Tiffany a year later. With weathered wood and green marble interiors, the store is still best described by Capote's fictional Holly Golightly: "It calms me down right away . . . nothing very bad could happen to you there." Breakfast at Tiffany's is now a reality; head for the Blue Box Café on the 4th floor (reservations recommended).

6

Paley Center for Media

📍 D3 🏛 25 West 52nd St
🚇 5 Av-53 St (E, M) 🕐 Noon-6pm Wed-Sun (to 8pm Thu)
🌐 paleycenter.org

In this one-of-a-kind repository museum, visitors can watch and listen to a collection of entertainment

7

Central Synagogue

📍 E2 🏛 652 Lexington Av
🚇 Lexington Av-53 St (E, M)
🕐 Noon-2pm Tue & Wed
🌐 centralsynagogue.org

This is New York's oldest building in continuous use as a synagogue. It was designed in 1870 by Silesian-born Henry Fernbach, America's first prominent Jewish architect. He also designed some of SoHo's

←

EAT

21 Club
An institution since 1929, surviving Prohibition, when staff pulled hidden levers to sweep bottles from shelves and down a chute. Head here for history, and both classic and contemporary American cuisine.

📍 D3 🏛 21 West 52nd St
🕐 Sun 🌐 21club.com

💲💲💲

Palm Court
Soaring palms under an elegant stained-glass dome mark this iconic spot for afternoon tea.

📍 D2 🏛 Fifth Ave at Central Park South (The Plaza)
🌐 theplazany.com

💲💲💲

The Pool
Replacing the legendary Four Seasons in 2017, this sophisticated spot serves quality seafood. Tables are arranged around a small marble pool festooned with foliage depending on the season.

📍 E3 🏛 99 East 52nd St
🕐 Sun 🌐 thepool newyork.com

💲💲💲

finest cast-iron buildings. Restored after a 1999 fire, the synagogue is considered the city's best example of Moorish-Islamic Revival architecture. The congregation was founded in 1846 as Ahawath Chesed (Love of Mercy) by 18 immigrants, most of them from Bohemia, on Ludlow Street on the Lower East Side.

8

General Electric Building

📍 E3 🏠 570 Lexington Av Ⓢ 51 St (6) 🕐 Closed to the public

In 1931 architects Cross & Cross were challenged to design a skyscraper in keeping with neighboring St. Bartholomew's Church. It was not an easy task, but the result won acclaim. The colors were chosen to blend and contrast, and the tower complemented the church's polychrome dome. Viewing the pair from the corner of Park Avenue and 50th Street reveals how well it works. The General Electric is no mere backdrop to the church, but a work of art in its own right and a favorite part of the city skyline. It is an Art Deco gem, from its chrome and marble lobby to its spiky "radio waves" crown.

One block north, on Lexington Avenue, is a place much cherished by movie fans. Here is the spot where Marilyn Monroe memorably stood in a white frock, which billowed in the breeze from the Lexington Avenue subway grating in the movie *The Seven-Year Itch*.

↑ The Byzantine church of St. Bart's is flanked by Midtown skyscrapers

9

St. Bartholomew's Church

📍 E3 🏠 325 Park Av Ⓢ 51 St (6) 🕐 9am–6pm daily (to 7:30pm Thu, 8:30pm Sun) 🌐 stbarts.org

Known fondly to New Yorkers as "St. Bart's," this Byzantine structure, with its ornate detail, pinkish brick, open terrace, and a polychromed gold dome, brought color and variety to Park Avenue in 1919.

Architect Bertram Goodhue incorporated the Romanesque entrance portico created by Stanford White for the original 1903 St. Bartholomew's on Madison Avenue, and marble columns from that church were used in the chapel.

St. Bartholomew's program of concerts is well known, as is its theater group, which mounts three productions in the church each year.

10

Seagram Building

📍 E3 🏠 375 Park Av Ⓢ 5 Av-53 St (E, M) 🕐 9am–5pm Mon–Fri

Samuel Bronfman, the late head of Seagram distillers,

← The General Electric Building, crowned with Gothic spires and fanciful carvings

was prepared to put up an ordinary commercial building until his architect daughter, Phyllis Lambert, intervened and persuaded him to go to the best – Mies van der Rohe. The result, which is widely considered the finest of the many Modernist buildings of the 1950s, consists of two rectangles of bronze and glass that let the light pour in.

11

Citigroup Center

📍 E3 🏠 601 Lexington Av Ⓢ 5 Av-53 St (E, M) 🕐 7am–11pm daily. St. Peter's Lutheran Church: 619 Lexington Ave 🕐 8:30am–8pm daily 🌐 saintpeters.org

An aluminum-clad tower built on ten-story stilts and with a 45-degree angled roof, the Citigroup Center caused a sensation when it was completed in 1978. The slanting top never functioned as a solar panel as intended,

---

DRINK

King Cole Bar
The reputed birthplace of the Bloody Mary features a grand Maxfield Parrish mural. Patrons have included Marilyn Monroe and Joe DiMaggio.

📍 E2 🏠 St Regis Hotel, 2 East 55th St 🌐 kingcolebar.com

P.J. Clarke's
Open since 1884, this casual pub drips with history. This was where, in 1958, Buddy Holly proposed to his wife – 5 hours after they met.

📍 F2 🏠 915 Third Av 🌐 pjclarkes.com

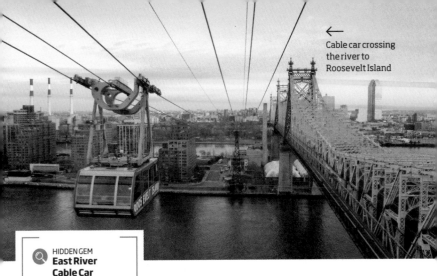

← Cable car crossing the river to Roosevelt Island

 HIDDEN GEM
East River Cable Car

Even if Roosevelt Island isn't on your bucket list, the breathtaking views on the three-minute aerial tramway ride, soaring rapidly to 250 ft (76 m) above the East River, make the visit worthwhile.

but it is an unmistakable landmark on the skyline.

The unusual base design accommodates St. Peter's Lutheran Church, which sits underneath the northwest corner of the building. Step inside to see the striking interior and the Erol Beker Chapel by sculptor Louise Nevelson. The church is well-known for its jazz vespers, theater presentations, and organ concerts (generally on Wednesdays at noon).

12

Lever House

📍 E3 🏠 390 Park Av
Ⓢ 5 Av-53 St (E, M)
🚫 Closed to the public

Imagine a Park Avenue lined with sturdy, residential buildings – and then imagine the sensation when they were suddenly reflected here in the first of the city's glass-walled skyscrapers, one of the most

influential buildings of the modern era. The Skidmore, Owings & Merrill design is simply two rectangles of stainless steel and glass, one horizontal, the other standing tall above it, to allow light in from every side. The crisp, bright design was intended to symbolize the Lever Brothers' soap products; in 1930, Lever merged to form Unilever.

Revolutionary in 1952, Lever House is now dwarfed by its many imitators, but its importance as an architectural pacesetter is undiminished. The Casa Lever restaurant is a VIP scene.

13

Roosevelt Island

📍 G2 Ⓢ 59 St Tram;
Roosevelt Island (F)
🌐 rioc.com

An often overlooked corner of New York, Roosevelt Island sits amid the East River, and is home to around 13,000 people. Known as Minnahannock by indigenous peoples, it was renamed Blackwell's Island when ownership passed to the English farmer Robert Blackwell in 1686.

Although it became known as Welfare Island in 1921, much of the island was deserted and forgotten by the 1950s.

It was redeveloped in the 1970s, and eventually became a popular residential neighborhood. Today, it has a breezy promenade with fabulous views of Midtown. A Swiss cable car departing from Second Avenue at 60th Street has offered a quick, thrilling ride across the river since 1976.

14

Franklin D. Roosevelt Four Freedoms Park

📍 G3 🏠 1 FDR Four Freedoms Park, Roosevelt Island Ⓢ Roosevelt Island (F) 🕐 Apr-Sep: 9am-7pm Mon, Wed-Sun; Oct-Mar: 9am-5pm Mon, Wed-Sun 🌐 fdrfourfreedomspark.org

Lying at the southern end of Roosevelt Island, the Franklin D. Roosevelt Four Freedoms Park was designed by architect Louis Kahn in the 1970s but was only completed in 2012. With 120 linden trees lining the park, the triangular expanse ends with a bronze portrait of the 32nd president. Nearby, there is an engraving of his "four freedoms" on slabs of granite. In a speech delivered in 1941, these four tenets were described as the freedom of speech, freedom of worship, freedom from want, and freedom from fear.

A SHORT WALK
UPPER MIDTOWN

Distance 1 mile (1.5 km) **Nearest subway** 5 Av, 51 St **Time** 10 minutes

The luxury stores synonymous with Fifth Avenue first blossomed as society moved on uptown. In 1917, Cartier acquired the mansion of banker Morton F. Plant, supposedly in exchange for a string of pearls, setting the style for other retailers to follow. But this stretch of Midtown is not simply for shoppers looking to splash their cash. There are some distinctive museums and a diverse assembly of architectural styles to enjoy, too.

Carriage rides have long been replaced with rickshaws and iconic yellow taxis along Fifth Avenue, offering tourists more leisurely ways to view some of the main sights (p208).

The University Club was built in 1899 as an elite club for gentlemen.

The Museum of Modern Art (MoMA) is one of the world's finest collections of modern art (p202).

Much of the interior carving of St. Thomas Church was designed by sculptor Lee Lawrie.

Exhibitions, seasons of special screenings, live events, and a vast library of historic broadcasts are offered at the Paley Center for Media (p209).

5 Av subway (lines E, V)

Saks Fifth Avenue has offered goods in impeccable taste to generations of New Yorkers.

St. Patrick's Cathedral is one of the largest Catholic cathedrals in the United States and a magnificent Gothic Revival building (p206).

Olympic Tower combines offices, apartments and a skylit atrium within its sleek walls.

Villard Houses comprise five handsome brownstone houses that form part of the Lotte New York Palace Hotel.

↑ St. Patrick's Cathedral, incongruous in busy Upper Midtown

| 0 meters | | 100 |
| 0 yards | | 100 |

N ↑

Trump Tower is Donald Trump's signature tower and contains luxury residences.

START

A peaceful atrium can be found at the base of the polished black granite IBM Building.

Sony Building has a very distinctive "Chippendale" top.

Renowned for its discreet luxury, the iconic Tiffany & Co store contains many precious jewels (p208).

Paley Park is a tiny green oasis, known as a "vest-pocket" park.

53RD ST

MADISON AVENUE

Lever House is one of the most prominent "glass-box" buildings in New York (p211).

Park Avenue Plaza is a bulky glass prism containing an airy atrium.

Racquet and Tennis Club, a Renaissance palazzo-style building, provides squash and tennis courts for its members.

E 51ST ST

PARK AVENUE

The spiky pinnacle of the General Electric Building, built in 1931, is meant to symbolize electrical waves (p210).

A Byzantine dome sets St. Bartholomew's Church apart from other Midtown churches (p210).

S 51 St subway (line 6)

● **FINISH**

Old-world elegance has attracted many famous guests to the Waldorf Astoria, from movie stars to heads of state (p208).

Locator Map
For more detail see p200

UPPER MIDTOWN

UPPER EAST SIDE

An enclave of New York's upper class since the 1890s, the area was once home to dynasties such as the Astors, Rockefellers, and Whitneys. Many of their Beaux Arts mansions are now museums and embassies, such as the Met and the buildings on Museum Mile, but the well-to-do still occupy apartment buildings on Fifth and Park avenues. Chic stores and galleries line Madison Avenue. Farther east lies what is left of German and Hungarian Yorkville in the East 80s, and little Bohemia, with its Czech population, below 78th Street. Although many of these ethnic groups no longer occupy the area, their churches, restaurants, and stores still remain.

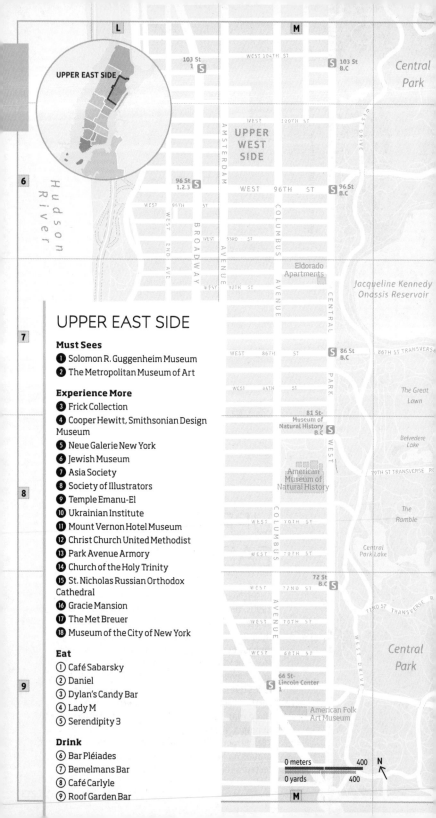

UPPER EAST SIDE

Must Sees

1. Solomon R. Guggenheim Museum
2. The Metropolitan Museum of Art

Experience More

3. Frick Collection
4. Cooper Hewitt, Smithsonian Design Museum
5. Neue Galerie New York
6. Jewish Museum
7. Asia Society
8. Society of Illustrators
9. Temple Emanu-El
10. Ukrainian Institute
11. Mount Vernon Hotel Museum
12. Christ Church United Methodist
13. Park Avenue Armory
14. Church of the Holy Trinity
15. St. Nicholas Russian Orthodox Cathedral
16. Gracie Mansion
17. The Met Breuer
18. Museum of the City of New York

Eat

1. Café Sabarsky
2. Daniel
3. Dylan's Candy Bar
4. Lady M
5. Serendipity 3

Drink

6. Bar Pléiades
7. Bemelmans Bar
8. Café Carlyle
9. Roof Garden Bar

UPPER EAST SIDE

UPPER WEST SIDE

Central Park

Hudson River

Eldorado Apartments

Jacqueline Kennedy Onassis Reservoir

86 St B.C

867H ST TRANSVERS

The Great Lawn

81 St-Museum of Natural History B.C

American Museum of Natural History

Belvedere Lake

79TH ST TRANSVERSE RD

The Ramble

Central Park Lake

72 St B.C

72ND ST TRANSVERSE R

Central Park

66 St-Lincoln Center

American Folk Art Museum

103 St 1

103 St B.C

96 St 1.2.3

96 St B.C

0 meters 400
0 yards 400

N

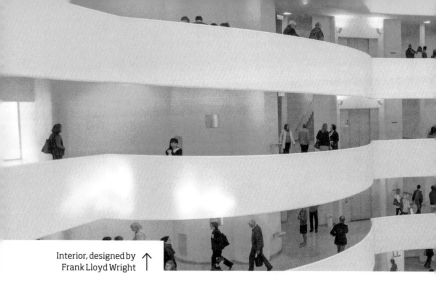

↑ Interior, designed by Frank Lloyd Wright

①

SOLOMON R. GUGGENHEIM MUSEUM

📍 N7 🏛 1071 Fifth Ave at 89th St Ⓢ 86 St (Q, 4, 5, 6) 🚌 M1-4 🕐 10am–5:45pm Fri–Wed (till 7:45pm Sat) 🌐 guggenheim.org

Home to one of the world's finest collections of modern and contemporary art, the building itself, designed by Frank Lloyd Wright, is perhaps the Guggenheim's greatest masterpiece. Inside, the spiral ramp curves down and inward from the dome, passing works by major 19th-, 20th-, and 21st-century artists along the way.

This seminal museum was named after its founder, mining magnate and abstract art collector Solomon R. Guggenheim. In 1937, he founded the Guggenheim Foundation, which displayed his art collection in rented spaces, before Frank Lloyd Wright was commissioned to design a permanent space in 1942. During his time, Wright was considered the great innovator of American architecture, though the Guggenheim commission was his only New York building. It was completed in 1959 after both his and Guggenheim's deaths. The museum has continued to grow since it opened, today housing works by the likes of Kandinsky, Calder, Picasso, Pollock, Degas, Cézanne, Van Gogh, and Manet.

↑ The museum's famous, shell-like facade is a veritable New York landmark

←

Woman Ironing (1904), from Picasso's Blue Period, conveys real hard work and fatigue

↑ *Black Lines* (1913) is one of Vasily
Kandinsky's "non-objective" works

MUSEUM GUIDE

The Great Rotunda features special exhibitions. The Small Rotunda shows some of the museum's Impressionist and Post-Impressionist holdings. The Tower galleries (also known as The Annex) hold exhibitions of work from the permanent collection, as well as contemporary pieces. The permanent collection is shown on a rotating basis, and only parts of it are on display at any one time.

↓ The Solomon R.
Guggenheim Museum

Tower

Great Rotunda

Small
Rotunda

Sackler Center for
Arts Education

Main entrance

The grand exterior of the Met ↑

2 🗡 🏍 🖥 🍴 🛍

THE METROPOLITAN MUSEUM OF ART

📍N8 🏠1000 Fifth Ave Ⓢ86 St (Q, 4, 5, 6) 🚌M1-4 🕐10am-5:30pm Sun-Thu, 10am-9pm Fri & Sat ⏲Thanksgiving 🌐metmuseum.org

The jewel in New York City's crown, and one of the most prestigious collections in the world, the Met houses more than two million treasures.

Generally referred to as "the Met," this museum's comprehensive collection was founded in 1870 by a group of artists and philanthropists who dreamed of an American art institution to rival those of Europe. The museum opened here in 1880 and today a staggering variety of objects and artifacts, dating from prehistoric times to the present, can be found across its sprawling galleries. You could spend days here, particularly as the museum also houses a number of excellent dining options. A guided tour is a great way to take in the museum and its stellar attractions. Tours are included with museum admission; visit the website for more information.

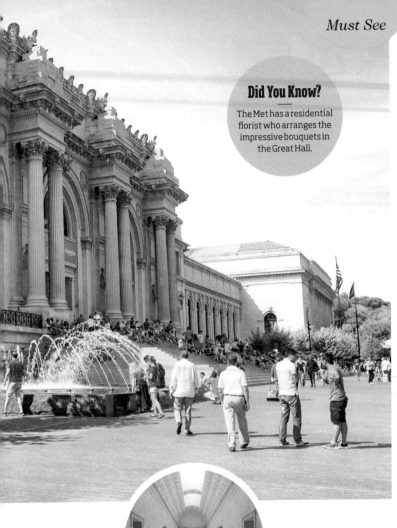

Did You Know?

The Met has a residential florist who arranges the impressive bouquets in the Great Hall.

Gallery Rooms

First Floor

▽ From the stunning Great Hall, visitors can explore Egyptian Art, Greek and Roman Art, Medieval Art, Modern and Contemporary Art, and the American Wing.

Third, Fourth, and Fifth Floors

▽ Asian Art and the American Wing both continue onto the third floor. The fourth floor is home to the Dining Room, and the fifth floor has the Cantor Roof Garden.

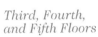

Second Floor

△ Modern and Contemporary Art and the American Wing both continue onto the second floor. Here visitors can also find galleries dedicated to European Paintings (1250-1800), Musical Instruments, Asian Art, and so much more.

17,000
—
drawings by the likes of Michelangelo and da Vinci are in the Met's collection.

↑ The Temple of Dendur is popular with visitors

MUSEUM'S LOWER LEVELS

The Great Hall is a suitably grand entrance to the Met, and the nerve center from which the wings and galleries are connected.

One of the museum's best-loved areas, just off the Great Hall, is the Egyptian Art wing, which displays every one of its holdings – from the prehistoric period to the 8th century AD. Objects range from the fragmented jasper lips of a 15th-century BC queen to the massive Temple of Dendur.

A Roman sarcophagus from Tarsus, donated in 1870, was the first work of art in the Met's collections. It can still be seen in the museum's Greek and Roman galleries, along with wall panels from a villa that was buried under the lava of Vesuvius in AD 79, Roman portrait busts, and Greek vases.

The Met's Medieval Art collection includes works dating from the 4th to the 16th centuries, roughly from the fall of Rome to the beginning of the Renaissance.

The collection is split between here and its uptown branch, the Cloisters (p290). In the Met, you'll find a chalice once thought to be the Holy Grail.

What had been one of the finest private art collections in the world, that of investment banker Robert Lehman, was donated to the museum in 1969. The Lehman Wing is a dramatic glass pyramid, crossing the ground and first floors, and houses an extraordinarily varied collection rich in Old Masters, drawings, and Post-Impressionists.

→ Marble statue of an old market woman

MUSEUM'S UPPER LEVELS

The Met's colossal collection continues upward. Spanning the first, second and third floors is the American Wing, which holds not only one of the world's finest collections of American painting and sculpture but also of decorative arts from Colonial times to the beginning of the 20th century. Period rooms, with their original decorative woodwork and furnishings, include the saloon hall in which George Washington celebrated his last birthday.

Also crossing the first and second floors are the Modern and Contemporary Art galleries. Since its foundation, the museum has been acquiring contemporary art,

but it was not until 1987 that a permanent home for 20th-century art was built – the Lila Acheson Wallace Wing. Other museums have larger collections of modern art, but this display space is considered among the finest. European and American works from 1900 onward are featured, including works by Picasso and Kandinsky. Each year the Cantor Roof Garden at the top of the wing features a new installation of contemporary sculpture, especially dramatic against the backdrop of the city and Central Park.

The second floor also houses Asian Art, including Chinese, Japanese, Korean, Indian, and Southeast Asian masterpieces, dating from the second millennium BC to the 20th century. The museum also has one of the finest collections of Song and Yuan dynasty paintings in the world, Chinese Buddhist monumental sculptures, Chinese ceramics and jade, and an important display of the arts of ancient China.

↑ *The Last Communion of Saint Jerome* (c. 1490), by Botticelli

> **MUSEUM GUIDE**
>
> We have collated the ground and first floors under "Lower Levels," and the second to fifth floors under "Upper Levels." Most artworks are housed on the first and second floors, with some additional collections featuring on the ground, third, and fifth levels. The fourth level doesn't feature any artworks.

TOP 5 UNMISSABLE ARTWORKS

Madonna and Child
Duccio (c. 1290–1300). Delicately crafted, early Renaissance piece.

Harvesters
Pieter Bruegel the Elder (1565). This captures an agricultural scene.

Washington Crossing the Delaware
Emanuel Leutze (1851). Shows Washington escaping in 1776.

Bridge over a Pond of Water Lilies
Claude Monet (1899). The Met's most popular Impressionist painting.

White Flag
Jasper Johns (1955). This was inspired by a dream.

↑ *Washington Crossing the Delaware* (1851) by Emanuel Leutze

EXPERIENCE MORE

3

Frick Collection

📍N9 🏛1 East 70th St
🚇68 St (6) 🕐10am–6pm
Tue–Sat, 11am–5pm Sun
🌐frick.org

The remarkable art collection of steel magnate Henry Clay Frick (1849–1919) is exhibited amid the furnishings of the opulent mansion built for him in 1914. The residential setting provides a rare glimpse of how the extremely wealthy lived in New York's gilded age. Henry Frick intended the collection to be a memorial to himself, and on his death he bequeathed the entire house to the nation.

The collection includes important Old Master paintings, major works of sculpture, French furniture, rare Limoges enamels, and beautiful Oriental rugs. Highlights include Vermeer's *Officer and Laughing Girl* (c. 1657) and the 18th-century Boucher Room, smothered in florid Rococo panels by François Boucher. The Living Hall contains a real masterpiece, Giovanni Bellini's *St. Francis in the Desert*. Stunningly well preserved, it depicts Francis' vision of Christ. Here also are two famous works by Hans Holbein the Younger, portraits of old adversaries Thomas Cromwell and Sir Thomas More. The

two are separated by El Greco's restrained *St Jerome*. In the West Gallery, the identity of the subject in *The Polish Rider*, by Rembrandt (around 1655), is unknown. The somber, rocky landscape creates an eerie atmosphere of unknown danger.

4

Cooper Hewitt, Smithsonian Design Museum

📍N7 🏛2 East 91st St
🚇86 St (Q, 4, 5, 6), 96 St (Q, 6) 🚌M1–4 🕐10am–6pm
(to 9pm Sat) 🌐cooper
hewitt.org

Housed in the former mansion of industrialist Andrew Carnegie, this museum underwent a massive redevelopment project, completed in 2014. The modern galleries are now scattered around the original staircase, with the mansion's wooden interiors and parquet floors still intact. On the second floor is the Carnegie Library, which features an array of intricate teak carvings.

The museum offers a varied and engaging range of displays, from digitally printed fruit to steel necklaces, rubber chairs, and porcelain chess sets. It also has the largest ensemble of paintings by the American artists Frederic Edwin Church and Winslow Homer. Aside from the permanent collection, the museum hosts a number of temporary exhibitions each year.

Modern piece by
Mathias Bengtsson at
Cooper Hewitt, Smith-
sonian Design Museum

Did You Know?

Portrait of Adele Bloch-Bauer I was bought by the Neue in 2006 for a record breaking $135 million.

5

Neue Galerie New York

📍N7 🏛1048 Fifth Av at
East 86th St 🚇86 St (Q, 4, 5, 6) 🚌M1–4 🕐11am–6pm
Thu–Mon 🌐neue galerie.
org

Founded by art dealer Serge Sabarsky and philanthropist Ronald Lauder, the Neue Galerie's objective is to collect, research, and exhibit early 20th-century fine and decorative arts of Germany and Austria.

The Louis XIII-style Beaux Arts structure was completed in 1914 by Carrère & Hastings, who also designed the New York Public Library *(p178)*. Once home to Mrs Cornelius Vanderbilt III, the mansion was purchased by Lauder and Sabarsky in 1994. The first floor has a bookstore and café; the second is devoted to works by Klimt and Schiele, and Wiener Werkstätte objects. The upper floors feature works from Der Blaue Reiter (Klee, Kandinsky), the Bauhaus (Feininger, Schlemmer), and Die Brücke (Mies van der Rohe, Breuer). Klimt's *Portrait of Adele Bloch-Bauer I* (1907) is the star of the museum. From his "Golden Period," the portrait depicts Adele Bloch-Bauer, a member of one of Vienna's richest Jewish families. Stolen by the Nazis in 1938, the painting's story was told in the 2015 movie *Woman In Gold*, starring Helen Mirren.

DRINK

Bar Pléiades

This stylish Art-Deco hotel bar and jazz venue is a homage to Chanel.

⑨N8 ⓐThe Surrey, 20 East 76th St
ⓦbar pleiades.com

Bemelmans Bar

Best known for Ludwig Bemelmans' exuberant murals and gold ceiling.

⑨P8 ⓐCarlyle Hotel, 35 East 76th St
ⓦrosewoodhotels.com

Café Carlyle

Clarinet-playing Woody Allen and jazz band on most Monday nights, with others performing throughout the week.

⑨P8 ⓐCarlyle Hotel, 35 East 76th St
ⓒSun, Jul-Dec
ⓦrosewoodhotels.com

Roof Garden Bar

Romantic spring and summertime spot, with the best views of Central Park and the city.

⑨N7 ⓐThe Met, 1000 Fifth Av
ⓒMid-Oct-Mid-Apr
ⓦmetmuseum.org

↑ The Asia Society bookstore and its wide range of books

6
Jewish Museum

⑨N6 ⓐ1109 Fifth Ave
ⓢ86 St (Q, 4, 5, 6), 96 St (6, Q) ⓒ11am-5:45pm Thu-Tue (to 8pm Thu; Mar-Nov: to 4pm Fri) ⓒJewish and Federal hols ⓦthejewish museum.org

The exquisite and châteaulike residence of Felix M. Warburg, financier and leader of the Jewish community, was designed by C. P. H. Gilbert in 1908. It now houses one of the world's largest collections of Jewish fine and ceremonial art, and historical Judaica. The stonework in an extension is by the stonemasons who built the Cathedral of St. John the Divine (p254) in Harlem.

The objects that form the collection have been brought here from all over the world, sometimes at great risk of persecution to the donors. Covering some 4,000 years of Jewish history, nearly 30,000 works of art and artifacts include Torah crowns, candelabras, kiddush cups, plates, scrolls, and silver ceremonial objects.

There is a Torah ark from the Benguiat Collection, the exquisite faience entrance wall of a 16th-century Persian synagogue, along with the powerful *Holocaust* by sculptor George Segal. Regularly changing exhibitions reflect Jewish life and experience around the world and the museum hosts talks and film screenings.

Admission to the museum is free on Saturday and "pay what you wish" on Thursday from 5–8pm.

7
Asia Society

⑨P9 ⓐ725 Park Ave
ⓢ68th St (6) ⓒ11am-6pm Tue-Sun (Sep-Jun: to 9pm Fri) ⓦasiasociety.org

Founded by John D. Rockefeller III in 1956 to increase understanding of Asian culture, the society is a forum for 30 countries in the Asia-Pacific region, from Japan to Iran and from Central Asia to Australia.

The 1981 eight-story building was designed by Edward Larrabee Barnes and constructed with red granite. After a renovation in 2001, the museum has increased gallery space. One gallery is devoted to Rockefeller's own collection of Asian sculptures, which he and his wife amassed on their frequent trips to Asia. It includes Chinese ceramics from the Song and Ming periods, and a copper Bodhisattva statue, inlaid with precious stones, from Nepal.

Changing exhibits show a wide variety of Asian arts, and the society has a full program of films, dance, concerts, and lectures. There is also a well-stocked bookstore.

↑ Exhibits at the Society of Illustrators include the signatures of some of its notable members *(inset)*

8 Ⓜ 🏛

Society of Illustrators

📍P9 📍128 East 63rd St
Ⓢ Lexington Av-63 St (F, Q)
🕙10am-8pm Tue & Thu,
10am-5pm Wed & Fri,
11am-5pm Sat Ⓦ society
illustrators.org

Established in 1901, this society was formed to promote the illustrator's art. Its notable members have included Charles Dana Gibson, N. C. Wyeth and Howard Pyle. At first concerned with education and public service, it still holds monthly lectures. In 1981, the Museum of American Illustration opened in two galleries. Changing thematic exhibitions show the history of book and magazine illustration, with an annual exhibition of the year's finest American illustrations.

9 Ⓜ 🏛

Temple Emanu-El

📍N9 📍1 East 65th St Ⓢ68
St (6), Lexington Av-63 St
(F, Q) 🕙10am-4:30pm Sun-
Thu Ⓦ emanuelnyc.org

This impressive limestone edifice of 1929 is one of the largest synagogues in the world, with seating for 2,500 in the main sanctuary alone. It is home to the city's longest established (and richest) Reform congregation.

Among many fine details are the Ark's bronze doors, which represent an open Torah scroll, and stained glass depicting biblical scenes and the tribal signs of the houses of Israel. These signs also appear on a great recessed arch framing the magnificent wheel window that dominates the Fifth Avenue facade.

The synagogue is on the site of the palatial home of famed society hostess Mrs William Astor, who moved to the Upper East Side after a feud with her nephew, who previously lived next door to her. Her wine cellar and three marble fireplaces remain at the synagogue.

10 🖼

Ukrainian Institute

📍N8 📍2 East 79th St
Ⓢ86 St (Q, 4, 5, 6) 🚌M1-4
🕙Noon-6pm Tue-Sat
Ⓦ ukrainianinstitute.org

Inevitably overshadowed by the Met up the road, this cultural center, with its intriguing art collection, is well worth a visit. Temporary exhibits from modern Ukrainian artists are on the second floor, while the upper levels exhibit abstract work from Alexander Archipenko, paintings from David Burliuk, the "father of Russian Futurism," and huge Soviet Socialist Realist canvases.

Built for the banker Isaac Fletcher in 1899, it is more famous for being the home, in the 1920s, of industrialist and scandal-prone oilman Harry Sinclair.

11

Mount Vernon Hotel Museum

📍 Q9 🏠 421 East 61st St
🚇 Lexington Av-59 St (N, R, W), 59 St (4, 5, 6) 🕐 11am-4pm Tue-Sun 🌐 mvhm.org

Built in 1799, the Mount Vernon Hotel Museum was once a retreat into the country for New Yorkers who needed an escape from the crowded city, then covering only the south end of the island. The stone building sits on land once owned by Abigail Adams Smith, daughter of President John Adams.

Acquired by the Colonial Dames of America, a women's patriotic society, in 1924 it was turned into a charming re-creation of a Federal home. Costumed guides show visitors through eight rooms, which exhibit Chinese porcelain, Sheraton chests, and a Duncan Phyfe sofa. One bedroom even contains a baby's cradle and children's toys. An attractive, 18th-century-style garden has also been planted around the house.

Park Avenue Armory, currently undergoing a $210-million renovation ↓

DYNASTIES OF NEW YORK

The Upper East Side has long been associated with New York's most wealthy and influential families. John Jacob Astor amassed a fortune, and in 1853 his grandson, William Backhouse Astor Jr., married Caroline Schermerhorn, of New York's Dutch aristocracy. In 1937 John D. Rockefeller Jr. moved to 740 Park Avenue (where Jacqueline Kennedy Onassis grew up) and his son Nelson lived at 810 Fifth Avenue. Eleanor Roosevelt moved to 49 East 65th Street in 1908, then to 55 East 74th in 1959. The Vanderbilt family had huge mansions on Fifth Avenue in the 19th century, and socialite Grace Vanderbilt later moved to what is now the Neue Galerie (p224).

 12

Christ Church United Methodist

📍 P9 🏠 524 Park Av 🚇 5 Av-59 St (N, R, W) 🕐 7am-6pm Mon-Fri, 8:30am-2pm Sun 🌐 christchurchnyc.org

With deceptively simple exteriors, this dazzling Romanesque structure was designed and built in 1931 by influential architect Ralph Adams Cram. Gold-leaf mosaics fill the stunning vaulted ceiling and apse, while parts of the choir screen date from 1660 and were once owned by Tsar Nicholas II of Russia. The altar is Spanish marble and the nave columns are veined, purple Levanto marble.

 13

Park Avenue Armory

📍 P9 🏠 643 Park Av 🚇 68th St (6) 🕐 For tours; days vary, check website for details 🌐 armoryonpark.org

From the War of 1812 through to two World Wars, the Seventh Regiment, an elite corps of "gentlemen soldiers" from prominent families, has played a vital role. Within the fortress-like exterior of their armory are extraordinary rooms filled with lavish Victorian furnishings, and objets d'art, along with a collection of regimental memorabilia.

The design, by Charles W. Clinton, a veteran of the regiment, had offices facing Park Avenue, with a vast drill hall stretching behind to Lexington Avenue. The reception rooms include the Veterans' Room and the Library by Louis Comfort Tiffany. The drill hall is now the site of the Winter Antiques Show and a favorite venue for charity balls. The Armory hosts a large number of cultural performances, from modern dance displays to concerts by the New York Philharmonic Orchestra.

Visitors are able to view the interiors of this landmark building as part of a tour. Check online for specific dates, and to make a reservation, which is compulsory.

The remarkable exterior of the Guggenheim

14 Church of the Holy Trinity

Q7 **316 East 88th St** **S** 86 St (Q, 4, 5, 6) **Opening times vary; check website for details** **w** holytrinity-nyc.org

Delightfully placed in a serene garden setting, this church was built in 1889 of glowing golden brick and terra-cotta and boasts one of New York's best bell towers, with a handsome wrought-iron clock. The arched doorway is richly carved with images of saints and prophets.

Serena Rhinelander was the benefactor, memorializing her father and grandfather, and the church is on part of their farmland. Farther down, at No. 350, the Rhinelander Children's Center is the head-quarters of the Children's Aid Society.

---

15 St. Nicholas Russian Orthodox Cathedral

N6 **15 East 97th St** **C** (212) 726-4229 **S** 96 St (Q, 6) **By appt**

A unique and unexpected find on a side street in this staid part of Manhattan, St. Nicholas Russian Orthodox

Cathedral (1902), in Muscovite Baroque style, has five onion domes crowned with crosses, and blue and yellow tiles on a red-brick and white-stone facade. Inside, the high central sanctuary has marble columns with blue and white trim above, and ornate wooden screens trimmed with gold enclose the altar.

Among the early worshipers here were White Russians, who had fled the Russian Revolution. They were mostly intellectuals and aristocrats who soon became a part of New York society. Later, there were further waves of refugees, dissidents, and defectors.

The cathedral now serves a scattered community, and the congregation is small. Mass is celebrated in Russian with great pomp and dignity.

16
Gracie Mansion

Q7 **East End Av at 88th St** **S** 86 St (Q, 4, 5, 6) **M31, M79, M86** **10am, 11am & 5pm Mon** **w** nyc.gov/gracie

This gracious, balconied wooden 1799 country home is the official mayor's residence. Built by wealthy merchant Archibald Gracie, it is one of the city's best Federal houses.

Acquired by the city in 1896, it was the first home of the Museum of the City of New York. When Fiorello La Guardia moved in after nine years in office, he said that even the modest Gracie Mansion was too fancy for him.

The mansion is open for pre-booked, guided tours only.

17
The Met Breuer

P8 **945 Madison Av** **S** 77 St (6) **10am-5:30pm Tue-Thu & Sun, 10am-9pm Fri & Sat** **w** metmuseum.org

An extension of The Metropolitan Museum of Art, The Met Breuer occupies the former premises of the Whitney Museum of American

 The dining room at Gracie Mansion featuring wallpaper made by Zuber in the 1830s

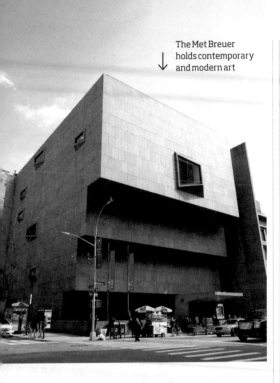

The Met Breuer holds contemporary and modern art

EAT

Café Sabarsky
Classic Viennese café with aromatic coffees and Austrian food.

⑨N7 **☖Neue Galerie, 1048 Fifth Av** **Ⓦkurtguten brunner.com**

$⑤⑤

Daniel
Opulent restaurant of chef Daniel Boulud.

⑨P9 **☖60 East 65th St** **☒Lunch, Sun** **Ⓦdanielnyc.com**

$$$

Dylan's Candy Bar
Iconic candy store, with a chocolate fountain.

⑨P9 **☖1011 Third Av** **Ⓦdylanscandy bar.com**

$$$

Lady M
Posh cake shop with a cult following.

⑨P8 **☖41 East 78th St** **Ⓦladym.com**

$$$

Serendipity 3
Café and ice-cream parlor, known for "frrozen" hot chocolate.

⑨P9 **☖225 East 60th St** **Ⓦserendipity3.com**

$$$

Created by architect Marcel Breuer, the building's Brutalist design was a controversial addition to the townhouses of the Upper East Side in 1966.

Art. Created by architect Marcel Breuer, the building's Brutalist design was a controversial addition to the townhouses of the Upper East Side in 1966. It provides exhibition space for 20th- and 21st-century art, along with educational programs and unique performances.

18

Museum of the City of New York

⑨N5 **☖1220 Fifth Av at 103rd St** **Ⓢ103 St (6)** **☉10am–6pm daily** **Ⓦmcny.org**

Founded in 1923, and at first housed in Gracie Mansion, this museum is dedicated to New York's development from its earliest beginnings to the present, and on to the future.

Housed in a handsome Georgian Colonial building since 1932, the museum has expanded its public space, with special exhibitions throughout the year on subjects such as fashion, architecture, theater, social and political history, and photography. In addition to all of this there is a fantastic and expansive collection of toys from different areas, including the famous Stettheimer Dollhouse, containing original works of art in miniature, painted by such luminaries as Marcel Duchamp and Albert Gleizes.

A core exhibition of the museum is the fascinating film *Timescapes: A Multimedia Portrait of New York*. Shown every 30 minutes, from 10:15am to 4:45pm, this uses various images from the museum's collection, along with historic maps charting the growth of New York City, from its earliest days as a tiny settlement to its current status as one of the largest cities in the world.

A SHORT WALK
MUSEUM MILE

Distance 1.25 mile (2 km) **Nearest subway**
96 St, 86 St-Lexington Av **Time** 25 minutes

Many of New York's museums are clustered on the
Upper East Side, in homes ranging from the former
Frick and Carnegie mansions to the modernistic
Guggenheim; it's worth exploring this neighborhood
for the palatial architecture of these world-famous
museums alone. If you're visiting the museums
themselves, you'll find the displays are as varied as
the architecture, running the gamut from Old Masters
to photographs, to decorative arts. Presiding over
the scene is the vast Metropolitan Museum of Art,
New York's answer to Paris's Louvre.

↑ Frank Lloyd Wright's
stunning Guggenheim
Museum

Did You Know?

Museum Mile has deals
on entry fees, with
"pay what you wish"
on specified days.

The most extensive collection
of Judaica in the world is
housed at the Jewish Museum.
It includes coins, archaeo-
logical objects, and
ceremonial and religious
artifacts (p225).

Ceramics, glass, furniture,
and textiles are well
represented at the Cooper
Hewitt, Smithsonian
Design Museum (p224).

The Church of the Heavenly
Rest was built in 1929 in the
Gothic style. The madonna in
the pulpit is by sculptor
Malvina Hoffman.

Architect Frank Lloyd Wright's
Guggenheim is in the form of a
spiral, and is floodlit at dusk.
To best appreciate one of the
world's premier collections of
modern and contemporary art,
take the elevator to the top and
walk down (p218).

Graham House is an
apartment building
with a splendid Beaux
Arts entrance. It was
built in 1892.

FIFTH AVENUE (MUSEUM MILE)

MADISON AVENUE

93RD S

92ND ST

91ST ST

90TH ST

89TH ST

FINISH

START

Locator Map
For more detail see p216

UPPER EAST SIDE

The facade of the Squadron A Armory is all that remains of the original building. It is now the west wall of the playground of Hunter College High School. The school was built to complement the style of the armory.

Public basketball court

The William G. Loew Mansion (1931), now part of the Spence School, is in the "American Adams" style.

The Synod of Bishops of the Russian Orthodox Church Outside of Russia is housed in a lovely 1918 mansion.

Night Presence IV (1972), a modern work in rusting steel, was created by Louise Nevelson. Some New Yorkers feel it is out of place among its staid, old-fashioned neighbors on Park Avenue.

PARK AVENUE

LEXINGTON AVENUE

At 120 and 122 East 92nd Street are two of the few wooden houses left in Manhattan. Built in 1859 and 1871, respectively, they have a charming Italianate air.

The Marx Brothers spent their childhood in a three-bedroom apartment in a modest rowhouse at 179 East 93rd Street.

← Manhattan's few remaining wooden houses, on East 92nd Street

CENTRAL PARK AND THE UPPER WEST SIDE

The city's "backyard" was officially opened in 1876 and it's difficult to imagine New York without it. Over the years Central Park has blossomed, with playgrounds, skating rinks, ball fields, and spaces for every other activity, not to mention hills, lakes, and meadows. In 1879, when the Ninth Avenue railroad made commuting to Midtown possible, the city streets were levelled and graded. Buildings sprang up on Central Park West and Broadway and the Upper West Side remains mainly residential today, with a blend of highrises and old brownstones. The Lincoln Center complex has made the area something of a cultural hub, while the American Museum of Natural History is one of the city's most popular family-friendly attractions.

110 St **S**
6

HARLEM AND
MORNINGSIDE HEIGHTS
p250

EAST 104TH ST

S 103 St
6

EAST 102ND ST

FRANKLIN D. ROOSEVELT DRIVE (EAST RIVER DRIVE)

Wards Island
Footbridge

5

CENTRAL PARK AND
THE UPPER WEST SIDE

EAST 99TH ST

EAST 98TH ST

Harlem

96 St **S** EAST 96TH ST
6

Mill
Rock Park

River

6

EAST 91ST ST

SECOND AVENUE

LEXINGTON AVENUE

THIRD AVENUE

FIRST AVENUE

YORK AVENUE

Gracie
Mansion

EAST 87TH ST

86 St **S**
4.5.6

PARK AVENUE

MADISON AVENUE

Carl
Schurz
Park

7

EAST 93RD ST

EAST END AVENUE

| 0 meters | | 500 | N |
| 0 yards | | 500 | ↗ |

UPPER
EAST SIDE
p214

77 St **S**
6

UPPER
EAST SIDE

PARK AVENUE

CENTRAL PARK AND
THE UPPER WEST SIDE

8

EAST 72ND ST

THIRD AVENUE

LEXINGTON AVENUE

SECOND AVENUE

S 68 St-
Hunter College
6

MADISON AVENUE

Park
Avenue
Armory

AVENUE

AVENUE

Must See
❶ Central Park
❷ American Museum of Natural History

Experience More
❸ Lincoln Center Theaters
❹ Columbus Circle
❺ Nicholas Roerich Museum
❻ The Dakota
❼ New York Historical Society
❽ Children's Museum of Manhattan
❾ American Folk Art Museum
❿ Riverside Drive and Park

Eat
① Per Se
② Jean-Georges
③ Absolute Bagels
④ Barney Greengrass
⑤ Jacob's Pickles
⑥ Zabar's Café

9

S

UPPER MIDTOWN
p198

❶ 🖥 🍴

CENTRAL PARK

📍M9 🚇Between 59th St, Fifth Av, 110th St and Eighth Av 🚇59 St-Columbus Circle (A, B, C, D, 1), 5 Av-59 St (N, Q, R), 72nd St (B, C) 🕐6am–1am daily
🌐centralparknyc.org

Few New Yorkers today could imagine their city without this expansive and beloved park, which lies at the heart of New York. With a wealth of green spaces, numerous sights to explore, and various activities to entertain, Central Park has something for everyone, and a different story to tell with each season.

Central Park is a green paradise for both New Yorkers and visitors to the city. It attracts bird-watchers and naturalists, swimmers and skaters, picnickers and sunbathers, runners and cyclists, and festival-goers in the summer. After a fierce competition, Frederick Law Olmsted and Calvert Vaux were chosen to create Central Park in the 1850s. The area had been largely desolate, pockmarked with shantytowns and pig farms, and the transformation was a huge undertaking. It opened to the public in 1876 under the proviso that it was a "people's park." Today the southern section of the park contains most of the popular attractions, including the Delacorte Theater, where Shakespeare in the Park is staged, and the Wollman Rink during the holiday season. But the northern tract (above 86th Street) is well worth a visit for its wilder natural setting and a dramatically quieter ambience.

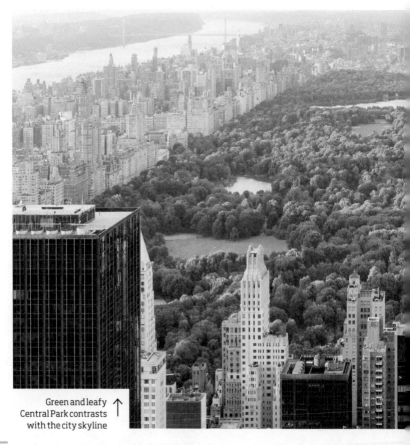

Green and leafy Central Park contrasts with the city skyline ↑

> 💬 **INSIDER TIP**
> ### The coolest spot in the city
> Central Park tends to be cooler than the rest of the city in the summer months, so it's good to head here if you're visiting June-August; it's also colder in winter, meaning photogenic snow lasts longer here than anywhere else.

↑ The Sheap Meadow, at the southern end of Central Park

Seasonal Guide

Spring

The park returns to life at the end of March, with cherry trees blossoming around The Reservoir and birds chirping on their spring migration. Check out model boat races at the Boat Pond (10am-1pm Sat).

Summer

The park becomes a shady respite in summer, while sunbathers bask in the Sheep Meadow. For many, it's all about the free festivals: Shakespeare in the Park, SummerStage, the Met Opera Summer Recital Series, and New York Philharmonic Concerts.

Fall

With 20,000 trees turning red and gold, plus milder temperatures, Central Park is at its most beautiful in the fall. Birds again visit, with hawks best spotted from Belvedere Castle.

Winter

Most of the trees are bare and the winds are biting cold, but winter can be a magical time in Central Park. Snow often blankets the lawns and woods long after it has melted from the streets, and you'll have large swaths of the park to yourself. Don't miss ice-skating at the Wollman Rink or Lasker Rink (Nov-Mar).

← Cycling is a great way to see Central Park during summer

The Dairy

🕐 **10am–5pm daily**

Central Park's visitor center is the place to begin. Maps and event information can be obtained here, and visitors can rent chess sets too.

② Strawberry Fields

This is Yoko Ono's tribute to her husband, John Lennon. Gifts for the garden came from all over the world.

↑ Pedestrians cross Bow Bridge, while boaters enjoy the lake

③ Belvedere Castle

🕐 **10am–5pm daily**

This stone castle atop Vista Rock, complete with tower and turrets, offers some of the best views of the park. Inside is the Henry Luce Nature Observatory, with a delightful exhibit telling inquisitive young visitors about the surprising variety of wildlife to be found in the park.

④ Bow Bridge

This is one of the park's original cast-iron bridges, and was designed as a bow tying together sections of the lake. In the 19th century, when the lake was used for skating, a hoisted red ball signalled that the ice was safe. The bridge offers expansive park views.

TOP 3 CENTRAL PARK BIKE RENTALS

Bike and Roll
451 Columbus Av, at W 82nd St; www.bikeandroll.com

Master Bike Shop
265 W 72nd St, between Broadway and West End Ave; www.masterbikeshop.com

Must See Central Park
56 W 56th St; www.mustseecentralpark.com

Bethesda Fountain and Terrace

Situated between the lake and the Mall, this is the architectural heart of the park, a formal element in the naturalistic landscape. The fountain was dedicated in 1873. The statue, *Angel of the Waters*, marked the opening of the Croton Aqueduct system in 1842, bringing the city its first supply of pure water; its name refers to a biblical account of a healing angel at the pool of Bethesda in Jerusalem.

 Conservatory Water

Better known as the Model Boat Pond, this is where model yacht races occur every week-end and birdwatchers gather here in spring to see the city's famous red-tailed hawk, Pale Male, nest on the roof of 927 Fifth Avenue. At the north end of the lake, a sculpture of Alice in Wonderland is popular with kids. It was commissioned by George T. Delacorte, who is immortalized as the Mad Hatter. Free story hours take place at H. C. Andersen's statue.

Did You Know?

The opening credits of sitcom *Friends* were filmed in LA, not in a Central Park fountain.

 Central Park Zoo

⏰ Apr–Oct: 10am–5pm Mon–Fri (until 5:30pm Sat, Sun & state hols); Nov–Mar: 10am–4:30pm daily

This imaginative zoo has won plaudits for its creative and humane use of small space. More than 150 species of animals are represented in three climate zones.

 Conservatory Garden

⏰ 8am–dusk

The Vanderbilt Gate on Fifth Avenue gives entry to three formal gardens, each reflecting a national landscape style; the Central Garden recreates an Italian style, the South Garden is English style, and the North Garden is French.

 Wollman Rink

⏰ Oct–Mar

The picturesque Wollman Rink has delivered the city's most atmospheric ice-skating since 1949. The location is perfect, providing thrilling views of the park and the skyscrapers along Central Park South. The rink transforms into Victorian Gardens, a small amusement park, June–September.

 Charles A. Dana Discovery Center & Harlem Meer

The Charles A. Dana Discovery Center has exhibits on the park's history and ecology. The center overlooks Harlem Meer, where catch-and-release fishing is allowed, and loans out free fishing poles and bait.

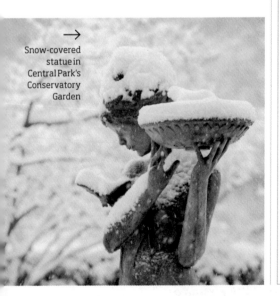

→ Snow-covered statue in Central Park's Conservatory Garden

EAT

Tavern on the Green
The park's most famous restaurant serves modern, seasonal cuisine to well-heeled locals and visitors.

🏠 Central Park West and 67th St 🌐 tavernonthe green.com

$$$

Loeb Boathouse Restaurant
Set by the Lake, Loeb Boathouse was funded by philanthropist Carl M. Loeb. The restaurant is popular with couples.

🏠 East 72nd St and Park Drive North 🕐 D Dec–Mar 🌐 thecentralpark boathouse.com

$$$

AMERICAN MUSEUM OF NATURAL HISTORY

2

📍 M8 🏛 Central Park West at 79th St Ⓢ 81 St (B, C)
🚌 M7, M10, M11, M79, M104 🕐 10am–5:45pm daily
🌐 amnh.org

Fossils, taxidermy, and skeletons galore – this encyclopedic collection of curiosities comprises one of the world's largest natural history museums, and houses the Rose Center for Earth and Space. Kids in particular will love exploring the museum's hoard of specimens, and getting their hands on the interactive exhibits.

↑ A parade of African elephants

Since the original building opened in 1877, the complex has grown to cover a whopping four city blocks and four floors, jam-packed with more than 30 million specimens and artifacts. The most popular areas are the Dinosaur Exhibit, housing the world's largest dinosaur collection, and the Milstein Hall of Ocean Life, which shows the drama of the undersea world. The Rose Center for Earth and Space includes the Hayden Planetarium, while the Hall of Gems and Minerals houses a stunning array of crystals. This barely scratches the surface – there's reptiles, amphibians, insects, African mammals, and much more.

← This enormous blue whale replica is based on a 1925 South American female

→ A young star-gazer

ROSE CENTER

When viewed from the street at night, the Rose Center is breathtaking, and the exhibits inside prove that, as Carl Sagan said, "We are starstuff." Housed within an 87-ft (27-m) sphere, the center contains the technologically advanced Hayden Planetarium; the Cosmic Pathway, a 350-ft (107-m) spiral ramp with a timeline chronicling 13 billion years of evolution; and the Big Bang Theater, where the origins of the universe are explained.

The museum *(inset)*, home
to the Hall of Biodiversity
and all its curiosities ↑

EXPERIENCE MORE

Lincoln Center Theaters

M9 **10 Lincoln Center Plaza (Columbus Av)** **66 St (1)** **lincolncenter.org**

The Lincoln Center is anchored by a series of spectacular performance venues, beginning with the Metropolitan Opera House. Designed by Wallace K. Harrison, it opened in 1966. Five great arched windows offer views of the opulent lobby and two murals by Marc Chagall. Inside there are curved white marble stairs, red carpeting, and exquisite starburst crystal chandeliers that are raised to the ceiling just before each performance.

Across the main plaza lies the David H. Koch Theater, by architects Philip Johnson and John Burgee, inaugurated in 1964. Gargantuan white marble sculptures by Elie Nadelman dominate the

vast four-story lobby. Because of its rhinestone lights and chandeliers both inside and out, it is sometimes described as "a little jewel box."

When David Geffen Hall opened in 1962 as the Philharmonic Hall, critics initially complained about the acoustics, but structural modifications have rendered the hall an acoustic gem, comparing favorably with other great classical concert halls around the world.

Three more intimate theaters make up the Lincoln Center theater complex, where eclectic and often experimental drama is presented. The theaters are the 1,000-seat Vivian Beaumont, the 280-seat Mitzi E. Newhouse, and

---

LEGENDARY COMPANIES OF THE LINCOLN CENTER

The thing that makes the Lincoln Center truly special is the caliber of its resident companies. The world-famous Metropolitan Opera Company is currently led by Yannick Nézet-Séguin. The American Ballet Theatre's most famous principal dancer is Misty Copeland. The New York City Ballet, at the David H. Koch Theater, performs Balanchine's *Nutcracker* every November and December. David Geffen Hall is home to the New York Philharmonic and the popular "Mostly Mozart" series. Alice Tully Hall hosts the Chamber Music Society.

The Lincoln Center is the world's most prestigious performing arts complex

building projects in New York City's history.

Multi-use skyscrapers have attracted national and international businesses. Global media company Time Warner has its headquarters in an 80-story skyscraper. The 2.8 million sq ft (260,000 sq m) building provides a retail, entertainment, and restaurant facility, with stores such as Hugo Boss, Williams-Sonoma, and Whole Foods Market; dining at Per Se and Masa; and a Mandarin Oriental hotel.

The Time Warner Center is also home to Jazz at the Lincoln Center. The three venues here – the Appel Room, the Rose Theater, and Dizzy's Club Coca-Cola – together with a jazz hall of fame and education center, comprise the world's first performing-arts facility dedicated to jazz.

Other notable buildings on Columbus Circle include Hearst House, designed by British architect Lord Norman Foster, Trump International Hotel, the Maine Monument, and the eye-catching Museum of Arts and Design (p182), formerly the American Craft Museum.

Did You Know?

West Side Story (1961) was filmed on Lincoln Center land before the complex was built.

the 112-seat Claire Tow. Works by some of New York's best modern playwrights have featured at the Beaumont. The size of the Newhouse suits Off-Broadway-style plays, while the Claire Tow features work written by emerging playwrights, directors, and designers.

④
Columbus Circle

Q M9 **S** 59 St-Columbus Circle (A, B, C, D, 1) **W** jazz.org

Presiding over this urban plaza at the corner of Central Park is a marble statue of explorer Christopher Columbus, perched atop a tall granite column in the center of a fountain and plantings. The statue is one of the few remaining original features in this circle, which has become one of the largest

⑤
Nicholas Roerich Museum

Q L5 **Q** 319 West 107th St **S** Cathedral Parkway-110 St (1) **Q** Noon-4pm Tue-Fri, 2-5pm Sat-Sun **W** roerich.org

The often overlooked Nicholas Roerich Museum occupies a handsome brownstone near Riverside Park. It contains a small and quirky collection of around 150 original paintings by Nicholas Roerich (1874–1947), a Russian-born

EAT

Per Se
Chef Thomas Keller's restaurant remains one of the most feted in the city. There are two (very pricey) nine-course tasting menus featuring superlative Californian-influenced cuisine, a great wine list, and spectacular views of Central Park. Jackets required for men.

Q M9 **Q** Time Warner Center, 10 Columbus Circle **Q** Lunch Mon-Thu **W** thomaskeller.com/perseny

$$$$$$

Jean-Georges
The jewel in the crown of famed chef Jean-Georges Vongerichten. Organic ingredients go into the contemporary French cuisine, with a three-course prix-fixe dinner menu (or more pricey tasting menus) and a two-course lunch menu. Reservations required.

Q M9 **Q** Trump International Hotel, 1 Central Park West **W** jean-georges restaurant.com

$$$$$$

artist who lived in India from the 1920s. Much of his work focuses on nature scenes from the Himalayas, influenced by Buddhist mysticism.

Born in St. Petersburg, his early art was promoted in Europe by Sergei Diaghilev. His association with New York began on an extended visit in 1920; he founded the Agni Yoga Society and Master Institute of United Arts in the city.

6
The Dakota

M9 **1 West 72nd St** **72 St (1, 2, 3)** **To the public**

The name and style reflect the fact that this apartment building was truly "way out West" when Henry J. Hardenbergh, the architect responsible for the Plaza Hotel, designed it in 1880–84. It was New York's first luxury apartment house and was originally surrounded by squatters' shacks and wandering farm animals. Commissioned by Edward S. Clark, heir to the Singer

HIDDEN GEM
The Boat Basin

Tucked away off Riverside Park, the 79th Street Boat Basin is a surprisingly tranquil hideaway on the Hudson River. The small marina features the relaxed Boat Basin Café, open from lunch to late evening (Apr–Oct).

sewing machine fortune, it is one of the city's most prestigious addresses.

The Dakota's 65 luxurious apartments have had many famous owners, including Judy Garland, Lauren Bacall, Leonard Bernstein, and Boris Karloff, whose ghost is said to haunt the place. The setting for the movie *Rosemary's Baby*, it was also where the tragic murder of John Lennon took place. His widow, Yoko Ono, still lives here.

7
New York Historical Society

M8 **170 Central Park West** **81 St (B, C)** **Galleries: 10am-6pm Tue-Sat (to 8pm Fri), 11am-5pm Sun; Library: 9am-3pm Tue-Fri, 10am-4:45pm Sat (varies by season)** **nyhistory.org**

Founded in 1804, this society houses a distinguished research library and the city's oldest museum. Its collections include historical material

> Riverside Drive is one of New York City's most attractive streets; broad, and with lovely shaded views of the Hudson River, this is a much desired street.

relating to slavery and the Civil War, an outstanding collection of 18th-century newspapers, all 435 water-colors of Audubon's *Birds of America*, and the world's largest collection of Tiffany lamps and glasswork. There are also fine displays of American furniture and silver.

8
Children's Museum of Manhattan

L7 **212 West 83rd St** **79 St or 86 St (1), 81 St (B, C)** **10am-5pm daily (to 7pm Sat)** **cmom.org**

This particularly imaginative museum is based on the premise that children learn best through play. The exhibit called "Eat, Sleep, Play" links food, the digestive system, and healthy living, while in "Block Party" children can build castles, towns, and bridges out of wooden blocks. Kids also delight in the exhibits on cartoon favorites Curious George and Dora the Explorer and her adventurous cousin Diego, where they learn about travel and cultures around the world.

On weekends and holidays the 150-seat theater hosts performers, from puppeteers to storytellers. There's also a gallery for free events, like "Pajama Day," as well as lively, theme-based museum tours.

←

Exclusive and expensive, The Dakota apartment building

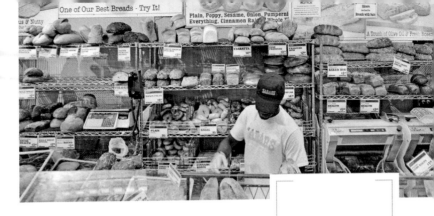

One of Our Best Breads - Try It!

Plain, Poppy, Sesame, Onion, Pumperni Everything, Cinnamon Rai

American Folk Art Museum

📍M9 🏛2 Lincoln Sq
🚇66 St (1) 🕐11:30am–7pm Tue-Thu & Sat, noon-7:30pm Fri, noon-6pm Sun
🌐folkartmuseum.org

The home for the appreciation and study of American folk art is conveniently located opposite the Lincoln Center complex. Founded in 1961, the museum comprises 7,000 artworks dating from the 18th century to the present day.

With colorful quilts, impressive portraits, and major works by self-taught, contemporary artists, the selection is remarkable. Especially worth seeking out are Henry Darger's water-colors, and the incredible urban commentaries of Ralph Fasinella. Exhibitions usually revolve, but the permanent collection is always on display.

↑ Locals enjoying the Upper West Side's leafy Riverside Park

↑ An array of tempting baked goods at Zabar's Café

Riverside Drive and Park

📍L5 🚇79 St or 86 St (1), 96 St (1, 2, 3)

Riverside Drive is one of New York City's most attractive streets; broad, and with lovely shaded views of the Hudson River, this is a much desired street. It is still lined with the opulent original townhouses, in addition to some more modern apartment buildings. At numbers 40–46, 74–77, 81–89, and 105–107 Riverside Drive are houses designed in the late 19th century by local architect Clarence F. True. The curved gables, bays, and arched windows seem to mirror the curves of the road and the flow of the river.

The bizarrely named Cliff Dwellers' Apartments at 243 (between 96th and 97th streets) is a 1914 building with a frieze featuring early Arizona cliff dwellers, complete with masks, buffalo skulls, and rattlesnakes.

Riverside Park, stretching for 4 miles (2.5 km) along the Hudson River, was designed by Frederick Law Olmsted, who also laid out Central Park (p238), and is one of only eight official "scenic landmarks" in the city.

EAT

Absolute Bagels
Some of the freshest, chewiest bagels in the city.

📍L5 🏛2788 Broadway 📞(212) 932-2052

💲💲💲

Barney Greengrass
Operating since 1908, the "Sturgeon King" serves up excellent lox, pastrami, salmon, and, of course, sturgeon.

📍M7 🏛541 Amsterdam Av 🕐Dinner, Mon 🌐barneygreen grass.com

💲💲💲

Jacob's Pickles
Southern fare like pancakes and fried chicken, plus tangy pickles await at this Upper West Side classic.

📍M7 🏛509 Amsterdam Av 🌐jacobspickles.com

💲💲💲

Zabar's Café
Takeout heaven for smoked fish, pickles, and bagels-and-lox sandwiches since 1934.

📍L8 🏛2245 Broadway 🌐zabars.com

💲💲💲

A SHORT WALK
LINCOLN CENTER

Distance 0.6 mile (1 km) **Nearest subway** 59 St, 72 St
Time 15 minutes

Lincoln Center was conceived when both the Metropolitan Opera House and the New York Philharmonic required homes, and a large tract on Manhattan's west side was in dire need of revitalization. The notion of a single complex where different performing arts could exist side by side seems natural today, but in the 1950s it was considered both daring and risky. Today Lincoln Center has proved itself by drawing audiences of five million each year. Proximity to its halls prompts both performers and arts lovers to live nearby.

Composer Leonard Bernstein, who based West Side Story in this neighborhood, was later instrumental in setting up the large music complex that we see here today.

The Vivian Beaumont and the Mitzi E. Newhouse theaters, part of Lincoln Center, are both housed in this building (p245).

The Guggenheim Bandshell in Damrosch Park is the site of free concerts.

Lincoln Center's focus is the Metropolitan Opera House. The cafe at the top of the lobby offers wonderful plaza views (p244).

The David H. Koch Theater is the home of the New York City Ballet, and is also a venue for American Ballet Theater (p244).

Dance, music, and theater come together in the fine Lincoln Center for the Performing Arts. It is also a great place to sit around the fountain and people-watch.

The College Board Building is an Art Deco delight that now houses condos and the administrative offices of the College Board, developers of the college entrance exam.

↑ Fountains outside the Metropolitan Opera House, Lincoln Center

Locator Map
For more detail see p236

Head to the American Folk Art Museum for amazing quilt exhibits (p247).

Artists Isadora Duncan, Noël Coward, and Norman Rockwell once lived at Hotel des Artistes.

James Dean once lived in a one-room apartment on the top floor at 19 West 68th Street.

W 67TH STREET

FINISH

Did You Know?

The stage of the Metropolitan Opera House is the size of a football field.

W 65TH STREET

CENTRAL PARK WEST

An ABC-TV sound stage for soap operas is housed in this castle-like building, formerly an armory.

55 Central Park West is an Art Deco apartment building, which featured in the film Ghostbusters, as the home of Dana Barrett, played by Sigourney Weaver.

The Society for Ethical Culture was one of the city's first Art Nouveau buildings. It also houses a school.

The Twin Towers of Central Park West are just one of a group of twin towers. The Century building is visible from Central Park.

START

Central Park West is home to many celebrities, who like the privacy of its highly exclusive apartments.

| 0 meters | 100 |
| 0 yards | 100 |

N ↑

HARLEM AND MORNINGSIDE HEIGHTS

Harlem has been at the heart of African-American culture since the 1920s, when poets, activists, and jazz musicians came together during the Harlem Renaissance. Today, the neighborhood is home to fabulous West African eateries, Sunday gospel choirs, a vibrant local jazz scene, and some of the prettiest blocks in the city. Morningside Heights, near the Hudson River, is home to Columbia University and two of the city's finest churches. Hamilton Heights is further uptown – primarily a residential area, it also contains a Federal-style historic mansion and the City College of New York.

251

HARLEM AND MORNINGSIDE HEIGHTS

Must Sees
1 Cathedral of St. John Divine
2 Schomburg Center

Experience More
3 Hamilton Grange National Memorial
4 Riverside Church
5 Grant's Tomb
6 Marcus Garvey Park
7 Langston Hughes House
8 Striver's Row (St. Nicholas District)
9 Studio Museum in Harlem
10 Mount Morris Historic District
11 Museo del Barrio
12 National Jazz Museum in Harlem
13 Apollo Theater
14 Graffiti Wall of Fame
15 City College of the City University of New York
16 Columbia University

Eat
① Patsy's Pizzeria
② Rao's
③ Red Rooster
④ Sylvia's Restaurant
⑤ Amy Ruth's

Stay
⑥ Harlem Flophouse
⑦ Mount Morris House
⑧ San Fermín Apartments

1 Ⓜ️ ▣

CATHEDRAL OF ST. JOHN THE DIVINE

📍M4 🏛️1047 Amsterdam Av at West 112th St Ⓢ Cathedral Pkwy-110 St (1)
🚌M4, M11, M60, M104 🕖7:30am–6pm daily 🌐stjohndivine.org

This Gothic cathedral is truly one of a kind. It will be the largest cathedral in the world when it is completed – over 100 years since construction first began – and hosts music, theater, and avante-garde art under its semi-finished roof.

Started in 1892, and still only two-thirds finished, the Cathedral of St. John the Divine will be the world's largest cathedral, surpassing St. Peter's Basilica in Vatican City. The interior is over 600 ft (183 m) long and 146 ft (45 m) wide. It was originally designed in Romanesque style by Heins & LaFarge; Ralph Adams Cram took over the project in 1911, devising a Gothic nave and west front. Medieval construction methods, such as stone-on-stone supporting buttresses, continue to be used to complete the cathedral. The cathedral plays an important role in the community, with various social and cultural events taking place here.

↓ The Cathedral of St. John the Divine

↑ Portals by stonemason Joe Kincannon show an apocalyptic New York City

The rose window symbolizes the many facets of the Christian Church.

Timeline

1823
▽ Cathedral planned for Washington Square.

1888
Competition to design cathedral won by Heins & LaFarge.

1891
Site chosen and designated Cathedral Parkway.

1892
△ December 27 (St. John's Day), cornerstone laid.

1941
▽ Work is halted by World War II and does not resume until 1978.

Rising to a height of over 100 ft (30 m), the piers of the nave are topped by graceful stone arches.

Each of the choir's columns is 55 ft (17 m) tall and made of polished gray granite.

THE FINISHED DESIGN

The north and south transepts, the crossing tower, and the west towers of the cathedral have yet to be finished. When the money to fund their construction is raised, the proposed design will still take at least another 50 years to complete.

The Bishop's Chair is a copy from the Henry VII chapel in Westminster Abbey, in London.

The pulpit

The bay altar windows are devoted to human endeavor. The sports window shows feats of skill and strength.

↑ The beautiful nave offers a calm, reflective space for worshipers

1982

▽ Daredevil aerialist Philippe Petit crosses a high wire between cathedral and a building on Amsterdam Ave.

2001

Major fire destroys interior and roof of north transept.

2017

▽ Cathedral and grounds designated a New York City Landmark.

1978–89

Third phase of building. Stonemasons' Yard opened, and south tower heightened.

2008

Reopens after seven-year closure for renovations.

2

SCHOMBURG CENTER

N2 515 Malcolm X Blvd, at West 135th St 135 St (2, 3) 10am–8pm Tue & Wed, 10am–6pm Thu–Sat nypl.org/locations/schomburg

The largest research center dedicated to black and African culture in the United States, the pioneering Schomburg Center is one of Harlem's premier cultural attractions.

The Home of African-American History

Housed in a sleek contemporary complex, the Schomburg Center is part of the New York Public Library family, and a key research hub. The center, formally called the Schomburg Center for Research in Black Culture, opened in 1991. Its immense collection was assembled by Arturo Schomburg (1874–1938), a black man of Puerto Rican descent. As a child, Schomburg was told by a teacher that there was no such thing as "black history," which inspired him to prove the teacher wrong by documenting African-American history and its heroes. The Carnegie Foundation bought the collection in 1926 and donated it to the NYPL; Schomburg, who lived in Harlem, was made curator in 1932. Today the Schomburg Center holds some 10 million items, from film and music recordings to African, Caribbean, and African-American literature, and hosts superb temporary exhibitions covering a range of themes based around the African-American experience. The center also houses a number of stunning murals by Aaron Douglas, a key artist in the Harlem Renaissance. Douglas stayed in Harlem en route from Kansas City to Paris and was convinced to stay for longer.

Guided tours are a great way to learn more about the history of the Schomburg Center and its brilliant collection. Tours are available from 10am to 3pm, Monday through Friday, and must be booked at least 30 days in advance. Visit the website for more information and to reserve a place on a tour.

↓ Murals by Aaron Douglas include *From Slavery Through Reconstruction*

INSIDER TIP
Aaron Douglas murals

From the Latimer/Edison Gallery you can glimpse the main reading room below, and admire the four haunting murals painted by Harlem Renaissance artist Aaron Douglas in 1934. These abstract artworks portray subjects from African-American history and experience.

1 The exterior of the Schomburg Center for Research in Black Culture.

2 In the center's main hall, the *Black Power!* exhibition tracks the ten-year movement that followed the Civil Rights Movement. Ignited by the assassination of activist Malcolm X in 1965, Black Power demanded immediate, physical action in response to white supremacy.

3 Visitors engage with exhibits on display at the center's popular *Black Power!* exhibition.

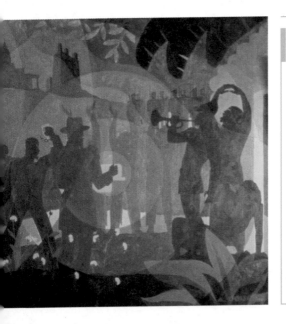

LANGSTON HUGHES

Seminal poet Langston Hughes was born in Missouri, in 1902. He moved to Harlem in 1929, where he became a key voice in the Harlem Renaissance, writing poetry, plays, and short stories up to his death in 1967. His ashes are interred here, beneath the terrazzo and "cosmogram" in the atrium beyond the main library entrance. This is inscribed with lines from his signature poem *The Negro Speaks of Rivers*: "My soul has grown deep like the rivers."

EXPERIENCE MORE

↑ The "family room" in Alexander Hamilton's home, The Grange

❸ Ⓜ 🏛
Hamilton Grange National Memorial

📍M1 🚇St. Nicholas Park, 414 West 141st St 🚉137 St-City College (1) 🕐9am–5pm Wed–Sun 🌐nps.gov/hagr

The subject of the highly successful Broadway musical, and the face on the $10 bill, Alexander Hamilton was one of the architects of the federal government system, First Secretary of the treasury and founder of the National Bank. Completed in 1802, this was his country home. Hamilton lived here for the last two years of his life, prior to being killed in a duel with political rival Aaron Burr in 1804.

In 1889, St. Luke's Episcopal Church acquired the site, and the building was moved four blocks west. A second move in 2008 brought it to its current site in St. Nicholas Park.

❹ 💻 Ⓜ
Riverside Church

📍L3 🚇490 Riverside Dr at 122nd St 🚉116 St-Columbia University (1) 🕐7am–10pm daily 🌐theriversidechurchny.org

A 21-story steel frame with a Gothic exterior, the church design was inspired by the cathedral at Chartres, France. It was lavishly funded by John D. Rockefeller Jr., in 1930. The Laura Spelman Rockefeller Memorial Carillon (in honor of Rockefeller's mother) is the largest in the world, with 74 bells. The 20-ton Bourdon, or hour bell, is the largest and heaviest tuned carillon bell ever cast. The organ, with its 22,000 pipes, is among the largest in the world.

At the rear of the second gallery is a figure by Jacob Epstein, *Christ in Majesty*, cast in plaster and covered in gold leaf. Another Epstein statue, *Madonna and Child*, stands in the court next to the cloister. The panels of the chancel screen honor eight men and women whose lives have exemplified the teachings of Christ. They range from Socrates and Michelangelo to Florence Nightingale and Booker T. Washington.

For quiet reflection, enter the small, secluded Christ Chapel, patterned after an 11th-century Romanesque

↑ Glowing stained glass backs the cross on the altar in Riverside Church

church in France. The church is particularly welcoming during the Christmas season, as the public is invited to a host of festive activities such as caroling by candlelight. The church also offers guided tours at 12:15pm on Sundays.

❺ Ⓜ
Grant's Tomb

📍L3 🚇West 122nd St and Riverside Dr 🚉116 St-Columbia University (1) 🚌M5 🕐9am–5pm Wed–Sun 🌐nps.gov/gegr

This grandiose monument honors America's 18th president, Ulysses S. Grant, the commanding general of the Union forces in the Civil War. The mausoleum contains the coffins of General Grant and his wife, Julia, in accordance with the president's last wish that they be buried together. After Grant's death in 1885, more than 90,000 Americans contributed $600,000 to build the sepulcher, which was inspired by Mausoleus's tomb at Halicarnassus (now Bodrum), one of the Seven Wonders of the Ancient World.

The tomb was dedicated on what would have been Grant's 75th birthday, April 27, 1897. The parade of 50,000 people, along with a flotilla of ten American and five European warships, took more than seven hours to pass in review.

The interior was inspired by Napoleon's tomb at Les

HARLEM GOSPEL AT ABYSSINIAN CHURCH

New York's oldest black church became famous through its charismatic pastor Adam Clayton Powell Jr. (1908–72), a congressman and civil-rights leader who made it the most powerful black church in America. The 1923 Gothic building is known for the uplifting gospel music of its Sunday services; arrive by 11am at the entrance, at the south-east corner of West 138th Street and Powell Boulevard.

←

The imposing Grant's Tomb, and its spectacular domed ceiling *(inset)*

Invalides in Paris. Each sarcophagus weighs 8.5 tons. Two exhibit rooms feature displays on Grant's personal life and his presidential and military career. Surrounding the north and east sides of the building are 17 sinuously curved mosaic benches that seem totally out of keeping with the formal architecture of the tomb. They were designed in the early 1970s by the Chilean-born Brooklyn artist Pedro Silva and were built by 1,200 local volunteers, who worked under his supervision. The benches were inspired by the work of Spanish architect Antoni Gaudí in Barcelona. The mosaics depict subjects ranging from the Inuit to New York taxis to Donald Duck.

A short walk to the north of Grant's Tomb is another, much simpler but equally poignant monument. An unadorned urn on a pedestal marks the resting place of a young child who fell from the riverbank and drowned. His grieving father placed a marker that simply reads: "Erected to the memory of an amiable child, St. Claire Pollock, died 15 July 1797 in his fifth year of his age."

 6

Marcus Garvey Park

9 N3 **🚇** 120th–124th streets **🚇** 125 St (2, 3, 4, 5, 6) **🌐** nycgovparks.org

This hilly, rocky, two-block square of green is the site of New York's last fire watchtower, an open cast-iron structure built in 1857, with spiral stairs leading up to the 47-ft- (14-m-) high observation deck. The bell below the deck was used to sound the alarm. The tower was temporarily dismantled in 2015 for reconstruction, and the $5.7 million project, which includes work on the surrounding plaza, was completed in 2018.

Previously known as Mount Morris Park, it was renamed in 1973 in honor of Marcus Garvey. He came to Harlem from Jamaica in 1916 and founded the Universal Negro Improvement Association, which promoted self-help, racial pride, and a back-to-Africa movement.

7

Langston Hughes House

9 N3 **🚇** 20 East 127th St **🚇** 125 St (4, 5, 6) **🕐** Noon–5pm Tue, Thu, Sat **🌐** itoo arts.com

Celebrated African-American poet Langston Hughes *(p257)* lived at this house in Harlem from 1948 until his death in 1967. It was here he penned classics such as *Montage of a Dream Deferred.* His aging 1869 brownstone was left virtually derelict for years, but was leased by the local I, Too, Arts Collective in 2016. The Collective has since opened parts of it to the public, in conjunction with running their poetry salons and creative conversations series. Hughes' typewriter and piano are displayed in the parlor, and the second and third floors may be open in future.

Overlooking colorful streets and an intersection in Harlem

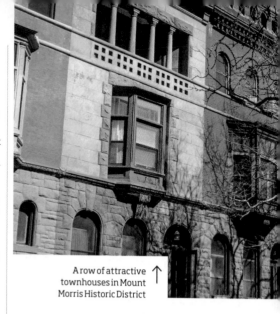

8

Striver's Row (St. Nicholas District)

📍 M1 🏠 202-250 West 138th & West 139th streets
Ⓢ 135 St (2, 3)

The two blocks here were built in 1891, when Harlem was being promoted as a neighborhood for New York's gentry. Officially designated the St. Nicholas Historic District, they are still among the city's most distinctive examples of row townhouses. McKim, Mead & White were responsible for the northernmost row of solid brick Renaissance palaces, while the Georgian buildings by Price and Luce are of buff brick with white stone trim. James Brown Lord's buildings feature outstanding red-brick facades and brownstone bases. In the early 20th century, this came to be the desirable residence for ambitious professionals within Harlem's burgeoning black community – hence the "Strivers" nickname.

9

Studio Museum in Harlem

📍 N3 🏠 144 West 125th St
Ⓢ 125 St (2, 3) 🕐 Noon-6pm daily 🌐 studiomuseum.org

The museum was founded in 1967 in a loft on upper Fifth Avenue with the mission of becoming the world's premier

 A row of attractive townhouses in Mount Morris Historic District ↑

center for the collection and exhibition of the art and artifacts of African-Americans.

The present premises, a five-story building on Harlem's main commercial street, was donated to the museum by the New York Bank for Savings in 1979. There are galleries on two levels for changing exhibitions featuring artists and cultural themes, and three galleries are devoted to the permanent collection of works by major black artists.

The photographic archives comprise one of the most complete records in existence of Harlem in its heyday. A side door opens onto a small sculpture garden. In addition to its excellent exhibitions, the Studio Museum also

maintains a national artist-in-residence program, and offers regular lectures, seminars, children's programs, and film festivals. An excellent store sells a range of books, unique prints, and African crafts.

10

Mount Morris Historic District

📍 N3 🏠 West 119th-West 124th streets
Ⓢ 125 St (2, 3)

Despite many of the buildings being in need of renovation, it is still clear that the late 19th-century townhouses near Marcus Garvey Park were once grand, favored by German Jews moving up in the world from the Lower East Side. After a long period of neglect, redevelopment is underway.

A few impressive churches, such as St. Martin's Episcopal Church, remain and interesting juxtapositions of faiths can be seen: the columned Mount Olivet Baptist Church, at 201 Malcolm X Boulevard, was once Temple Israel, one of the most imposing synagogues in the city; and at the Ethiopian Hebrew Congregation, 1 West 123rd

---

LIVE JAZZ IN HARLEM

Jazz remains a fundamental part of Harlem's appeal. Classic joints such as Showman's (with veteran Hammond organist Seleno Clarke) and Minton's are still going strong, while sax man Bill Saxton still plays Fridays and Saturdays at Bill's Place. Although no relation to the famous original, the Cotton Club offers good swing, blues, jazz, and a Sunday Gospel brunch.

> Duke Ellington, Thelonious Monk, Charlie Parker, Count Basie, John Coltrane, and Billie Holiday all got their start in Harlem clubs and speakeasies.

Street, housed in a former mansion, the choir sings in Hebrew on Saturdays.

Museo del Barrio

📍N5 🏠1230 Fifth Av
🚇103 St (6) 🕐11am-6pm
Wed-Sat, noon-5pm Sun
🌐elmuseo.org

Founded in 1969, this was North America's first museum devoted to Latin American art, specializing in the culture of Puerto Rico. Exhibitions show contemporary painting and sculpture, folk art, and historical artifacts. About 240 wooden Santos (carved figures of saints) and a reconstructed *bodega*, or Latino convenience store, are highlights. Exhibits change, but Santos are often on display. The Pre-Columbian collection contains rare artifacts from the Caribbean. At the far end of Museum Mile, the museum aims to bridge the gap between the lofty

Upper East Side and Spanish Harlem. A store sells eye-catching items by artists from all over Latin America.

National Jazz Museum in Harlem

📍N2 🏠58 West 129th St
🚇125 St (2, 3) 🕐11am-5pm
Thu-Mon 🌐jazzmuseumin harlem.org

This tiny museum honors Harlem's important role in the history of jazz. Duke Ellington, Thelonious Monk, Charlie Parker, Count Basie, John Coltrane, and Billie Holiday all got their start in Harlem clubs and speakeasies. The small gallery contains rare jazz memorabilia, including Duke Ellington's white 1920s piano, and a scarf he bought for his wife, as well as Ralph Ellison's collection of jazz recordings. The museum also arranges jazz-related programs, classes, and live events.

EAT

Patsy's Pizzeria
This rare remnant of Italian Harlem is where the pizza slice concept was invented. Cash only.

📍Q4 🏠2287 First Av
🌐thepatsyspizza.com

$$$

Rao's
This authentic Italian restaurant is in high demand, with only ten tables (nine standing only). Cash only.

📍Q4 🏠455 East 114th St 🕐Lunch 🌐raos restaurants.com

$$$

Red Rooster
Southern-style comfort food includes steak with fried green tomatoes, roast pork loin, and fiery jerk chicken.

📍N3 🏠310 Malcolm X Blvd 🌐redrooster harlem.com

$$$

Sylvia's Restaurant
The best soul food – from fried chicken with waffles to BBQ ribs and candied yams. The peach cobbler is divine.

📍N3 🏠328 Malcolm X Blvd 🌐sylvias restaurant.com

$$$

Amy Ruth's
Soul food at its most comforting. The waffle breakfasts and desserts are equally enticing.

📍N4 🏠113 West 116th St 🌐amyruths.com

$$$

The Apollo Theater, a long-established Harlem venue

1980s, the Apollo once again features top entertainers and hosts amateur nights.

 14

Graffiti Wall of Fame

P5 Park Av and East 106th St **103rd St (6)**

Founded in 1980 by street artist Ray Rodríguez, the Graffiti Wall of Fame honors the street art that exploded in the 1970s. The inner side of the concrete wall is actually located in the Junior High School 13 Jackie Robinson playground, so the gates are sometimes locked (ask at the school along 106th Street for a closer look). The wall features art from many of the city's best-known graffiti writers, including Dez, Crash, Flight, Delta, Tats Cru, and Skeme.

 15

City College of the City University of New York

M2 Main entrance at West 138th St and Convent Av **137 St-City College (1)** ccny.cuny.edu

High on a hill adjoining Hamilton Heights, the original Gothic quadrangle of this

13

Apollo Theater

M3 253 West 125th St **125 St (A, B, C, D)** For performances only apollotheater.org

Opened in 1913 as a whites-only opera house, the Apollo's great fame came when entrepreneur Frank Schiffman took over in 1934 and opened it to all. It became Harlem's best-known showcase, with artists such as Bessie Smith, Billie Holiday, Duke Ellington, and Dinah Washington.

Wednesday Amateur Nights (begun in 1935), with winners determined by audience applause, were famous, and there was a long waiting list for performers. These amateur nights helped launch the careers of Sarah Vaughan, Pearl Bailey, James Brown, and Gladys Knight. The Apollo was *the* place during the swing band era; following World War II, a new generation of musicians, such as Charlie "Bird" Parker, Dizzy Gillespie, Thelonious Monk, and Aretha Franklin, continued the tradition. Refurbished in the

HARLEM RENAISSANCE

The Harlem Renaissance of the 1920s was inspirational for generations of African-American musicians, writers, and performers. Jazz musicians such as Duke Ellington, Count Basie, and Cab Calloway electrified the Cotton Club, Savoy Ballroom, Apollo Theater, and Smalls Paradise. But the Harlem Renaissance wasn't just about music. It was also marked by a rich body of literature produced by Langston Hughes, Jean Toomer, and Zora Neale Hurston, among many others. Hughes declared the movement over in 1931 after the death of noted African-American socialite and patron A'Lelia Walker.

Students relax on the lawns of Columbia University's Morningside Heights campus

college, built between 1903 and 1907, is very impressive. The material used for the buildings is Manhattan schist, a stone that had been excavated in building the IRT subway. Later, contemporary buildings were added to the school, which enrolls nearly 15,000 students.

Once free to all residents of New York, City College still offers low tuition rates. Most of the students are from minority groups, and many of them are the first in their families to attend college.

16

Columbia University

L4 **West 116th St and Broadway** **116 St-Columbia University (1)**
Visitors' Center: 213 Low Library, 535 West 116th St
9am–5pm Mon–Fri
columbia.edu

Columbia is noted for its law, medicine, and journalism schools and its distinguished faculty and alumni, past and present, include over 50 Nobel laureates. Famous alumni include J. D. Salinger, James Cagney, and Joan Rivers. Across the street is the affiliated Barnard College. Columbia's Morningside Heights campus is the third location of one of America's oldest universities. Visitors can join free tours of the Morningside Heights campus; ask at the visitor center for information.

Founded in 1754 as King's College, it was first located close to where the World Trade

Center stood. In 1814, when a move uptown was proposed, the university approached the authorities for funding but was instead given a plot of land valued at $75,000 on which to build a new home. The university never built on the land itself, but leased it out and spent the years from 1857 to 1897 in buildings nearby. It finally sold the plot in 1985 to the leaseholders, Rockefeller Center Inc., for $400 million.

The present campus was begun in 1897 on the site of the Bloomingdale Insane Asylum. Architect Charles McKim placed the university on a terrace, serenely above street level. Its spacious lawns and plazas still create a sense of contrast in the busy city.

Opened in 2017 about one mile (1.6 km) north of the original Morningside Heights campus, the stylish new **Manhattanville campus** is a showcase for celebrated architect Renzo Piano. His nine-story glass-and-steel Jerome L. Greene Science Center is the largest building ever constructed for Columbia University. It serves as a hub for the neuroscience researchers of the Mortimer B. Zuckerman

Mind Brain Behavior Institute. Piano also designed the eight-story metal panel Lenfest Center for the Arts, containing the Wallach Art Gallery and performance spaces for theater, music, and dance. Piano's University Forum acts as a gateway to the campus and as a multipurpose venue. All the new buildings are glass-enclosed and open to view at street level. The Nash Building, originally built as an automobile showroom, now contains the campus historical interpretive exhibit.

Manhattanville campus
L2 **West 125th St to 133rd St, between Broadway and 12th Av** **125 St (1)**

STAY

Harlem Flophouse
Beautiful, artist-owned B&B based in a 1890s brownstone.

M3 **242 West 123rd St** **harlemflophouse.com**

$$$

Mount Morris House

Elegant brownstone overlooking Marcus Garvey Park, with five luxurious suites.

N3 **12 Mt Morris Park West** **mountmorrishousebandb.com**

$$$

San Fermín Apartments

Set in a lovely 1910 brownstone in Sugar Hill, featuring three en-suite doubles.

M1 **195 Edgecombe Ave** **sanferminapartmentsny.com**

$$$

A SHORT WALK
COLUMBIA UNIVERSITY

Distance 1.25 mile (2 km) **Nearest subway**
116 St-Columbia University **Time** 25 minutes

Columbia University's Morningside Heights campus should not be underestimated as a place of interest. After admiring the architecture, linger awhile on Columbia's central quadrangle in front of the Low Library, where you will see the future leaders of America mingling between classes. Across from the campus on both Broadway and Amsterdam Avenue are the coffee-houses and cafés where students engage in lengthy philosophical arguments, debate the topics of the day, or simply unwind.

116 St-Columbia University subway (line 1)

BROADWAY

START

The School of Journalism is one of Columbia's many McKim, Mead & White buildings. Founded in 1912 by publisher Joseph Pulitzer, it is the home of the Pulitzer Prize, awarded for the best in letters and music.

Alma Mater was sculpted by Daniel Chester French in 1903 and survived a bomb blast in the 1968 student demonstrations.

114TH ST

With its imposing facade and high dome, the Low Library dominates the main quadrangle. McKim, Mead & White designed it in 1895–7.

Butler Library is Columbia's main library.

Columbia University's first buildings were designed by McKim, Mead & White and built around a central quadrangle (p265).

AMSTERDAM AVENUE

← Graduation day at Columbia University's Morningside Heights Campus

The Sherman Fairchild Center was built in 1977 to house the university's life sciences departments.

Designed by the architects Howells & Stokes in 1907, St. Paul's Chapel is known for its fine woodwork and magnificent vaulted interior. It is full of light and has fine acoustics.

HARLEM AND MORNINGSIDE HEIGHTS

Locator Map
For more detail see p252

0 meters — 100
0 yards — 100
N ↑

FINISH

Student demonstrations put Columbia University in the news in 1968. The demonstrations were sparked by the university's plan to build a gymnasium in nearby Morningside Park. The protests forced the university to build elsewhere.

W 116TH ST

W 115TH ST

MORNINGSIDE DRIVE

W 113TH ST

→
Facade of the
Église de
Notre Dame

The Église de Notre Dame was built for a French-speaking congregation. Behind the altar is a replica of the grotto at Lourdes, France – the gift of a woman who believed her son was healed there.

If the Neo-Gothic Cathedral of St. John the Divine is ever finished, it will be the largest in the world. Although one-third of the structure has not yet been built, it can hold 10,000 parishioners (p254).

Did You Know

Columbia University's second campus, Manhattanville, opened in 2017.

BROOKLYN

Brooklyn became a New York borough in 1898, and for decades after served primarily as a residential and industrial neighborhood. Three times bigger than Manhattan, it has changed dramatically since the start of the 21st century. Districts such as Fort Greene, Williamsburg, Bushwick, and Cobble Hill are now among the most fashionable in the city, popular for their bars, flea markets, and hipster culture. Brooklyn offers a multitude of experiences. Its brownstone townhouses and tree-lined streets give way to encyclopedic museums, inventive restaurants, and innovative cultural hubs.

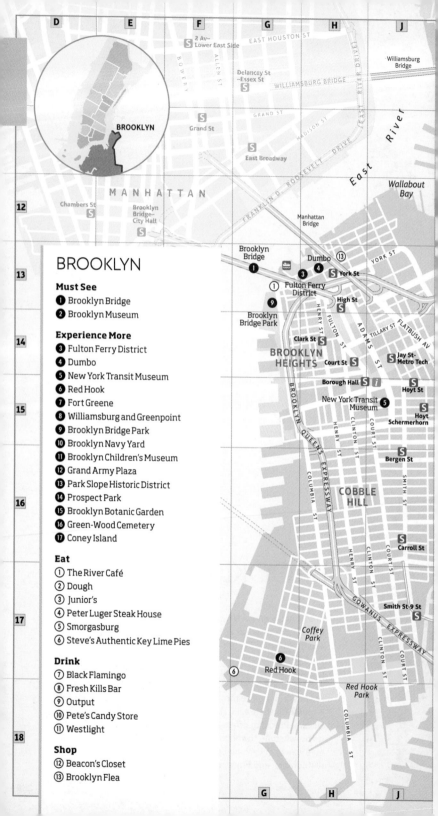

BROOKLYN

Must See
1 Brooklyn Bridge
2 Brooklyn Museum

Experience More
3 Fulton Ferry District
4 Dumbo
5 New York Transit Museum
6 Red Hook
7 Fort Greene
8 Williamsburg and Greenpoint
9 Brooklyn Bridge Park
10 Brooklyn Navy Yard
11 Brooklyn Children's Museum
12 Grand Army Plaza
13 Park Slope Historic District
14 Prospect Park
15 Brooklyn Botanic Garden
16 Green-Wood Cemetery
17 Coney Island

Eat
1 The River Café
2 Dough
3 Junior's
4 Peter Luger Steak House
5 Smorgasburg
6 Steve's Authentic Key Lime Pies

Drink
7 Black Flamingo
8 Fresh Kills Bar
9 Output
10 Pete's Candy Store
11 Westlight

Shop
12 Beacon's Closet
13 Brooklyn Flea

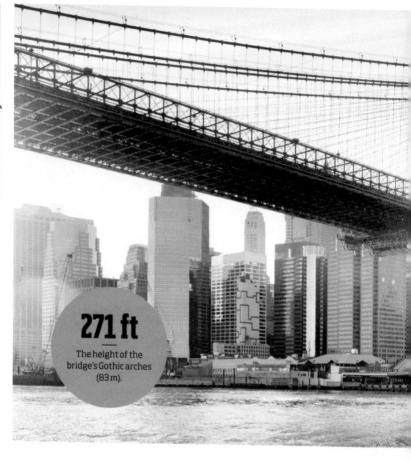

271 ft

The height of the bridge's Gothic arches (83 m).

❶

BROOKLYN BRIDGE

🅿 G13 🅂 Chambers St (J, Z), Brooklyn Bridge-City Hall (4, 5, 6), High St (A, C) to Manhattan side; High St (A, C) to Brooklyn side 🚌 M9, M15, M22, M103

The Brooklyn Bridge is one of New York City's oldest icons. Connecting the boroughs of Manhattan and Brooklyn, it is a vital commuter link, an architectural treasure, and a potent symbol of the American Dream.

Completed in 1883, the Brooklyn Bridge was the largest suspension bridge in the world for 20 years, and the first to be made of steel. Engineer John A. Roebling conceived of a bridge spanning the East River while ice-bound on a ferry to Brooklyn, which was then a separate city. The bridge took 16 years to build, required 600 workers, and claimed over 20 lives, including Roebling's. Most died of caisson disease (known as "the bends") after coming up from the underwater excavation chambers. The bridge used new and revolutionary building techniques, from making the cable wires to sinking the supports. When finished, the bridge linked the boroughs of Manhattan and Brooklyn, signaling the birth of one great metropolis. New Yorkers themselves were in awe of the Brooklyn Bridge upon completion. Aside from providing new commuter links, the bridge offered a dramatic addition to the landscape long before skyscrapers punctuated the skyline.

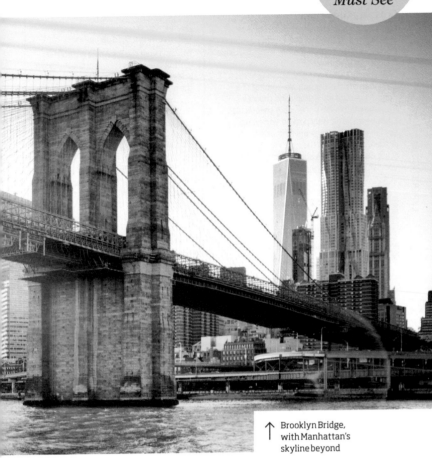

↑ Brooklyn Bridge, with Manhattan's skyline beyond

Timeline

1872

Roebling's son takes over construction, but is partly paralyzed by "the bends." His wife oversees the bridge's completion.

1883

Panic breaks out on Memorial Day after a woman trips; of the 20,000 on the bridge, 12 are crushed to death.

1869

△ Engineer Roebling crushes his foot between an incoming ferry and the ferry slip. He dies three weeks later.

1885

◁ Robert Odlum is the first to jump off the bridge, on a bet. He later dies from internal bleeding.

1983

△ The bridge's centennial is celebrated with a spectacular fireworks display.

Crossing the Bridge

Brooklyn Bridge remains an object of awe and beauty as much as a convenient commuter link between the boroughs – as many Brooklyn cyclists use the bridge to go to work as pedestrians and cars today. Strolling across this landmark has become something of a right of passage for visitors, and the views from the middle are undeniably spectacular. From here the densely packed skyscrapers of the Financial District seem to soar straight out of the water, while to the north the Empire State Building towers above Midtown. Today you can access the bridge's wooden walkway,

> **Strolling across this landmark has become something of a right of passage for visitors, and the views from the middle are undeniably spectacular.**

PICTURE PERFECT
Brooklyn Bridge

You can't visit the Big Apple without getting that perfect photo of the Brooklyn Bridge. You'll get the best close-ups of the bridge from the Fulton Ferry District (on the Brooklyn side); for full-length shots, walk up South Street north of the bridge (on the Manhattan side).

which is shared with cyclists, from Centre Street in Manhattan. From here, you can meander all the way to Downtown Brooklyn, or exit at the first set of stairs for Brooklyn Heights (p284), and the Fulton Ferry District (p278). The first section of the bridge does tend to get very crowded, especially in summer – go early if you can, or consider crossing the bridge from Brooklyn to Manhattan instead, which provides spectacular skyline views.

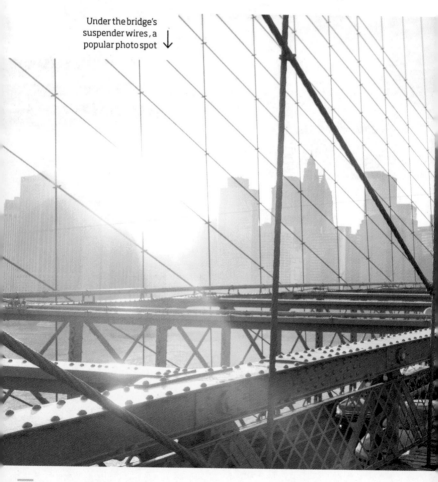

Under the bridge's suspender wires, a popular photo spot ↓

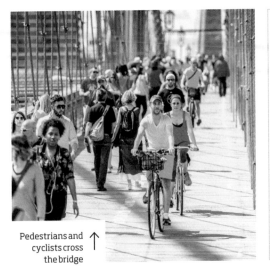

Pedestrians and ↑
cyclists cross
the bridge

EAT

The River Café
Linger at this idyllic spot after crossing from Manhattan. Set charmingly by the water, on the Brooklyn side, this Michelin-star restaurant offers exceptional food and spectacular bridge views.

📍G13 🏠1 Water St
🌐rivercafe.com

$ $ $

Did You Know?

Elephants marched across the bridge, as a demonstration of its safety, in 1884.

2 ⚡ Ⓜ 🖥 🏛

BROOKLYN MUSEUM

📍 M16 🏠 200 Eastern Pkwy Ⓢ Eastern Pkwy-Brooklyn Museum (2, 3)
🚌 B41, B45, B67, B69 🕐 11am–6pm Wed–Sun (to 10pm Thu), 11am–11pm
1st Sat of each month (except Sep) 🌐 brooklynmuseum.org

This cultural institution houses an encyclopedic collection of some one million objects, including an outstanding assemblage of Native American art, exquisite pieces of ancient Egyptian and Islamic art, and important American and European paintings.

When it opened in 1897, the Brooklyn Museum building, designed to be the largest cultural edifice in the world, was the greatest achievement of New York architects McKim, Mead & White. Today its five floors of galleries, covering 560,000 sq ft (50,025 sq m), house a collection to rival that of the Met. The Connecting Cultures exhibition can be found on the first floor; Arts of Asia and the Islamic World on the second; Egyptian, Classical, and European painting and sculpture on the third; the decorative arts on the fourth; and American art on the fifth. Among its treasures is a sacred ibis coffin, probably recovered from the animal cemetery of Tuna el-Gebel in Middle Egypt, works by great artists like Monet, and a 19th-century deerskin worn by a chief of the Blackfoot tribe. Judy Chicago's *The Dinner Party* installation can be found in the Elizabeth A. Sackler Center for Feminist Art.

←
Downtown is depicted in Francis Guy's *A Winter Scene in Brooklyn* (1820)

↑ John Singer Sargent's *An Out-of-Doors Study* (1889) shows artist Paul Helleu

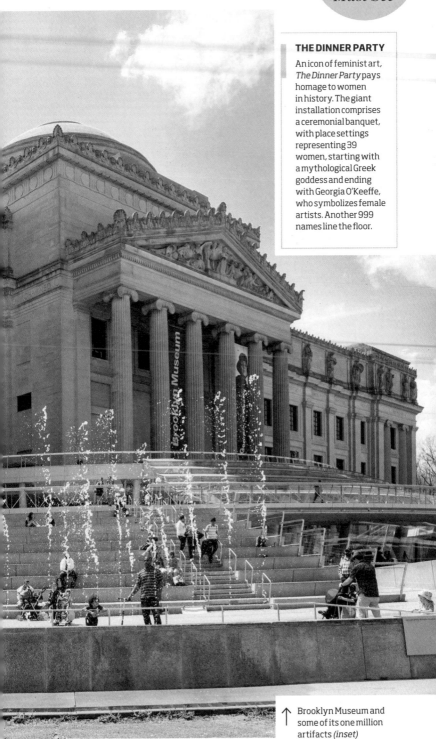

THE DINNER PARTY

An icon of feminist art, *The Dinner Party* pays homage to women in history. The giant installation comprises a ceremonial banquet, with place settings representing 39 women, starting with a mythological Greek goddess and ending with Georgia O'Keeffe, who symbolizes female artists. Another 999 names line the floor.

↑ Brooklyn Museum and some of its one million artifacts *(inset)*

EXPERIENCE MORE

③

Fulton Ferry District

📍 H13 🚇 High St (A, C)

This small historic district at the foot of the Brooklyn Bridge was once the busiest section of the East River, thanks to Robert Fulton's steamboat ferries. Among the landmarked 19th-century buildings is the Eagle Warehouse, built in Romanesque Revival style for the *Brooklyn Eagle* newspaper in 1893, which was edited for a while by poet Walt Whitman. Today, it is occupied by expensive apartments.

The old pier area still receives New York Water Taxis from Manhattan, and there are popular classical music concerts at Bargemusic. The original Grimaldi's pizza recipe can be enjoyed at Juliana's Pizza (not to be confused with Grimaldi's restaurant, on the same street), while the Brooklyn Ice Cream Factory offers freshly made ice creams in just eight delectable flavors.

④

Dumbo

📍 H13 🚇 York St (F), High St (A, C)

Dumbo – "Down Under the Manhattan Bridge Overpass" – is a ritzy area of converted brick factories between the Manhattan and Brooklyn bridges. The spacious lofts were colonized by artists in the 1970s, and since the 1990s the neighborhood has been transformed by art galleries, hip restaurants, luxury condominiums, and bars.

The redeveloped waterfront park offers an unmissable view of Manhattan, and St. Ann's Warehouse, a revered arts institution, occupies an old warehouse on the park's edge.

⑤

New York Transit Museum

📍 J15 🏛 Boerum Pl and Schermerhorn St
🚇 Borough Hall (2, 3, 4, 5), Jay St-MetroTech (A, C, F, R)
🕐 10am–4pm Tue–Fri, 11am–5pm Sat & Sun
🌐 nytransitmuseum.org

Charting the evolution of the city's public transit system,

BARGEMUSIC

Chamber music on a river barge? It might seem an odd concept, but the acoustics at Bargemusic are first-class. Concerts featuring performers from around the world are held five days a week on the converted coffee barge, moored just under the Brooklyn Bridge, at 1 Water St. Purchase tickets online (bargemusic.org) or call (800) 838-3006. Concerts run for 1 hour to 1 hour and 30 minutes.

Amazing views of
Manhattan from Fulton
Ferry State Park

this museum appropriately
occupies the former Court
Street shuttle station.

Exhibits include models,
photographs and maps, as
well as aged turnstiles and a
few interactive displays of
fuel technologies. Visitors can
explore various models of the
restored subway trains and
tram carts on the old station
platforms. There's also a small
exhibition space and store in
Grand Central Terminal (p188)
in Manhattan.

Red Hook

🚇 H17 🚊 Smith St–9th St
(F, G)

Settled by the Dutch in 1636,
Red Hook ("Roode Hoek") got
its name from the color of the
soil and the *hoek* (corner)
shape of the land where the
New York and Gowanus bays
meet. It became one of the
busiest and toughest dock-
lands in the US, inspiring the
1954 film *On the Waterfront*,
and Arthur Miller's play *A View
from the Bridge* (1955).

Today, Red Hook's water-
front is a surprising blend of

↑ A converted town-
house in Brooklyn's
Fort Greene

brick warehouses, cycle paths,
cobblestoned blocks and
stores, and its laid-back vibe
makes it unlike any other part
of the city. A few independent
stores and places to eat dot
Van Brunt Street, the area's
busiest strip. The Red Hook
Ball Fields host soccer tournaments, and Latino food stands
on summer weekends.

Fort Greene

🚇 K14 🚊 Atlantic Av (B, D,
N, Q, R, 2, 3, 4, 5), Fulton St
(G) 🌐 bam.org

Home to Saturday's Brooklyn
Flea, Fort Greene is full of
beautiful Italianate and East-
lake townhouses built in the
mid-19th century. At its heart
is Fort Greene Park, designed
by Frederick Law Olmsted and
Calvert Vaux in 1867, crowned
by the Prison Ship Martyrs'
Monument (1908), commem-
orating the estimated 11,500
Americans who died in British
floating prison camps during
the Revolutionary War.

Fort Greene is home to the
Brooklyn Academy of Music
(BAM), at 30 Lafayette Av, a
leading cultural venue where
outstanding performances
often lean toward the avant-
garde. BAM's main building,
the 1908 Howard Gilman
Opera House, is a Beaux Arts
gem, designed by Herts &
Tallant. The nearby 1904
Harvey Theater stages most
of BAM's plays.

Williamsburg and
Greenpoint

🚇 K10 & M10 🚊 Bedford
Av (L) for Williamsburg,
Greenpoint Av or Nassau
Av (G) for Greenpoint

One of the city's trendiest
neighborhoods, Williamsburg
occupies much of northeast
Brooklyn, its main strip at
Bedford Avenue crowded with

SHOP

Beacon's Closet

Massive used-clothing
paradise for modern
and vintage attire.
Smaller branches in
Park Slope, Bushwick,
and Greenwich Village.

🚇 M10 📍 74 Guernsey
St, Greenpoint
🌐 beanscloset.com

Brooklyn Flea

In Fort Greene (Sat) and
Williamsburg (Sun), this
market has over 200
stands, artisanal food,
and arts and crafts.

🚇 H13 📍 176 Lafayette
Av, Fort Greene; 50 Kent
Av, between North 11th
and North 12th streets,
Williamsburg
🌐 brooklynflea.com

boutiques, record stores, bars,
coffee shops, and restaurants.
Big on nightlife, this area is a
noted indie rock venue.

Culinary attractions include
the Brooklyn Brewery, Mast
Brothers chocolate factory
(tours available) and
Smorgasburg, an outdoor
food market that runs April
through to October (p282).
Another Brooklyn Flea is
based here on Sundays.

Greenpoint is a traditional
Polish stronghold with an artsy
crowd. The Russian Orthodox
Cathedral of the Transfigur-
ation is at North 12th Street
on Driggs Avenue, a Byzantine
Revival landmark with five
patinated-copper onion domes
that loom above McCarren
Park's trees. The park forms
an unofficial boundary
between the two neighbor-
hoods and contains a historic
(1936) swimming pool and the
renowned McCarren Hotel.

9

Brooklyn Bridge Park

📍 G13 🚇 From Manhattan Bridge to Atlantic Av Ⓢ High St (A, C), York St (F), Clark St (2, 3) 🌐 brooklyn bridgepark.org

A series of playgrounds, sports amenities, stellar viewpoints, and reclaimed docks stretch along the rejuvenated waterfront from Dumbo to Brooklyn Heights. The section of the park just east of the Brooklyn Bridge features the traditional Jane's Carousel, spacious open lawn, and giant steps for picnicking.

On the other side of the bridge, Pier One offers free kayaking on summer weekends, while Pier Two features shuffleboard courts and a roller rink. Pier Five has sports fields and a picnic area, while Pier Six is brilliant for kids, with a popular water park, climbing area, and a giant slide.

10

Brooklyn Navy Yard

📍 K12 🚇 From Manhattan Bridge to Williamsburg Bridge ℹ BLDG 92, 63 Flushing Av Ⓢ High St (A, C), York St (F) 🌐 brooklyn navyyard.org

Transformed in recent years from a near-derelict site, the Brooklyn Navy Yard now has over 300 businesses, from Brooklyn Grange Farms to Steiner Studios (where *Boardwalk Empire* and *Girls* were filmed). Get oriented at the Brooklyn Navy Yard Center at BLDG 92, which charts the history of the site, and includes models of well-known ships built here, such as the USS *Ohio*).

↑ Looking out over Brooklyn Navy Yard, a frequent film set

Other highlights include Kings County Distillery, making craft bourbon.

11

Brooklyn Children's Museum

📍 N15 🚇 145 Brooklyn Av Ⓢ Kingston Av (3), Kingston-Throop Av (C) 🕐 10am–5pm Tue–Fri (till 6pm Thu), 10am–7pm Sat-Sun 🌐 brooklynkids.org

Founded in 1899, the Brooklyn Children's Museum was the first to be designed especially for children. Since then, it has been a model, inspiration, and consultant for the development of more than 250 museums for children across the country and all over the world. Housed in a hi-tech underground building dating from 1976, it is one of the most imaginative children's museums anywhere. In 2008, a "green" renovation by Uruguayan architect Rafael Viñoly added solar panels and other energy-saving devices, and expanded the museum space.

Galleries contain hands-on exhibitions that focus on the environment, science, and local neighborhood life – which highlights various multicultural districts around Brooklyn. The "Totally Tots" area is dedicated to children under the age of five, with a "Water Wonders" play quarter. The live animals on display downstairs will especially thrill the little ones. There are also play stores and restaurants where children can buy, sell, and even make (fake) pizza. Special events and classes, such as Zumba for kids, workshops, and art projects, take place daily.

→ The sun sets over Manhattan, as seen from Brooklyn

⑫ Grand Army Plaza

◾M16 ◾Plaza St at Flatbush Av ◾Grand Army Plaza (2, 3)

Frederick Law Olmsted and Calvert Vaux laid out this grand oval in 1870 as an imposing gateway to Prospect Park. The Eastern Parkway, the world's first parkway, also begins here.

The Soldiers' and Sailors' Arch and its sculptures were added in 1892 as a grand tribute to the Union Army. Designed by John H. Duncan, the arch is reminiscent of Imperial Roman monuments, with its intricate carving and detail. Stanford White modified the arch between 1894 and 1901 to accommodate the bronze sculptures by Philip Martiny and Frederick MacMonnies, along with the columns. The bust of John F. Kennedy here is, somewhat surprisingly, the only official New York City monument to the 35th president of the United States. The arch itself is occasionally open for special exhibitions.

⑬ Park Slope Historic District

◾L16 ◾From Prospect Park West below Flatbush Av, to 8th/7th/5th Avs ◾Grand Army Plaza (2, 3), 7 Av (F)

This wonderful enclave of beautiful Victorian town houses on the edge of Prospect Park dates from the 1880s, when it served upper-middle-class professionals who could commute into Manhattan after the Brooklyn Bridge opened in 1883. The shady streets are lined with houses in every architectural style popular in the late 19th century, some with the towers, turrets, and curlicues so representative of the era. Particularly fine examples are in Romanesque Revival style, with rounded entry arches.

The Montauk Club at 25 Eighth Avenue combines the style of Venice's Ca' d'Oro palazzo with the friezes and gargoyles of the Montauks, for whom this popular 19th-century private social club was named.

DRINK

Black Flamingo
Latin and 1970s theme bar with dance floor below.

◾L10 ◾168 Borinquen Pl ◾Mon ◾black flamingonyc.com

Fresh Kills Bar
Best of Williamsburg's hand-crafted cocktails.

◾M10 ◾161 Grand St ◾freshkillsbar.com

Output
Williamsburg's popular warehouse dance club.

◾M10 ◾74 Wythe Av ◾Mon & Tue ◾outputclub.com

Pete's Candy Store
Friendly local pub, with free live music.

◾M10 ◾111 12th St ◾Tue ◾petes candystore.com

Westlight
Soak up sensational city views.

◾M10 ◾111 North 12th St ◾westlightnyc.com

EAT

Dough

Fabulous, enormous doughnuts, including a delicious hibiscus option.

📍M13 🏠 448 Lafayette Av
🌐doughbrooklyn.com

Junior's

Venerable Brooklyn diner most famous for classic NY cheesecake.

📍K14 🏠 386 Flatbush Av Extension, at DeKalb Av 🌐juniors cheesecake.com

Peter Luger Steak House

Heavenly porterhouse (the only cut served) since 1887. Cash only.

📍L10 🏠 178 Broadway 🌐peterluger.com

Smorgasburg

America's largest open-air food market has over 100 tempting stands on Saturdays (Apr–Oct).

📍M10 🏠 East River State Park, 90 Kent Av 🕐Mon–Fri, Sun, mid-Nov–Apr 🌐smorgasburg.com

Steve's Authentic Key Lime Pies

Some of the tastiest key lime pies in the Northeast.

📍G17 🏠 Pier 40, 185 Van Dyke St 🌐stevesauthentic.com

14

Prospect Park

📍M17 🚇Grand Army Plaza (2, 3), Prospect Park (B, Q) 🌐prospectpark.org

Olmsted and Vaux considered this park, which opened in 1867, better than their earlier Central Park *(p238)*. The Long Meadow, a sweep of broad lawns and grand vistas, is the longest unbroken swath of green space in New York.

Olmsted's belief was that "a feeling of relief is experienced by entering them" (the parks) "on escaping from the cramped, confining, and controlling circumstances of the streets of the town." That vision is still as true today as it was a century and a half ago.

Notable features include Stanford White's colonnaded Croquet Shelter, and the pools and weeping willows of the Vale of Cashmere. The Music Grove bandstand hosts summer concerts.

A favorite feature of the park is the Camperdown Elm, an old and twisted tree planted in 1872, which has inspired many poems and paintings. Ranger-led tours are the best way to see the park and its wide variety of landscapes, from Classical gardens with statues to rocky glens with running brooks.

15

Brooklyn Botanic Garden

📍M15 🏠900 Washington Av 🚇Prospect Park (B, Q), Eastern Pkwy (2, 3) 🕐Tue–Sun; times vary, check website for details 🌐bbg.org

Though not vast, this garden has many delights. Designed by the Olmsted Brothers in 1910, it features an Elizabethan-style "knot" garden and one of North America's largest collections of roses.

The central showpiece is a Japanese hill-and-pond garden, with a teahouse and Shinto shrine. In late April and early May the promenade is aglow with delicate Japanese cherry blossoms, celebrated in an annual festival of Japanese culture. April is also the time to visit the Magnolia Plaza, where some 80 trees display their beautiful, creamy blossoms against a backdrop of daffodils on Boulder Hill.

The Fragrance Garden has raised beds of heavily scented

Visitors seeking traditional beachside fun on Coney Island ↑

> **In the mid-1800s, Brooklyn poet Walt Whitman composed many of his works on Coney Island, which was at that time purely untamed Atlantic coastline.**

and textured plants all labeled in Braille. The conservatory has a large bonsai collection and some rare rain forest trees.

 16

Green-Wood Cemetery

📍 L18 🏠 500 25th St at Fifth Av Ⓢ 25 St (R) 🕐 Apr-Sep: 7am-7pm; Oct-Mar: 7am-5pm 🌐 green-wood.com

This 478-acre (193-ha) cemetery was founded in 1838, and today it is almost a city park, both sprawling and beautiful. Several famous citizens are interred here, including the street artist Jean-Michel Basquiat (1960–88), abolitionist Henry Ward

 ←

Stunning blossom in the Japanese Garden, Brooklyn Botanic Garden

Beecher (1813–87), composer Leonard Bernstein (1918–90), and glass artist Louis Comfort Tiffany (1848–1933). The whole Steinway family of the piano-making dynasty also lie at rest in a 119-room mausoleum.

 17

Coney Island

📍 N13 Ⓢ Stillwell Av (D, F, N, Q), W 8 St (F, Q) 🌐 coney island.com

New Yorkers have been visiting Brooklyn's Coney Island for seaside fun – at the cost of a single journey – since 1867. Crowds continue to flock to this peninsular neighborhood to revel in its kitsch amusement parks, plummeting rollercoasters, and candy floss stands, away from the hubbub of Manhattan.

In the mid-1800s, Brooklyn poet Walt Whitman composed many of his works on Coney Island, which was at that time

purely untamed Atlantic coastline. By the 1920s, Coney Island was billing itself as the "World's Largest Playground," home to three huge fairgrounds. The subway arrived in 1920, and the 1921 boardwalk ensured Coney Island's popularity throughout the Great Depression.

Coney Island has been modernized, much to the chagrin of local residents, who feared that its character would be lost. However, the boardwalk still yields lovely ocean views, and the modern Luna Park features a number of spine-tingling rides, including the Cyclone roller-coaster, which at roughly 90 years old has been designated an official city landmark. The more faint-hearted might prefer the Wonder Wheel, which also has an official landmark status, and offers beautiful views of the city. Opening times vary – check the park's website for detailed opening times and price lists.

Further attractions on Coney Island include the New York Aquarium, home to over 350 species. There's also the Coney Island Museum, which has memorabilia, souvenirs, and relics of old rides from the amusement park. The Mermaid Parade in June (see p54) is also a major annual event.

A SHORT WALK
BROOKLYN HEIGHTS

Distance 1 mile (1.5 km) **Nearest subway** Clark St
Time 20 minutes

Facing Lower Manhattan, across the East River, Brooklyn Heights is one of New York's most elegant and historic neighborhoods. The city's wealthy elites built brownstone townhouses here in the 1820s, when the Heights became the city's first commuter suburb. The completion of the Brooklyn Bridge in 1883 intensified development. Today, Brooklyn Heights is an affluent neighborhood, and the perfect place to admire Manhattan's famous skyline.

Brooklyn Bridge Park/Dumbo Ferry Terminal

START

Bargemusic, moored just under the Brooklyn Bridge, is a renovated coffee barge dating from the late 19th century, and holds nightly chamber music performances (p278).

Brooklyn Ice Cream Factory is based in an early 20th-century fireboat house on the Fulton Ferry Pier, and serves just eight flavors of ice cream.

FURMAN ST

COLUMBIA HEIG

↑ Brooklyn Ice Cream Factory, based in an early 20th-century fireboat house

BROOKLYN QUEENS EXPY

COLUMBIA HEIGHTS

WILLO

70 Willow Street is said to be where Truman Capote wrote Breakfast at Tiffany's.

Brooklyn Heights Promenade is a pedestrian path providing sensational views of the Statue of Liberty, Lower Manhattan's skyscrapers, and the Brooklyn Bridge.

COLUMBIA HEIGHTS

CLARK ST

| 0 meters | 75 |
| 0 yards | 75 |

N ↑

FINISH ●

Just below the Brooklyn Bridge, Fulton Ferry District is a historic wharf area named after Robert Fulton, the steamboat king. It features iconic landmarks such as the Eagle Warehouse with its large, glass clock-window (p278).

Juliana's Pizza is the original location of Patsy Grimaldi's famous coal-oven pizzas, not to be confused with the newer Grimaldi's next door.

Locator Map
For more detail see p270

Did You Know?

Brooklyn Heights, or "America's first suburb," was one of the first areas outside of Manhattan to be settled.

24 Middagh St is the area's oldest house, erected in 1824. Other examples of old buildings can be found along Middagh and Willow.

Plymouth Church was the base of pastor Henry Ward Beecher, abolitionist and campaigner for women's rights. It was also a stop on the Underground Railroad, where slaves were hidden on their way to freedom.

Clark St subway
Ⓜ (lines A,C)

↑ Fulton Ferry District, a wharf area with spectacular views across the river

Must Sees

1 Cloisters Museum
7 New York Botanical Garden
8 Bronx Zoo

Experience More

2 Hispanic Society
3 Morris-Jumel Mansion
4 George Washington Bridge and Fort Washington Park
5 Shabazz Center
6 Ralph Ellison Memorial
9 Poe Cottage
10 Woodlawn Cemetery
11 Belmont and Arthur Avenue
12 Yankee Stadium
13 The Bronx Musuem of the Arts
14 Flushing Meadows-Corona Park
15 Queens Museum
16 Louis Armstrong Museum
17 Steinway & Sons
18 Noguchi Musuem and Socrates Sculpture Park
19 Museum of the Moving Image and Kaufman Astoria Studio
20 MoMA PS1, Queens
21 Historic Richmond Town
22 Jacques Marchais Museum of Tibetan Art
23 The Snug Harbor Cultural Center and Botanic Garden
24 Alice Austen House
25 Little Sri Lanka

BEYOND
THE CENTER

Though officially part of New York City, Upper Manhattan and the outer boroughs (the Bronx, Queens, and Staten Island) are quite different in feel. Largely residential, and without the world-famous sights that are typically associated with New York, these calmer areas are well worth exploring for their countless attractions. Here you'll discover the country's biggest zoo, idyllic botanical gardens, ground-breaking museums, iconic sports arenas, and a restaurant scene representing almost every ethnicity.

GETTING TO KNOW
BEYOND THE CENTER

Leave the hubbub of downtown Manhattan behind you and experience the city beond the center. Explore suburban Upper Manhattan and, to the north, the Bronx, which is the only borough on the mainland. Across the East River lies multicultural Queens, while suburban Staten Island sits in the harbor.

PAGE 290

UPPER MANHATTAN

Once a Dutch settlement, now a suburban area with little of the bustle of downtown, Upper Manhattan is perfect for escaping the inner city. Here you'll find relaxed museums, idyllic green spaces, and beautiful houses.

Best for
History, medieval art, escaping the crowds

Home to
The Cloisters Museum, Fort Washington Park

Experience
The peaceful gardens of the Cloisters Museum

PAGE 294

THE BRONX

This once prosperous suburb became a byword for urban decay in the mid-20th century, but the Bronx is slowly gentrifying. There are large pockets of beauty waiting to be discovered in this borough, comprising historic mansions, tranquil parks, an outstanding botanic garden and zoo, and the famous Yankee Stadium.

Best for
Baseball, green spaces

Home to
New York Botanical Garden, Bronx Zoo, Yankee Stadium

Experience
The thrill of a baseball game at Yankee Stadium

QUEENS

Queens, the city's largest borough, has a trove of cultural attractions – from piano showrooms and sculpture parks to a museum dedicated to the art of filmmaking, and Louis Armstrong's house. It's a real melting pot of cultures, and there's a huge array of ethnic restaurants here, with the aromas of Greek, Thai, and Indian food lingering in its streets. Queens is also one of the epicenters of New York's craft beer renaissance, and breweries operate tasting or "tap" rooms.

Best for
Mulitcultural New York, diverse cuisines, craft beer, unique museums

Home to
Queens Museum, Museum of the Moving Image, Steinway & Sons, Louis Armstrong Museum

Experience
Seasonal pours at one of Queens' craft breweries

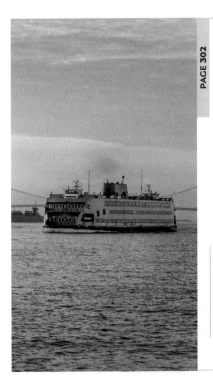

STATEN ISLAND

Its famous ferry ride aside, Staten Island and its attractions are not well known to New Yorkers in general but it would be a mistake to dismiss the "forgotten borough" so readily. Visitors who venture beyond the ferry terminal will be pleasantly surprised to find hills, lakes, and greenery, with expanses of open space, amazing harbor views, and well-preserved early New York buildings. One of the biggest surprises here is a cache of Tibetan art that is hidden away in a replica of a Buddhist temple.

Best for
A different view of Manhattan, history of the city, Sri Lankan food, Tibetan art

Home to
Historic Richmond Town, Jacques Marchais Museum of Tibetan Art, Little Sri Lanka

Experience
Life in the 19th century at Historic Richmond Town

$\rightarrow$

❶ 🛡️ ⚡ 🖥️ 🛍️

THE CLOISTERS MUSEUM

🏛️ Fort Tryon Park 🚇 190 St (A) 🚌 M4 🕙 10am–5:15pm daily (Nov–Feb: to 4:45pm) 🚫 Thanksgiving 🌐 metmuseum.org/visit/met-cloisters

Crowning a hilltop in Upper Manhattan, this extraordinary museum transports visitors to a European monastery thanks to its authentic, medieval-style building, reconstructed cloisters, and rich art collection.

Despite appearances, the Met's museum of medieval art resides in a building constructed in the early 20th century. Sculptor George Grey Barnard founded the museum in 1914 before John D. Rockefeller Jr. funded the Metropolitan Museum of Art's 1925 purchase of the collection. Rockefeller also donated the site at Fort Tryon Park for the museum's construction. Designed by modern architect Charles Cullens, who was responsible for Riverside Church *(p258)*, the stunning building reflects the content of its collection, incorporating medieval cloisters, chapels, and halls from Europe that were then rebuilt here. The cloisters, for example, are named Cuxa, Saint-Guilhem, Bonnefont, and Trie, after their French origins. The museum is organized roughly in chronological order, starting with the Romanesque period (AD 1,000) and moving to the Gothic (1150–1520). Sculptures, stained glass, and paintings are on the lower floor and the Unicorn Tapestries are on the upper floor. There are also gardens to enjoy.

Monastic in appearance, Upper Manhattan's Cloisters Museum

UNICORN TAPESTRIES

This set of seven beautiful tapestries (also known as "The Hunt of the Unicorn"), woven in Flanders around 1500, depicts the quest for, capture, sacrifice, and ultimate resurrection of the mythical unicorn. Its incredible detailing and mysterious symbolism – critics still argue about its meaning – make it one of the greatest medieval artworks. The tapestries have been interpreted both as complicated metaphors for Christ and a celebration of matrimony.

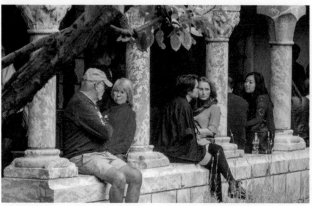

← Visitors enjoy the Benedictine Cuxa cloister gardens, surrounded by marble columns

1934
—
The year construction of this unique museum began.

↑ The beautiful sanctuary at the Cloisters Museum

EXPERIENCE MORE

Hispanic Society

📍 Broadway at 155th St
Ⓢ 155 St (C), 157 St (1)
🕐 For renovations
🌐 hispanicsociety.org

The Hispanic Society of America owns one of the greatest collections of Hispanic art outside of Spain. The extensive collections include Spanish sculpture, decorative arts, prints, and photographs, with changing exhibits throughout the year. The main gallery, in Spanish Renaissance style, holds Goya's famous *Duchess of Alba*. The adjacent Bancaja Gallery contains Joaquín Sorolla y Bastida's *Vision of Spain*, commissioned in 1911. Its 14 large murals depict people and life in Spain. The balcony above offers some of the best works: paintings by El Greco, such as *Holy Family*, and portraits by Velázquez.

The Hispanic Society is based in Audubon Terrace, a complex of Classical Revival buildings in Washington Heights, completed in 1908 by Charles Pratt Huntington. Funded by the architect's cousin, civic benefactor Archer Huntington, the entrance plaza contains statues by Archer's wife, Anna Hyatt Huntington. The majority of the complex is occupied by Boricua College, and the society is the only museum here.

Morris-Jumel Mansion

📍 65 Jumel Terrace at West 160th St and Edgecombe Ave Ⓢ 163 St-Amsterdam Av (C) 🕐 10am–4pm Tue–Fri, 10am–5pm Sat & Sun
🌐 morrisjumel.org

This is one of New York's few pre-Revolutionary buildings and it has a long and, at times,

↑ The beautifully restored exterior of Morris-Jumel Mansion

scandalous history. Now a museum with nine restored period rooms, it was built in 1765 for Roger Morris. In 1810 it was bought and updated by Stephen Jumel, a merchant of French-Caribbean descent, and his wife Eliza. The museum exhibits include many original Jumel pieces. Tours take place at noon on Saturday and 2pm on Sunday.

The pair furnished the house with souvenirs of their many visits to France. Her boudoir has a "dolphin" chair, reputedly bought from Napoleon. Eliza's social climbing and love affairs scandalized New York society. It was rumored that she let her husband bleed to death in 1832 so she could inherit his fortune. She later married Aaron Burr, aged 77, and divorced him three years later on the day he died.

The exterior of the Palladian-style, wood-sided Georgian house, with a Classical portico and octagonal wing, has been restored.

George Washington Bridge and Fort Washington Park

Ⓢ 175 St (A), 181 St (1)
🌐 panynj.gov

French architect Le Corbusier called this "the only seat of grace in the disordered city." While not as famous a landmark as its Brooklyn equivalent, this bridge by engineer Othmar Ammann and his architect Cass Gilbert has its own individual character and history. Plans for a bridge linking Manhattan to New Jersey had been in the pipeline for more than 60 years before the Port of New York Authority raised the necessary $59 million to fund the project. It was Ammann who suggested a road bridge rather than a more expensive rail link. Work began in 1927, and the bridge was opened in 1931. Today it is a vital link for commuter traffic between Manhattan and New Jersey's Fort Lee, and is in constant use, carrying over 53 million vehicles per year.

Gilbert planned to clad the bridge's two towers with masonry but funds did not permit it, leaving an elegant skeletal structure 600 ft (183 m) high and 4,760 ft (1,451 m) long. The lower deck was added in 1962.

Below the eastern tower in Fort Washington Park is a lighthouse that dates from 1889, and was saved from demolition in 1951 by public pressure. Many thousands of young New Yorkers and children all around the world have loved the bedtime story *The Little Red Lighthouse and the Great Gray Bridge* (1942), and wrote letters to save the lighthouse. Author Hildegarde Hoyt Swift wove the tale around her two favorite New York landmarks.

The Little Red Lighthouse Festival is held here every September and includes a special guest reading of the famous book.

5

Shabazz Center

🏠 3940 Broadway, at West 165th Street 🚇 168 St (A, C, 1) 🕐 10am–4pm Tue–Fri, 10am–5pm Sat & Sun 🌐 theshabazzcenter.org

In Washington Heights, the Shabazz Center, or, to quote its full name, the Malcolm X and Dr Betty Shabazz Memorial and Educational Center, commemorates the life of the influential African-American minister and political activist Malcolm X. The center holds events and film screenings honoring the work of Malcolm X, while the first floor contains touch-screen panels that highlight key phases of his life via interviews and videos.

The center occupies what's left of the Audubon Ballroom, the scene of Malcolm X's assassination in 1965. It is now part of the Columbia-Presbyterian Hospital.

Born Malcolm Little in Nebraska, in 1925, Malcolm X spent much of his later life in New York as a committed follower of Elijah Muhammad's Nation of Islam. He was a key inspiration for the Black Power movement.

6

Ralph Ellison Memorial

🏠 West 150th St and Riverside Dr 🚇 145 St (1)

African-American author Ralph Ellison is commemorated by this small but poignant memorial. The bronze structure, with a cut-out male figure, was created by Elizabeth Catlett and dedicated in 2003. The four surrounding stone markers are engraved with Ellison quotes, notably the opening lines of *Invisible Man* (1952): "I am invisible, understand, simply because people refuse to see me."

Born in the segregated Deep South in 1913, Ralph Ellison moved to Harlem in 1936, living nearby at 730 Riverside Drive.

→ George Washington Bridge, linking New York with New Jersey

7 🖋️ Ⓜ️ 🖥️ 🏛️

NEW YORK BOTANICAL GARDEN

📍 Kazimiroff Blvd, Bronx River Parkway (Exit 7W) 🚇 Bedford Pk Blvd (4, B, D) 🚌 Bx26 🕐 10am–6pm Tue–Sun (until 5pm mid-Jan–Feb) 🌐 nybg.org

One of the oldest and largest botanical gardens in the world, this lush park provides a nature escape in the heart of the bustling Bronx.

The New York Botanical Garden offers 250 acres (100 ha) of dazzling beauty and hands-on enjoyment. From the nation's most glorious Victorian glasshouse to the Everett Children's Adventure Garden, this green space is alive with things to discover. Perhaps most importantly, the New York Botanical Garden has 50 gardens and plant collections, and 50 acres (20 ha) of uncut woodland in the Thain Family Forest. This is some of the most important woodland in the city; it follows the same trails used by the Lenape tribe and is home to trees that date back to the American Revolution. A great way to see the garden is by joining the tram tour. This 20-minute, narrated ride includes nine stops, so visitors can hop on and off.

① The Enid A. Haupt Conservatory is a stunning Victorian-style glasshouse, and consists of eleven interconnecting glass galleries. These house "A World of Plants," which comprises rain forests, deserts, aquatic plants, and seasonal exhibitions.

② The Peggy Rockefeller Rose Garden contains over 2,700 rose bushes, and is best visited in early summer when the roses are in bloom. Named by David Rockefeller, for his horticulturalist wife, the garden was laid out in 1988.

③ Blossoming trees in the Japanese Garden.

Did You Know?

The grounds are free to enter all day Wednesday and 10am-noon Saturday.

↑ Fall colors and falling leaves in the Thain Family Forest

8

BRONX ZOO

⌂ 2300 Southern Blvd, Bronx Ⓢ E Tremont Av (2, 5) 🚌 Bx9, Bx12, Bx19, Bx22, Bx39, BxM11, Q44 🕐 10am–5pm Mon–Fri, 10am–5:30pm Sat & Sun 🌐 bronxzoo.com

America's biggest urban wildlife park is right here in the Bronx. Popular with little and big kids alike, the zoo's residents include bears, bison, baboons, and everything in between.

A Day at the Zoo

Opened in 1899, the Bronx Zoo is home to more than 4,000 animals of 500 species, which live in realistic representations of their natural habitats. The zoo is a leader in the perpetuation of endangered species, such as the Indian rhinoceros and the snow leopard.

Its 265 acres (107 ha) of woods, streams, and parklands accommodate, in season, a children's zoo, the Butterfly Garden, and the Wild Asia Monorail; other attractions include World of Reptiles, a one-of-a-kind bug carousel, and a 4-D theater experience. Tours take place at 10:15 and 11:45am, and last an hour.

The attractive Wildlife Conservation Society building, Bronx Zoo ↓

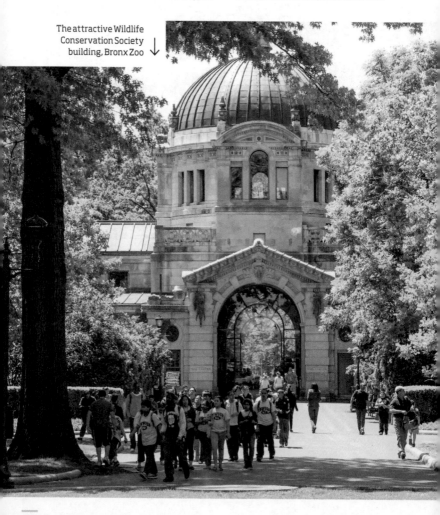

💬 INSIDER TIP
Children's Zoo

If the little ones need to let off steam, head to the Children's Zoo, which can be found near the Zoo Center and Madagascar! exhibit. Here, kids can monkey around by crawling through prairie dog tunnels, trying on turtle shells, and even petting and feeding some animals. Check the website for opening times.

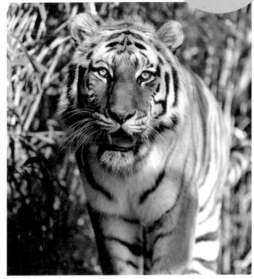

↑ Magnificent Amur tigers are on view all year at Tiger Mountain

↑ Visitors look for residents at the tropical rain forest JungleWorld

THE CONGO GORILLA FOREST

This award-winning replica of a central African rain forest is home to the largest population of Western Lowland gorillas in the US, as well as a family of pygmy marmosets, the world's smallest monkeys.

Edgar Allan Poe's cottage, where the writer lived and wrote for three years

Poe Cottage

🅰 2640 Grand Concourse
🚇 Kingsbridge Rd (D, 4)
🕐 10am–3pm Thu & Fri, 10am–4pm Sat, 1–5pm Sun
🌐 bronxhistorical society.org

Built as a modest laborer's dwelling around 1812, this white-clapboard house, set incongruously today in the midst of working-class Latino housing blocks, was Edgar Allan Poe's rural home from 1846 to 1849. The charming house originally stood on farmland a short distance away on East Kingsbridge Road, but it was moved here (at the northern tip of the specially created Poe Park) in 1913.

Although Poe was already relatively successful as the writer of The Raven, he was dogged by financial problems in the mid-1800s. He moved here with his wife, Virginia, and her mother, Maria, in search of fresh rural air. Sadly, soon after they arrived at the cottage, Virginia died of tuberculosis, aged just 24. Heartbroken, Poe managed to write a few revered works while in mourning, including the moving poem Annabel Lee, which was written in memory of his wife. Maria outlived them both, and moved out of the cottage shortly after Poe's mysterious death in Baltimore two years later.

Today, the restored cottage contains several rooms set up to look as they did during Poe's time. There is also a small gallery of artwork from the 1840s within the vicinity.

The elegant Poe Park Visitor Center stands separate from Poe Cottage itself, at 2650 Grand Concourse. Designed by the Japanese architect Toshiko Mori, the educational facility features rotating exhibitions of art. Open Tuesday through Saturday, its sharply angled roof was inspired by a raven's outstretched wings, in honor of the writer's most famous literary work.

Woodlawn Cemetery

🅰 Webster Av and East 233rd St 🚇 Woodlawn (4)
🕐 8:30am–4:30pm daily
🌐 thewoodlawn cemetery.org

Established in 1863, Woodlawn Cemetery is the burial place of many a wealthy and distinguished New Yorker. Memorials and tombstones are set on beautiful grounds. F. W. Woolworth and many members of his family are interred in a mausoleum only a little less ornate than the building that carries the family name. The pink marble vault of meat magnate Herman Armour is oddly reminiscent of a ham.

Other New Yorkers who are buried here include Mayor Fiorello La Guardia; Rowland Hussey Macy, the founder of the great Macy's department store; author Herman Melville; and jazz legend Duke Ellington.

Belmont and Arthur Avenue

🚇 Fordham Rd (B, D, S), then 🚌 Bx12 🌐 arthuravenue bronx.com

Within walking distance of the botanical garden and zoo, Belmont is home to one of New York's largest Italian-American communities. This is a more authentic and much larger alternative to Little Italy in Manhattan, and its main thoroughfare, Arthur Avenue, is lined with Italian bakeries, pizzerias, and restaurants.

The Arthur Avenue Retail Market includes pastry shops, butchers, pasta-makers, places selling Italian sausages, fish stands, and coffee shops. Every September, the neighborhood celebrates Ferragosto, a traditional harvest festival, with dancing, food stalls, live performances, and a cheese-carving contest.

Hero sandwiches are among treats in store along Arthur Avenue

12

Yankee Stadium

East 161st St at River Av, Highbridge 161 St (B, D, 4) 10am–12:40pm daily (except game days) newyork.yankees.mlb.com

This was first home of the New York Yankees baseball team in 1923. Among Yankee heroes are two of the greatest players of all time: Babe Ruth and Joe DiMaggio (also famous for marrying actress Marilyn Monroe in 1954). In 1921 left-hander Babe Ruth hit the stadium's first home run – against the Boston Red Sox, his former team. The stadium was completed two years later, and became known as "the house that Ruth built."

One of the largest annual gatherings has been that of the Jehovah's Witnesses, and in 1950, 123,707 attended on one day. In 1965 Pope Paul VI celebrated mass before more than 80,000 people – the first visit to North America by a pope; in 1979 John Paul II also visited the stadium.

In 2009, the Yankees moved to a stadium constructed parallel to the old site. This remains one of the most expensive venues built on US soil, estimated at around $1.5 billion, and honors aspects of the 1923 stadium, such as the granite and limestone facade.

The Yankees remain one of the top teams in the American League. Multiple Yankee Clubhouse stores in New York sell tickets for tours and games.

13

The Bronx Museum of the Arts

1040 Grand Concourse 167 St (B, D) 11am–6pm Wed, Thu, Sat & Sun, 11am–8pm Fri bronxmuseum.org

Founded in 1971, the museum showcases contemporary works by Asian, Latino, and African-American artists, with over 1,000 works. It also hosts readings, performances, and other events.

Among artists represented are Romare Bearden (1911–88), a multimedia artist known for his depictions of everyday African-American life; Bronx-born Whitfield Lovell (b. 1959), renowned for his African-American figures in pencil and charcoal; Cuban installation and performance artist Tania Bruguera (b. 1968); lauded photographer Seydou Keïta (1921–2001) from Mali; Brazilian visual artist Hélio Oiticica (1937–80); contemporary African-American artist Kara Walker (b. 1969); and the Chinese artist Xu Bing (b. 1955).

Since 1982, the museum has been housed in a former synagogue, donated by the City of New York. In 2006 the museum, with a striking new jagged steel-and-glass "accordion" facade, was reopened after an expansion completed by Miami-based company Arquitectonica.

BIRTHPLACE OF HIP HOP TOUR

New York is the home of hip hop. The Bronx scene emerged in the mid-1970s with pioneers such as DJ Kool Herc (Run-DMC formed in Queens in 1981 and Fab Five Freddy hailed from Brooklyn). Hush Hip Hop Tours (hushtours.com) runs the "Birthplace of Hip Hop Tour" through Harlem and the South Bronx, hosted by the likes of Grand Master Caz, Rahiem, and Kurtis Blow.

International icon, the Yankee Stadium in the Bronx

14

Flushing Meadows-Corona Park

S Mets-Willets Point (7)

The site of New York's two World's Fairs offers expansive waterside picnic grounds and a multitude of attractions. The 41,000-seat Citi Field stadium is home to the New York Mets baseball team, and is a popular rock concert venue. Flushing Meadows is also home to the National Tennis Center, where the US Open is played. The courts are available the rest of the year.

The Unisphere, symbol of the 1964 fair, still dominates the remains of the fairground. The giant hollow ball of green steel, 12 stories high and weighing 350 tons, is at the center of a circular fountain, and is always busy with casual photographers and families.

15

Queens Museum

A New York City Building, Flushing Meadows-Corona Park **S** 111 St (7) **O** 11am-5pm Wed-Sun **W** queensmuseum.org

Next to the Unisphere, the museum occupies the only remaining building from the 1939 World's Fair, designed as the New York City Pavilion. There are temporary exhibitions and three long-term installations. The Neustadt Collection of Tiffany Glass has pieces by Louis Comfort Tiffany, whose design studios were in Corona in the 1890s. "From Watersheds to Faucets: The Marvel of the NYC Water Supply System" features a large wood-and-plaster relief map, created for the 1939 World's Fair. Other World's Fair artifacts are also on display.

The other major attraction is the Panorama of the City of New York, from the 1964 World's Fair. At 9,300 sq-ft (864 sq m), it is the world's largest architectural model, with 895,000 buildings carved out of wood, plus harbors, rivers, bridges.

16

Louis Armstrong House Museum

A 34-56 107th St **S** 103 St-Corona Plaza **O** 10am-5pm Tue-Fri, noon-5pm Sat & Sun **W** louisarmstronghouse.org

Legendary trumpeter Louis Armstrong (1901–71) lived here from 1943 until his death in 1971, and is buried in nearby Flushing Cemetery. The jazz artist's home is preserved just as he and his fourth wife, singer Lucille Wilson, left it. Audio recordings reveal everyday goings-on, casual conversations with friends and relatives, and impromptu trumpet practice sessions. Guided tours, which take place hourly until 4pm, provide context. Concerts are held in the garden.

The visitors' center across the street displays more of Armstrong's personal archives.

17

Steinway & Sons

A 1 Steinway Place, 19th Av **S** Ditmars Boulevard (N, W) **W** steinway.com

Heinrich Steinweg (1797–1871) emigrated from Germany in 1850, anglicized his name to Henry Steinway, and founded Steinway & Sons in 1853.

Recognized for producing the finest pianos, and winning prizes at international trade fairs, the company rapidly grew and about 1,250 grand pianos a year are built here. Among the most complex objects still made by hand, the pianos, made of maple, walnut, pear, or spruce wood, are assembled from over 12,000 parts, a process that takes a year. Visitors can join a tour at 9:30am on Tuesdays (Sep–Jun). Reservations essential.

18

Noguchi Museum and Socrates Sculpture Park

A 9-01 33rd Rd **S** Broadway (N, W), then **Q104** **O** Noguchi Museum: 10am-5pm Wed-Fri, 11am-6pm Sat & Sun **W** noguchi.org

Devoted to Japanese-American abstract sculptor Isamu Noguchi (1904–88), this museum and garden provides an artistic space for visitors to

CRAFT BREWERIES

Thirsty? Head for Queens and its craft breweries. Long Island City is home to Rockaway Brewing (English ales and stouts; www.rockawaybrewco.com) and tiny Transmitter Brewing (farmhouse ales; www.transmitterbrewing.com). SingleCut Beersmiths in Astoria (www.singlecutbeer.com) is a lager specialist, while out in Ridgewood, Finback Brewery (www.finbackbrewery.com) offers seasonal pours.

↑ Queens Museum offers free tours, in English and Spanish, on Sundays.

experience his creative vision. Probably best remembered for his work with the Herman Miller company in 1947, when he created the iconic Noguchi table, Noguchi also designed the Red Cube outside the Marine Midland Building in Lower Manhattan.

Nearby, on Vernon Boulevard, Socrates Sculpture Park was created in 1986, when abstract expressionist sculptor Mark di Suvero converted an old landfill into an outdoor studio. Several artists have used the space to exhibit their work on a massive scale. The park is open from 9am until sunset daily, and tours take place at 2pm, Wednesday through Sunday.

⑲ Museum of the Moving Image and Kaufman Astoria Studio

🏠 36-01 35th Av at 36th St, Astoria ⑤ 36 St (N, W), Steinway St (R) 🕐 10:30am–5pm Wed–Thu, 10:30am–8pm Fri, 10:30am–6pm Sat & Sun 🌐 movingimage.us

In New York's filmmaking heyday, Rudolph Valentino, W. C. Fields, the Marx Brothers, and Gloria Swanson all made movies in the Astoria Studio,

which was opened in 1920 by Paramount Pictures. When the movies went west, the army made training films here from 1941 to 1971.

In 1977 the Astoria Motion Picture and Television Foundation was created to preserve the studios. *The Wiz*, a musical starring Michael Jackson and Diana Ross, was made here, helping to pay for restoration. Today, the studios house the largest moviemaking facilities on the East Coast.

One of the studio buildings houses the Museum of the Moving Image, with displays of memorabilia, from Ben Hur's chariot to *Star Trek* costumes. Its main gallery draws from the permanent collection of over 130,000 movie artifacts. State-of-the-art amenities include a 254-seat theater, a video-screening amphitheater, and an educational screening room, with screenings taking place on Friday through Sunday. Tours take place at 2pm on Saturday and Sunday.

⑳   MoMA PS1, Queens

🏠 22-25 Jackson Av at 46th Av, Long Island City ⑤ 23 St-Court Sq (E, F, M), 45 Rd-Courthouse Sq (7), Court Sq (G), 21 St-Van Alst (G) 🚌 B61, Q67 🕐 Noon–6pm Thu–Mon 🌐 momaps1.org

In a former elementary school, PS1 was founded in 1971 under a scheme to transform abandoned city buildings into exhibition, performance, and studio spaces. It is affiliated with the Museum of Modern Art *(p202)* and is one of the oldest art organizations in the US devoted solely to contemporary art. Exhibitions are hosted alongside permanent works and many interactive pieces. On Saturdays in summer, the outdoor courtyard hosts a daytime dance party, with live performers.

EAT

Empanadas Café
Tasty Latin American meat pies (try the beef and cheese).

🏠 56-27 Van Doren St, Corona 🌐 empanadas cafe.com

💲💲💲

Jackson Diner
The best-known Indian restaurant in Jackson Heights, with outstanding curries.

🏠 37-47 74th St, Jackson Heights 🌐 jacksondinerny.com

💲💲💲

M. Wells Dinette
Cafeteria-style place, offering Quebecois-fusion dishes in a classroom-themed space.

🏠 22-25 Jackson Av, in MoMA PS1, Long Island City 🕐 Tue, Wed 🌐 magasinwells.com

💲💲💲

SriPraPhai
Truly authentic Thai food, light years ahead of anything over the river in Manhattan. Cash only.

🏠 64-13 39th Av, Woodside 🌐 sripraphai restaurant.com

💲💲💲

Taverna Kyclades
Friendly and popular Greek taverna specializing in seafood.

🏠 33-07 Ditmars Blvd, Astoria 🌐 taverna kyclades.com

💲💲💲

EXPERIENCE Staten Island

The Snug Harbor Cultural Center and Botanical Garden

⌂1000 Richmond Terrace
🚌S40 from ferry to Snug
Harbor Gate ⏰Grounds:
dawn-dusk daily
🌐snug-harbor.org

Founded as an affluent retirement community for "aged, decrepit, and worn-out sailors" in 1801, this became a complex of museums, galleries, gardens, and art centers in 1975. With an 83-acre (34-ha) leafy campus, the center has 28 buildings, which range from grand Greek Revival-style halls to sophisticated Italianate structures. The oldest is the beautiful, restored Main Hall (Building C), which functions as the Visitor Center. The adjacent Newhouse Center for Contemporary Art showcases the work of local artists, and is open Thursday to Sunday in March through to November.

Other buildings here house attractions such as the award-winning Staten Island Children's Museum (open Tuesday to Friday), and the Noble Maritime Collection, which features prints and paintings created by the nautical painter John Noble (1913–83); visitors can view his houseboat studio as well. The Staten Island Museum, which relocated to this complex in 2016, has a major exhibition on Staten Island history, spanning three centuries.

Most of the Snug Harbor grounds belong to the charming **Botanical Garden**. Attractions here include an exhibit designed to attract butterflies, a charming antique rose garden, other themed areas, and various events throughout the year. The tranquil Chinese Scholar's Garden, with its goldfish ponds, pagoda-roofed halls, and bamboo groves, was built in 1999 by artists from Suzhou, China.

Historic Richmond Town

⌂441 Clarke Av 🚌S74
from ferry ⏰1–5pm Wed-
Sun 🌐historicrichmond
town.org

There are 29 buildings here, around 14 of which are open to the public, in New York's only restored village and living history museum. The village was first named Cocclestown, after the local shellfish, but this was soon corrupted to "Cuckoldstown," much to the annoyance of the residents. By the end of the Revolutionary War, the name Richmondtown had been adopted.

The community was the county seat until Staten Island was made part of the city in 1898, and has been preserved as an example of an early New York settlement.

The Voorlezer's House, built in Dutch style around 1695, is the oldest elementary school in the country. The Stephens General Store, which opened in 1837, doubled as the local post office – it has been well restored, right down to the contents of the shelves. The complex, on 100 acres (40 ha), includes wagon sheds, an 1837 courthouse, houses, several stores, and a tavern. There are also seasonal workshops where traditional crafts are demonstrated. St. Andrew's Church (1708) and its graveyard are just across the Mill Pond stream. The Historical Society Museum, in the County Clerk's and Surrogate's Office, has a delightful toy room.

↑ Historic Richmond Town recalls Staten Island's past

Jacques Marchais Museum of Tibetan Art

⌂338 Lighthouse Ave
🚌S74 from ferry ⏰1–5pm
Wed-Sun (Dec: Fri-Sun only)
🌐tibetanmuseum.org

On a tranquil hilltop is one of the largest privately owned collections of Tibetan art of the 15th to the 20th centuries outside Tibet, completed in 1947 by Mrs Jacques Marchais, a dealer in Asian art. The main building is a replica of a mountain monastery, with an authentic altar in three tiers, crowded with gold, silver and bronze figures. The second building is a library.

Stone sculptures in the garden include life-size Buddhas. The Dalai Lama paid his first visit here in 1991.

> The tranquil Chinese Scholar's Garden, with its goldfish ponds, pagoda-roofed halls, and bamboo groves, was built in 1999 by artists from Suzhou, China.

EAT

Denino's Pizzeria & Tavern

Staten Island's favorite pizzeria since 1937. It still slings pizzas with a slightly thicker, chewier crust than most brick-oven spots in New York. Try the signature clam pie or garbage pie (sausage, meatballs, pepperoni, mushrooms, onions). Cash only.

🏠 524 Port Richmond Av 🌐 deninossi.com

$ ⑤ ⑤

Ralph's Famous Italian Ices

In business since 1928, this spot is handily just across from Denino's Pizzeria – an ideal dessert stop off. The specialty of this small takeout is Italian "water ices," made with fruit or other flavorings.

🏠 501 Port Richmond Av 🕐 Summer only; reserve ahead 🌐 ralphsices.com

$ ⑤ ⑤

Alice Austen House

🏠 2 Hylan Blvd 🚌 S 51 from ferry to Hylan Blvd 🕐 House: 1–5pm Tue–Fri, 11am–5pm Sat & Sun; grounds: to dusk daily 🌐 aliceausten.org

This small, charming cottage, built around 1690, has the delightful name of Clear Comfort. It was the home of the prolific photographer Alice Austen, who was born in

1866 and who lived in this house for most of her life. Her photography documented life on Staten Island, across the water in Manhattan, on trips to other parts of the country, and on her travels to Europe. She lost all her money in the stock market crash of 1929, and her poverty forced her into a public poorhouse in 1950, at the age of 84.

One year later, Austen's photographic talent was finally recognized by *Life* magazine. The publication printed an article about her, which earned her enough money to enter a nursing home. When she died in 1952, she left 3,500 photographic negatives dating from 1880 to 1930.

Her house was rescued and restored, and the Friends of Alice Austen House mount exhibitions of her best work.

Little Sri Lanka

🏠 2 Hylan Blvd 📞 (718) 816-4506 🚌 S 51 from ferry to Hylan Blvd 🕐 11am–5pm Tue–Sun

New York's Little Sri Lanka is centered along Victory Boulevard (at Cebra Avenue), in the Tompkinsville neighborhood of Staten Island, a 20-minute stroll from the ferry terminal. It's one of the largest Sri Lankan communities outside of Sri Lanka itself. Cheap hoppers (a type of pancake) and curries are available at New Asha (322 Victory Boulevard), while Lanka Grocery at 353 Victory Boulevard is piled high with a range of Ceylon teas, chutneys, spices, candy, and other delicacies.

→ Alice Austen House, also called Clear Comfort

NEED TO KNOW

Heading to Manhattan from Queens

BEFORE
YOU GO

Forward planning is essential to any successful trip. Be prepared for all eventualities by considering the following points before you travel.

AT A GLANCE

CURRENCY
US Dollar (USD)

AVERAGE DAILY SPEND

ON A BUDGET	MODERATE SPENDER	SPLASH OUT
$120	$250	$350+

BOTTLED WATER	COFFEE	BEER	DINNER FOR TWO
$1.50	$2	$7	$75

CLIMATE

 The longest days occur Jun–Aug. Nov–Feb sees the shortest daylight hours.

 Temperatures average 84°F (29°C) in summer, and fall below freezing in winter.

 The heaviest rainfall is in March and August; showers occur all year round.

ELECTRICITY SUPPLY
The standard US electric current is 110 volts and 60 Hz. Power sockets are type A and B, fitting plugs with two flat pins.

Passports and Visas

Canadian and Mexican visitors require valid passports to enter the US. Citizens of Australia, New Zealand, and the EU do not need a visa, but must apply to enter in advance via the Electronic System for Travel Authorization (**ESTA**) and have a valid passport.

Visitors from all other regions will require a tourist visa and passport to enter, and will be photographed and have their fingerprints checked. Be sure to allow plenty of time for the US border agency's thorough passport and visa checks at the airport.

A return airline ticket is required to enter the country. Entry regulations may change, so always check well in advance of travel with the **US Department of State** (see below) for the most up-to-date visa and travel information.
ESTA
W esta.cbp.dhs.gov/esta
US Department of State
W travel.state.gov

Travel Safety Advice

Visitors can get up-to-date travel safety information from the US Department of State, the UK Foreign and Commonwealth Office, and the Australian Department of Foreign Affairs and Trade.
Australia
W smartraveller.gov.au
UK
W gov.uk/foreign-travel-advice

Customs Information

Nonresident travelers need to complete a **Customs and Border Protection Agency** form when crossing the US border. Passengers may carry $100 in gifts; one liter of alcohol as beer, wine or liquor (if aged 21 years or older); and one carton of cigarettes, 50 cigars (not Cuban) or two kilograms (4.4 lbs) of smoking tobacco into the US without incurring tax.
Customs and Border Protection Agency
W cbp.gov/travel

Insurance

Emergency medical insurance is highly recommended for international travelers to the US, as costs for medical and dental care can be high. Travel insurance for cancellations, delays, theft, and loss of belongings is recommended. Car rental agencies offer vehicle and liability insurance; check your policy before traveling.

Vaccinations

No inoculations are required for visiting the United States.

Booking Accommodation

With over 115,000 hotel rooms available, New York offers something for everyone. The city's top hotels are among the most expensive in the US, but there are also many budget and mid-priced hotels, family-run B&Bs, and hostels.

Hotels are busiest during the week, when business travelers are in the city, so most of them offer budget weekend packages. Hotel rooms are subject to a total 14.75% tax, plus a $3.50 room fee per night.

Money

Most establishments accept major credit, debit, and prepaid currency cards. Contactless payments are becoming increasingly common, with plans underway to introduce a contactless payment system on the subway and some bus routes by 2020.

Cash is still required on buses and by some smaller businesses and street vendors. ATMs (Automated Teller Machines) are available at nearly every bank and street corner.

Travelers with Specific Needs

New York City law requires that all facilities built after 1987 provide entrances and accessible restroom facilities for the disabled. All city buses now have steps that can be lowered to allow wheelchair access, and most street corners also have curb cuts for wheelchairs.

The **Mayor's Office for People with Disabilities** is the liaison between New York City government and the disabililty community.

It offers a range of support services and provides information on accessibility in the city.

The **Theater Development Fund** offers the superb Theater Access Project, which aims to increase access to theater for those who are hearing- and visually-impaired, as well as for those with other disabilities. The **Lighthouse Guild** offers tips on exploring New York for the visually impaired.

Lighthouse Guild
W lighthouseguild.org
Mayor's Office for People with Disabilities
W nyc.gov/mopd
Theater Development Fund
W tdf.org

Language

New York City is a cosmopolitan city in which you will hear multiple languages spoken. Many tour companies cater for those with limited English by offering foreign language headsets and guided tours in a range of languages.

Closures

Mondays and Tuesdays Some museums close on Monday, Tuesday, or both, though the majority are open daily.
Sundays Most banks close in the afternoon and many smaller businesses close for the day.
Federal and State Holidays Museums, attractions and many business close, especially for major holidays. It is best to check with individual venues for specific closures ahead of your visit.

FEDERAL HOLIDAYS 2019	
1 Jan	New Year's Day
21 Jan	Martin Luther King, Jr. Day
18 Feb	President's Day
27 May	Memorial Day
4 Jul	Independence Day
2 Sept	Labor Day
28 Nov	Thanksgiving Day
25 Dec	Christmas Day

GETTING
AROUND

Whether exploring New York City by foot or public transportation, here is all you'll need to know to navigate the city like a pro.

PUBLIC TRANSPORT COSTS

The following tickets are valid on bus and subway services operated by MTA.

ONE-WAY TICKET

$3

1 transfer permitted within 2 hours of first use

PAY-PER-RIDE METROCARD

$2.75

1 transfer permitted within 2 hours of first use

METROCARD 7-DAY PASS

$32

Unlimited travel on bus and subway services

SPEED LIMIT

RURAL FREEWAYS

65
mph
(100 kmph)

URBAN FREEWAYS

55
mph
(90 kmph)

URBAN AREAS

30
mph
(48 kmph)

NEIGHBORHOOD SLOW ZONE

20
mph
(30 kmph)

Arriving by Air

Three major airports serve New York City. The two main international airports in the New York City area are John F. Kennedy International (JFK) and Newark Liberty International (EWR) in New Jersey. Both also handle domestic flights. The third major airport is LaGuardia (LGA), which mostly handles domestic flights. All three airports offer connecting flights to most US cities.

Be sure to allow plenty of extra time at the airport, both at arrival and departure, as there are often long lines for passport control and thorough security checks.

For a list of transport options, approximate journey times, and travel costs for transport between each of New York City's Airports and Midtown Manhattan, see the table opposite.

Train Travel

Amtrak, the US passenger rail service, Long Island Rail Road (**LIRR**), and New Jersey Transit (**NJT**) commuter trains all pull in to Penn Station, situated on Seventh and Eighth Avenues and 31st and 34th Streets, beneath Madison Square Garden. Amtrak has its own designated area in Penn Station for ticket sales, and separate waiting rooms for coach and high-speed passengers.

Metro-North regional trains use Grand Central Terminal (often referred to as Grand Central Station) located at 42nd Street and Park Avenue in Midtown Manhattan.

Tickets can be bought on the day of travel, or ahead of your trip online or over the phone. Pre-paid tickets can be collected at ticket windows or automated kiosks at the station. If you collect tickets at the window, photo ID will be requested. Ensure you get the cheapest fares by booking in advance.

You can buy tickets for multiple journeys with Amtrak's USA Rail Pass, which allows eight journeys over a 15-day period for $459; children pay half-fare.

The most popular train service from New York is Amtrak's Northeast Corridor route between

Airport	Transport to Midtown	Journey Time	Price
John F. Kennedy	AirTrain JFK + LIRR	1 hr 30 mins	$23
	NYC Airporter	1 hr 45mins–2 hrs	$19
	SuperShuttle	1–2 hrs	from $25
	Taxi	1 hr–1 hr 45 mins	from $52
Newark Liberty	AirTrain Newark + NJ Transit	40 mins	$13
	Newark Airport Express	45 mins–1 hr	$18
	SuperShuttle	1–2 hrs	from $23
	Taxi	45 mins – 1 hr	$70–95
	National Express Coach	1 hr 40 mins	from $5
	Taxi	1 hr 10 mins	from $75
La Guardia	LaGuardia Link + subway	50 mins	$2.75
	NYC Airporter	1 hr 30 mins	$16
	SuperShuttle	1–2 hrs	from $20
	Taxi	1hr–1 hr 30 mins	$30–$40

Boston, New York, Philadelphia, and Washington, DC. Most of the trains on this route have unreserved seating, but Amtrak's high-speed **Acela Express** trains offer an hourly service with reserved first- and business-class seating plus electrical outlets for laptops.

Amtrak also offer a Northeast Corridor sleeper service, which is often preferable to flying as it avoids traveling long distances to and from the airport. Included in the service is a private cabin and restroom, a complimentary meal onboard, and private lounge access.

Acela Express
W amtrak.com/acela-express-train
Amtrak
W amtrak.com
LIRR
W mta.info/lirr
Metro-North
W mta.info/mnr
NJT
W njtransit.com

Long-Distance Bus Travel

Intercity buses are a great, economical way to get to New York City, or to travel further afield with New York as your base.

Coach and intercity buses from all over the US, as well as New York City commuter lines, arrive at the **Port Authority Bus Terminal** (PABT), which is the central hub for interstate buses in New York City.

Taxis can be found on the Eighth Avenue side of the terminal; the A, C and E subway stops are located on the lower floors in the terminal; and a one-block-long tunnel leads to Times Square station and other subway connections.

Buses from the Port Authority connect with all three airports, and the terminal also serves many busy commuter bus lines to New Jersey. With over 6,000 buses arriving and departing daily, the atmosphere can be hectic at rush hour.

Greyhound offer low-cost routes between New York and Philadelphia (2 hours), Washington, DC (4 hours), Boston (4.5 hours), Toronto (11.5 hours), and Montreal (8.5 hours), among many other cities. Discount long-distance bus services, such as **Megabus** and **Bolt Bus**, depart and arrive at 34th Street between 11th and 12th Avenues.

Bolt Bus
W boltbus.com
Greyhound
W greyhound.com
Megabus
W megabus.com
Port Authority Bus Terminal
W panynj.gov/bus-terminals/port-authority-bus-terminal.html

Public Transportation

New York City's extensive bus and subway transportation system is operated by the Metropolitan Transportation Authority (**MTA**). Timetables, ticket information, transport maps, and a useful route planner can be found on the MTA website. Subway maps are also available for free at any station fare booth.

MTA
w mta.info

Planning Your Journey

Buses and subways are busiest during the rush hours: 7–9.30am and 4:30–6pm, Monday to Friday. Throughout these periods, it may be much faster and easier to face the crowds on foot than attempt any journey by bus, taxi, or subway. At other times of day and during certain holiday periods, the traffic is often much lighter, and you should reach your destination more quickly. Note that public transport runs a reduced service during major holidays.

Tickets

MetroCards and SingleRide tickets are valid on buses and the subway. Cards may be purchased for any number of individual rides. One free transfer ride is allowed between the subway and bus (and vice versa), or between two different bus lines. This must be used within 2 hours of first use.

A single trip costs $3 with a SingleRide paper ticket and a SingleRide MetroCard, or $2.75 with a Pay-Per-Ride MetroCard, no matter how far you travel. If you are making several trips, buy a weekly unlimited ticket for $32 and the cost per journey will work out to be less.

MetroCards and tickets are sold at news stands, drug stores, and all subway stations. They can be purchased for amounts from $5.50 to $80. Seven-day ($32) or 30-day. ($121) unlimited-ride options are also available. If you put $5.50 or more on a MetroCard, you receive a 5% bonus.

The MTA charges a $1.00 "new card fee" for the purchase of a new MetroCard. By refilling and reusing your current MetroCard, you will avoid this additional fee.

Subway

The subway is the fastest way to get around, with over 470 stations across all five boroughs, and routes that fan out to the farthest reaches of New York City. The subway runs 24 hours a day, though late night service patterns change.

Generally, the 1, 2, 3, 4, 5, 6, A, B, C, D, Q trains cover the main parts of the city, running north–south, originating in upper Manhattan or the Bronx and, with the exception of the 1 and 6, all continue east to Brooklyn. The L train runs

east–west across Manhattan along 14th Street to Brooklyn. The 7 train runs along 42nd Street to Queens. The E, F, M, N, R, and W originate in Queens and make a few stops in the city before continuing into Brooklyn (except for the E which terminates in lower Manhattan).

Bus

Most buses run every 3–5 minutes during the morning and evening rush hours, and every 7–15 minutes from noon to 4:30pm and from 7–10pm. Bad traffic or adverse weather conditions can cause delays. A reduced service operates on weekends and holidays.

Certain buses on the busiest crosstown routes require you to enter the MetroCard into the kiosks at the bus stop to get a receipt for your journey. Inspectors do check occasionally, and riders without a receipt are fined.

Many lines run 24 hours, but be sure to check the schedule posted at your stop. After 10pm, many buses run every 20 minutes or so. From midnight to 6am, expect to wait 30–60 minutes for a bus.

Bus Tours

One of the most popular ways to see the sights is aboard a hop-on-hop-off bus tour. Get off wherever you like, stay as long as you want, and catch another bus when you are ready.

Gray Line is the best-known company offering these tours aboard double-decker buses. Routes include a Downtown loop, Uptown loop, Brooklyn loop, as well as night and holiday lights tours (not hop-on-hop-off). Buy a 48- or 72-hour pass, and you can see a great deal of New York this way.

Gray Line
w grayline.com

Taxis

Manhattan's iconic yellow taxis can be hailed anywhere and can be found waiting outside most hotels and stations. The light atop the cab goes on when it is available. All cabs accept cash and some accept credit cards. For any taxi complaints, you can call 311.

The green Boro taxis operate in areas of New York not commonly served by yellow cabs – north of West 110th Street and East 96th Street in Manhattan, the Bronx, Queens (excluding the airports), Brooklyn, and Staten Island. They can drop you off anywhere in the city, but cannot pick up passengers in Manhattan below 96th and 110th Streets.

All taxis are metered and can issue printed receipts. The meter starts ticking at $3. The fare increases 50 cents after each additional fifth of a mile or every 60 seconds of waiting time. There is an additional 50-cent charge from 8pm–6am, and an extra $1 charge from 4–8pm on week days. Tolls are extra and are added to the fare. There is no extra charge for luggage.

The base fare for an Uber is $2.55, with an additional $1.75 per mile. Lyft and Gett offer similar rates.

Driving

Heavy, slow-moving traffic, lack of parking, and expensive rental cars make driving in New York a frustrating experience that is best avoided. To get around stress-free, opt for public transport outside of rush hour.

Car Rental

Rental car companies are located at airports, major stations, and other locations in the city.

To rent a car in the US you must be at least 25 years old with a valid driving license and a clean record. All agencies require a major credit card. Damage and liability insurance is recommended just in case something unexpected should happen. It is advisable always to return the car with a full tank of gas; otherwise you will be required to pay the inflated fuel prices charged by the rental agencies. Be sure to check for any pre-existing damage to the car and note this on your contract before you leave the rental lot.

Parking

If you do decide to drive in the city, check with your hotel to see if they offer parking; this will usually add at least $25 per night to your bill.

Otherwise, there are parking meters across the city, where you can park for up to 12 hours, starting at $3.50 per hour (meters do not have to be paid on Sundays), and you will have to return every 1 or 2 hours to top up. If not, a parking fine will set you back $65.

New York also has numerous parking lots, but these can be expensive, starting from an average of $50 per day.

Rules of the Road

All drivers are legally required to carry a valid driver's license and must be able to produce registration and insurance documents. Most foreign licenses are valid, but if your license is not in English, or does not have a photo ID, apply an International Driving Permit (IDP)

Traffic drives on the right-hand side of the road, and the speed limit is usually 30 mph (48 kmph) in Midtown unless otherwise stated.

Seat belts are compulsory in front seats and are suggested in the back. Children under 3 years old must ride in a child seat in back. Seat belts are also compulsory in cabs.
Most streets are one-way, and there are traffic lights at almost every corner. Unlike the rest of New York State, you can never turn right on a red light unless there is a sign indicating otherwise.

If a school bus stops to let passengers off, all traffic from both sides must stop and wait for the bus to drive off.

A limit of 0.08 per cent blood alcohol is strictly enforced at all times. For drivers under the age of 21 there is a zero tolerance policy for drink-driving. Driving while intoxicated (DWI) is a punishable offense that incurs heavy fines or even a jail sentence. Avoid drinking altogether if you plan to drive.

In the event of an accident or breakdown, drivers of rental cars should contact their car rental company first. Members of the American Automobile Association (**AAA**) can have their vehicle towed to the nearest service station to be fixed. For simple problems like a flat tire or a dead battery, the AAA will fix it or and install a new battery on site for a fee.
AAA
ⓦ aaa.com

Walking and Biking

New York City is always busy, so streets have pedestrian walk lights at most intersections; some also have audio cues. Exploring by foot is a great way to experience the city, but central attractions are quite spread out, so pack a pair of comfortable shoes if you plan to walk from place to place.

It takes courage to cycle alongside busy traffic in Midtown. Bike trails along the East River and far west side offer a pleasant alternative, and are very popular, as are the many roads for bikers in Central Park.

Bike Rent NYC offer daily bike rentals and guided tours in the city. One-day, three-day, or monthly subscriptions are available.

Citibike has 12,000 bicycles at 750 stations all over the city; reserve at a particular address through the app (p311) or use a credit card at the pickup location.

There is no law requiring cyclists to wear a helmet, but it is highly recommended.
Bike Rent NYC
ⓦ bikerent.nyc
Citibike
ⓦ citibikenyc.com

Boats and Ferries

New York Waterway ferries connect New Jersey and Manhattan, providing transportation to New York Yankee and Mets baseball games. Buy tickets online or at the ferry terminal.

The 24-hour Staten Island Ferry is free and offers spectacular views of Lower Manhattan and the Statue of Liberty.
New York Waterway
ⓦ nywaterway.com

PRACTICAL
INFORMATION

A little local know-how goes a long way in New York City. Here you will find all the essential advice and information you will need during your stay.

AT A GLANCE

EMERGENCY NUMBERS

GENERAL
EMERGENCY

911

TIME ZONE
EST/EDT
Eastern Daylight Time
(EDT) runs 10 Mar–
3 Nov 2019
PST +3
GMT -5
AEDT +14

TAP WATER
Unless otherwise stated, tap water is safe to drink.

TIPPING

Waiter	15–20%
Bartender	$1 per drink
Hotel Porter	$2 per bag
Housekeeping	10% of room bill
Cab Driver	10–15%

Personal Security

New York is a large, cosmopolitan city. Petty crime does exist, so always be alert to your surroundings, and be wary of pickpockets on public transportation and in crowded areas.

If you have anything stolen, report the crime within 24 hours to the nearest police station and take ID with you. Get a copy of the crime report in order to claim on your insurance. Contact your embassy if you have your passport stolen, or in the event of a serious crime or accident.

Health

It is possible to visit a doctor or dentist in New York without being registered, but you will be asked to pay in advance. Keep receipts to make a claim on your insurance later.

There are plenty of walk-in medical clinics and emergency rooms, as well as 24-hour pharmacies. **Mount Sinai** offers convenient walk-in or by-appointment services for adults and children at locations around the city, from the West Village to Midtown. Another option is **NYC Health + Hospitals**.

Hospital emergency treatment is available 24 hours a day. If you are able, call the number on your insurance policy first, and check which hospitals your insurance company deals with. For immediate treatment in an emergency, call an ambulance.

Payment of hospital and other medical expenses is the patient's responsibility. As such it is important to arrange comprehensive medical insurance before traveling (p305).
Mount Sinai
🅦 roosevelthospitalnyc.org
NYC Health + Hospitals
🅦 nychealthandhospitals.org

Smoking, Alcohol, and Drugs

The legal minimum age for drinking alcohol in the USA is 21, and you will need photo ID as proof of age in order to purchase alcohol and be allowed into bars. It is illegal to drink alcohol in public parks or to carry an open container of alcohol in your car, and penalties for driving under the influence of alcohol are severe *(p309)*.

Smoking is prohibited in all public buildings, bars, restaurants, and stores. Cigarettes can be purchased by those over 18 years old; proof of age will be required.

Possession of narcotics is prohibited and could result in a prison sentence.

ID

It is not compulsory to carry ID at all times in New York City. If you are asked by police to show your ID, a photocopy of your passport photo page (and visa if applicable) should suffice. You may be asked to present the original document within 12 or 24 hours.

Local Customs

There is a knack to navigating New York City's busy streets. Always walk on the right side of the sidewalk and stairwells. If you want to take a picture or consult a map while walking, don't just stop, move to the side first. Avoid walking three or four abreast. The locals will be quick to tell you if you are doing something wrong.

Visiting Churches, Cathedrals, and Synagogues

Dress respectfully: cover your torso and upper arms. Ensure shorts and skirts cover your knees.

Cell Phones and Wi-Fi

Free Wi-Fi hotspots are widely available throughout the city, including in some MetroRail stations. Cafés and restaurants will usually let you use their Wi-Fi if you make a purchase.

Cell phone service in New York City is generally excellent. If you are coming from overseas and want to guarantee that your cell phone will work, make sure you have a quad-band phone.

In order to use your phone abroad you may need to activate the "roaming" facility, which is notoriously expensive. If you are planning on using your phone for Wi-Fi only, ensure that data roaming is turned off. Other options include buying a prepaid cell phone in the US or a SIM chip for a US carrier.

Post

Stamps can be bought from post offices, drugstores, and newsstands. On-street mailboxes are usually blue, or red, white, and blue. Mail is not collected on Sundays.

The city's main General Post Office is open from 10pm Monday to Friday, until 9pm on Saturdays, and 7pm on Sundays.

Taxes and Tipping

A sales tax of around 9% is added to most items, including meals. Waiters generally receive 15–20% of the bill, including tax. A quick way to calculate restaurant tips is simply to double the tax, which adds up to about 18%.

Discount Cards

New York City offers a number of visitor passes and discount cards for exhibitions, events, museum entry and even transport. These are available online and from participating tourist offices. The cards are not free, so consider carefully how many of the offers you are likely to take advantage of before purchasing.
City Pass
🅦 citypass.com
New York Explorer Pass
🅦 smartdestinations.com
The New York Pass
🅦 newyorkpass.com

WEBSITES AND APPS

Citibike
Find bike docking stations near you and receive real-time updates on bike and dock availability using this app.

NYC & Co.
Check out New York City's official tourist information website at nycgo.com.

NY Waterway
This App provides route maps, schedules, and transport links for New York's ferry services. The app also allows users to buy paperless tickets and present their phone as proof of purchase.

INDEX

Page numbers in bold refer to main entries

ACKNOWLEDGMENTS

DK Travel would like to thank the following people whose help and assistance contributed to the preparation of this book

Karissa Adams, Adam Brackenbury, Elizabeth Byrne, James Davis, Sarah Dennis, Matt Dobbin, Bridget Fuller, Pauline Giacomelli-Harris, Meryl Halls, George Hamilton-Jones, Catherine Hetherington, Debbie James, Tom Morse, Chris Rushby, Mike Sansbury

Cartographic Data ERA-Maptec Ltd (Dublin) adapted with permission from original survey and mapping by Shobunsha (Japan)

PICTURE CREDITS

Eataly: 155; Virginia Rollison 154clb; Evan Sung 154bl.

Getty Images: AFP / Kena Betancur 55cl, / Torsten Blackwood 24bl, / Timothy A Clary 40-1t, / Don Emmert 40tl, / Oliver Lang 219cla; Archive Photos 60t; Jon Arnold 34b, 221cb; Bettmann 254clb; Bruce Bi 188-9; Bloomberg 26cr, 31t, 54cra, 59bl; Andrew Burton 31cl; Buyenlarge 49cla; CBS Photo Archive 51br; Julie Dermansky 59tr; James Devaney 297tr; Dia Dipasupil 54crb; Keith Draycott 69cl; Krzysztof Dydynski 110tc; Elsa 44b; EyeEm / Ricardo Ramirez 89br; Fine Art 57tl; FPG 57tr; Victor Fraile Rodriguez 39t; Noam Galai 13t, 50-1t; Robert Giroux 58-9t; Steven Greaves 46bc; Heritage Images 49crb, / Brooklyn Museum 276bl; Gary Hershorn 55br; John Kobal Foundation 165tr; Dimitrios Kambouris 43cl; Stacy Kay 303br; Keystone-France 69tr; Library of Congress 95tr; Lonely Planet 47cl; Brad Mangin 299b; Maremagnum 34-5t, 212bl; Gonzalo Marroquin 51cla; MCNY / Gottscho-Schleisner 77cla; Mondadori Portfolio 204clb; John Moore 95ca; Hal Morey 188cl; Francis G. Mayer / Brooklyn Museum 276cl; National Archives 165crb; New York Daily News / James Keivom 59cra; New York Daily News Archive 58crb, 58bc, 167bl, 254cb, 255bc; The New York Historical Society 56tc, 167clb; Johnny Nunez 50b; Pacific Press 54cr; Andria Patino 241bl; Sean Pavone 46tl; Bob Peterson 58cr; Steve Kelley aka mudpig 273crb; Photolibrary / Toshi Sasaki 119t; Kyle Reid 23t, 268-9cl; Jason Carter Rinaldi 167br; Douglas Sacha 96cl; Mark Sagliocco 97; Steve Schapiro 60br; Merten Snijders 24clb; Sunset Boulevard 60crb, 60bl; Claire Takacs 26br; Mario Tama 43tr, 96cb; Tetra Images 68; Tony Shi Photography 156bl, 304-5b; Universal History Archive 70ca, 273clb; Jack Vartoogian 12t; Roger Viollet 254bl; Slaven Vlasic 54cla, 55tr; The Washington Post 13cr; Westend61 188cra; Barry Winiker 206cl.

Governors Island: Kreg Holt 77cra.

iStockphoto.com: 400tmax 73cra, 120tr; ablokhin 24tc; AlbertPego 289bl; AlexPro9500 218clb; Alija 166bl, 239cla; andykazie 55tl; andyparker72 221br; BirgerNiss 75tl; Boogich 26t, 166-7t, 239cra; Matt Burchell 10clb; c3nsored 28cr; chang 170cr; deberarr 132-3; dell640 238-9b; diego-grandi 134cl; Eloi_Omella 192bl, 240tr; espiegle 11t; ferrantraite 38-9b, 41clb; Frogman1484 59br; GCShutter 10-1b; iShootPhotosLLC 48-9t; JayLazarin 157tl; jejim 206cr; johnandersonphoto 32-3t; Juntaski 37t; kasto80 274-5b; littleny 19tl, 150-1; lucagavagna 35cla, 202bl; Lya_Cattel 45br; MaximFesenko 8cla; mbbirdy 62-3b; MBPROJEKT_Maciej_Bledowski 288cb; Meinzahm 291; mizoula 131bl, 231tl, 265bl; naphtalina 28bl; NicolasMcComber 112cl, 122cl, 272-3t; nuiiko 244br; OlegAlbinsky 227bl; Andrei Orlov 28t; peeterv 4bc, 111b; pidjoe 24crb; PJPhoto69 35bl; robertcicchetti 178cb; RolfSt 285br; S. Greg Panosian 71tr; sangaku 76-7b; santypan 52-3b; SeanPavonePhoto 86t; SergeYatunin 255crb; Snowshill 12bl; tatarac 260-1; tomeng 176br; Torresigner 32-3b; visualspace 72-3t, 131t, 239bc; wdstock 18t, 94-5b, 123br, 124-5, 142bl, 148bl, 149tl, 170tc, 249tl; xavierarnau 20tl, 172-3.

La Bernardin: Daniel Krieger 30br.

The Metropolitan Museum of Art: Water Lilies by Claude Monet (French, Paris 1840-1926 Giverny), 1916-19, Gift of Louise Reinhardt Smith, 1983 39br; Marble statue of an old woman (A.D. 14–68), Early Imperial, Julio-Claudian, Rogers Fund, 1909 222br; The Last Communion of Saint Jerome (early 1490s) by Botticelli (Alessandro di Mariano Filipepi) (Italian, Florence 1444/45–1510 Florence). Bequest of Benjamin Altman, 1913 223tr; Washington Crossing the Delaware (1851) by Emanuel Leutze (American, Schwäbisch Gmünd 1816–1868 Washington, D.C.) Gift of John Stewart Kennedy, 1897 223bl.

Museum at Eldridge Street: 96bl, 96br.

New Museum: Dean Kaufman 106-7; Benoit Pailley 106tc; Scott Rudd 106bl.

New York Botanical Garden: Robert Benson 295.

New York Public Library: 178-9b, 179cra.

Picfair.com: Dan Martland 196bl; Tetra Images 82-3.

The Public Theater / Tammy Shell: Photo of free Shakespeare in the Park 10ca.

Courtesy of Queens Museum: David Sundberg, Esto 301tl.

Rex by Shutterstock: Kobal / Warner Bros TV / Bright / Kauffman / Crane Pro / 61cb.

Robert Harding Picture Library: Wendy Connett 11cr; Richard Cummins 159cr, 206crb; Apocalypse of the Twin Towers by Joe Kincannon, St. John the Divine Cathedral, New York / Godong 254cl; KFS 16cb, 90-1; Tetra Images 16cl, 64-5.

Schomburg Center / NYPL: 257tr, 257cl, 257c.

SPiN: 44cla.

studio ai architects: Ed Caruso 135br.

SuperStock: 3LH 57cr; age fotostock / Jeff Greenberg 11br, / Spencer Grant 290bc, / Richard Levine 44-5t, 55clb, Riccardo Sala / MoMA, Museum of Modern Art, New York / Henri Matisse © Succession H. Matisse / DACS 2018 *Dance I* (1909) 202-3b; Album 58tl; Peter Barritt / Solomon R. Guggenheim Museum / Pablo Picasso © Succession Picasso / DACS, London 2018 *Woman Ironing* (1904) 218bc; Hemis / Patrice Hauser 41c; imageBROKER / Daniel Schoenen 8clb; Stock Connection 55cr, 242cl; Underwood Photo Archives 77tc; World History Archive 56bc.

Tenement Museum: 95tl, 95cla.

Whitney Museum of American Art: © Jasper Johns / DACS, London / VAGA, NY 2018, *Three Flags*, 1958. Encaustic on canvas, 30 5/8 × 45 1/2 × 4 5/8in. (77.8 × 115.6 × 11.7 cm). purchase, with funds from the Gilman Foundation, Inc., The Lauder Foundation, A. Alfred Taubman, Laura-Lee Whittier Woods, Howard Lipman, and Ed Downe in honor of the Museum's 50th Anniversary 80.32 129cra; George Bellows *Dempsey and Firpo* (1924), Oil on canvas, 51 1/8 × 63 1/4in. (129.9 × 160.7 cm); purchase, with, funds from Gertrude Vanderbilt Whitney 31.95 129crb; Ben Gancsos / Whitney Museum of American Art, 99 Gansevoort Street, New York, N.Y. 10014 by Renzo Piano Building Workshop, architects. Opened May 1, 2015 128-9.

Front flap: AWL Images: Jordan Banks cra; Getty Images: Alexander Spatari br; iStockphoto.com: Matt Burchell bl, espiegle t; Robert Harding Picture Library: Wendy Connett cb, Tetra Images cla.

Sheet map cover: Getty Images: Alexander Spatari.

Cover images:
Front and spine: Getty Images: Alexander Spatari. *Back:* AWL Images: Michele Falzone tr; iStockphoto.com: MaximFesenko c, Snowshill cl; Getty Images: Alexander Spatari b.

For further information see: www.dkimages.com

Penguin Random House

Main contributers
Stephen Keeling, Eleanor Berman

Senior Editor Alison McGill

Senior Designer Laura O'Brien

Project Editor Lucy Richards

Project Art Editors Bess Daly, Tania Gomes, Ben Hinks, Stuti Tiwari Bhatia, Bharti Karakoti, Priyanka Thakur, Vinita Venugopal

Factchecker Todd Obolsky

Editors Danielle Watt, Penny Phenix

Proofreader Kathryn Glendenning

Indexer Helen Peters

Senior Picture Researcher Ellen Root

Picture Research
Harriet Whitaker

Illustrators Richard Draper, Robbie Polley, Hamish Simpson

Cartographic Editor James Macdonald

Cartography Ashutosh Ranjan Bharti, Uma Bhattacharya, Zafar ul Islam Khan, Chez Picthall, Kunal Singh

Jacket Designers
Maxine Pedliham, Bess Daly

Jacket Picture Research Susie Peachey

Senior DTP Designer Jason Little

DTP Coordinator George Nimmo

Senior Producer Stephanie McConnell

Managing Editor Rachel Fox

Art Director Maxine Pedliham

Publishing Director Georgina Dee

First American edition 1993
Published in the United States by DK Publishing, 345 Hudson Street, New York, New York 10014.

Copyright 1993, 2018 © Dorling Kindersley Limited, London

A Penguin Random House Company

18 19 20 21 10 9 8 7 6 5 4 3 2 1

Published in Great Britain by Dorling Kindersley Limited.

A catalog record for this book is available from the Library of Congress.

ISSN: 1542-1554
ISBN: 978-1-4654-7162-8

Throughout this book, floors are referred to in accordance with European usage; i.e., the "first floor" is the floor above ground level.

Printed and bound in China

www.dk.com